C000068760

CREDIT MANAGEMENT

*how to manage credit effectively
and make a real contribution to profits*

R.M.V. BASS

Third Edition

Stanley Thornes (Publishers) Ltd

First published in 1979 by Hutchinson Education

Second edition 1988

Third edition 1991 by:
Stanley Thornes (Publishers) Ltd
Ellenborough House
Wellington Street
CHELTENHAM GL50 1YW
United Kingdom

98   99   00   /   10   9   8   7   6   5

British Library Cataloguing in Publication Data

Bass, R.M.V.
     Credit management: How to manage credit
     effectively and make a real contribution to
     profits. – 3rd ed.
     I. Title
     658.15

     ISBN 0–7487–1374–3

Typeset by Hope Services (Abingdon) Ltd
Printed and bound in Great Britain at
Redwood Books, Trowbridge, Wiltshire

CREDIT MANAGEMENT

*how to manage credit effectively
and make a real contribution to profits*

Contents

Part One   CREDIT MANAGEMENT

agencies — Banks — Agents — Credit contacts — Public buyers — Appendix: accounting terminology used in overseas balance sheets

Foreword

by **Dennis G.S. Williams**
European Credit Manager, Texas Instruments Inc.

I am very pleased to have the opportunity of writing a foreword to this book by my friend and former colleague Richard Bass. Regrettably, the bibliography available to the student of credit management in the United Kingdom is still relatively small, and a significant proportion of it is published in the USA and, therefore, directed to the North American reader rather than to his European counterpart. This volume will, I believe, prove an acceptable and useful addition to the bookshelves of credit managers and others concerned with the management of trade credit in the British Isles.

In commending this work to the intending reader, I am encouraged by the knowledge that Mr Bass is among those practitioners of credit management who recognise it for what it should be, namely comprehensive and professional management of what is frequently one of the largest, if not the largest, asset in the company's balance sheet. The successful running of a business organisation generally involves the co-ordinated management of a group of diverse assets. It is a matter for regret that in many companies which are otherwise capably managed, trade accounts receivable, though representing as much as 30–40 per cent of total asset value, do not receive their proper share of professional attention, but are relegated to a subordinate level of activity often carried out part-time by financial accounting personnel who do not always have the specialised training, or indeed the authority, to perform the function effectively.

The heavy commitment of company funds represented by trade debtors means that the amounts and periods of credit granted, the quality of the resulting accounts receivable and the techniques used to collect them can all affect sales, profitability, liquidity, the security of working capital and the return on investment of the whole enterprise. It follows that the responsibility for overall supervision of the receivables portfolio, particularly in a large company, is a heavy one which, if it is to be discharged effectively, must be entrusted to a well-trained and fully qualified credit manager.

It may be opportune here to outline briefly the qualities which such a person should possess. The key to a successful credit function in any company is primarily the calibre of the individual chosen to head the operation. The role, if fully developed, can be a demanding one. The first requirement, in addition to possession of the technical capability expected of him, is the understanding of marketing objectives and profit goals, coupled with a broad comprehension of the financial aspects of running a business. The credit manager should identify with overall company policies and be a convinced and enthusiastic proponent of the contribution which good credit management can make towards their achievement. He should be, both by nature and by virtue of the responsibility vested in him, a decision-maker whose judgements will be respected and opinions be sought by his directors and fellow-managers. He will be constantly searching for better ways of doing the job. Good interface with people at every level in his own and outside organisations is essential. Effective credit management is usually not achieved without good communication; the credit manager who frequently leaves his desk and visits customers, attends sales meetings and generally uses every opportunity to sell himself and the company's credit policies will (and so, therefore, will his company) always have a head start over the competition in the successful management of the receivables portfolio.

It is to this type of credit manager, profit-oriented, aware of the wider aspects of business, articulate and innovative, and also to the more junior staff who aspire to succeed him, that I believe this book is addressed. I wish it and its readers every success.

Foreword to Third Edition

by Dennis G. Williams
formerly European Credit Manager, Texas Instruments Inc.

Twelve years have passed since the foreword of the first edition of this book was written. I then hoped and believed (though I could not be certain) that the new book would, for the reasons set out in the foreword, soon find a place among the standard textbooks on credit management available in the British Isles. The appearance of the third edition at this time makes it possible to say with every confidence that those original expectations have been amply realised.

The passage of time has, if anything, increased the need for a book such as this. The growth of credit management as a recognised professional business discipline, and the appreciation of its importance to the financial health of business organisations large and small, have continued to increase substantially since the appearance of the first edition. They have fuelled an ever-growing need for training, both of new entrants to the profession, and of those already engaged in it who aim to enhance their skills and knowledge through study and formal qualification, as well as by the acquisition of on-the-job experience. It cannot be said too often that the key to establishing and maintaining a competent and professional credit management environment in any business organisation is, above all, sound training. In times of recession, such as those in which this book is relaunched, many companies have found, to their cost, that effective credit management is not something which can be installed and made to work at short notice when trading and financial conditions become difficult. By then, for many, it is too late. Time as well as resources are needed for good credit policies and practices to become effective; but once these are in place, the benefits are cumulative, and will do much to sustain the financial strength of the organisation through bad times as well as good. A consistently high level of training is essential to the maintenance of satisfactory standards of performance; public and in-house seminars, as well as distance-learning courses, all have a part to play. However, these must always be supplemented and reinforced by the availability of comprehensive, authoritative and up-to-date reference books to which both students and practitioners can turn for information and guidance. To such a select bibliography this book by Richard Bass surely belongs. I have every confidence in its continuing success in this new edition.

November 1991

Foreword from the Institute of Credit Management

by Peter Allen, FICM
Chairman of the Institute of Credit Management

It gives me great pleasure to welcome this third edition of Dick Bass' book on credit management. This book, first published in 1979, has now achieved the status of a standard work on the subject, and is an invaluable work of reference for the many practitioners and students of credit management.

There is no question that this new edition comes at a most opportune time, as credit management is now clearly recognised as a management discipline, with a crucial role to play in the profitability or, indeed, in the survival of companies. Efficient credit control can also make all the difference between cost-effective and wasteful administration in the public sector of a country's economy, and is being accorded a central role in that field. The 1990s will present many challenges to managers in all sectors, and there can be little doubt that the credit manager will be increasingly called upon to deal with these.

A professional credit management function requires professionally qualified people to direct it and Dick Bass' book will help to produce those people. It is required reading for students preparing for the examinations of the Institute of Credit Management, especially if they are studying by means of the Institute's Distance Learning Scheme. In addition, the study of credit management is now being included in business and finance courses in many universities and other higher education institutions, and this volume will find a worthy place on the shelves of libraries and of individual students in such places. From a mere trickle a decade ago, the number of serious students of credit management has increased dramatically, with more than 2000 registered to take ICM examinations in the United Kingdom alone.

Dick Bass has combined in a most effective way the general principles of credit management with an update on its practices. He thus deserves a wide audience not only in the United Kingdom, but also in those many other countries where credit management is establishing its importance as a management function. Experience shows that, although national cultures may differ, credit managers usually have the same fundamental problems to solve, and a strong common interest is developing, particularly among the member countries of FECMA (the Federation of European Credit Managers Associations) and similar national associations. They and their members could all learn much from this book, and I commend it to credit managers and students of credit management wherever they may be.

R. P. Allen
November 1991

Preface

Credit management is an art which has been practised since the earliest days of civilisation. Being an art — and not a precise science — its techniques have constantly changed according to the needs of the business community.

Credit management in the UK has developed a great deal over the last ten years. Yet whilst we may take pride in being ahead of the rest of Europe in recognising its importance, we are still decades behind the USA. This is strikingly illustrated by the fact that the National Association of Credit Management was founded in the USA in 1896, whereas our own Institute of Credit Management did not see the light of day until 1939.

I am conscious of the fact that in the UK today there are many practices and customs in different industries which result in countless differences in the way credit control operates. I can only draw on my personal experience, broadened by contact with credit managers from many industries and many countries over the last twenty years.

Within this limitation, I shall try to focus on the requirements of successful credit management in industry today. Consumer credit is not covered nor do I include any detailed examination of insolvency procedures. The emphasis that will, I hope, emerge is on credit management as a positive function, vital to the protection of assets but also contributing to profitability.

A substantial part of the book is devoted to export credit because comparatively little has been published on a topic which has become of increasing interest to credit people in recent years.

Preface to Third Edition

Once again the UK is in the depths of a recession, with each new set of insolvency figures setting a record. At such a time the credit manager is tested and stretched to the limit of his or her abilities. On the home front he has to walk a tightrope, minimizing losses and reducing overdues, whilst striving to find ways of accepting such new business as is available. Looking abroad, into a Europe which is supposedly soon to be regarded as an extended domestic market, the problem of how to assess and manage business with Eastern Europe is added to the difficulties of trading with the Third World.

I hope this new edition, extensively revised and updated, will be of help to trainee credit managers and to those already established.

Dick Bass
July 1991

Preface to 1998 revision

In this second revision to the third edition, I have endeavoured to remove most of the out-dated references, to remedy errors and omissions that have accumulated over nearly twenty years and to include coverage of what I believe to be 'current best practice' in credit management.

Dick Bass
July 1998

Acknowledgements

First and foremost I must thank my wife and family for their patience during the twelve months this book was in preparation. Secondly, I owe a great deal to Irene who typed (and re-typed) without complaint.

Many friends and colleagues have helped me, especially in the chapters concerned with export credit. I should particularly like to mention Graham Findlay of Grindlay Brandts Ltd, Nigel Allington and others from Credit Insurance Association Ltd, George Volsik of Bank of America, John Gallagher of Dun & Bradstreet Ltd, David Webb of GKN Ltd, Joe Binns of Fenchurch, Credit Insurance Services Ltd, Tom Hewson of Oxy Metal Industries Europe, Richard Evans and others from ECGD and Denzil Davos of Amalgamated Metal Corporation Ltd.

Finally — my thanks to the authors of the many publications I have consulted for information. A list of these is given in 'Further reading'.

Part One
Credit Management

Chapter 1

The nature and cost of credit

'Credit, like the honour of a female, is of too delicate a nature to be treated with laxity — the slightest hint may inflict an injury which no subsequent effort can repair.' (*The Morning Chronicle*, 1825.) There can hardly be a credit man unable to quote from his own experience an example of the truth of this aphorism.

The right to receive trade credit is very often taken for granted, which goes a long way towards explaining the need for tact and diplomacy. Industry and commerce would rapidly come to a halt if goods could only be sold to buyers able to pay cash on delivery, and indeed the whole concept of a mass production economy depends on continuous buying activity. The result of this need to give credit is that a substantial amount of cash is tied up in accounts receivable (otherwise known as debtors or sales ledger). This simple fact is the crux of all credit management problems. Successful business depends on money flowing through the company fast enough to meet all commitments. Profits derive from the efficient use of assets, but if the cash-flow is sluggish, the profits may never be realised.

The cost of credit

The starting point for efficient credit control is recognition of the cost of credit and its potential effects on profit and liquidity.

The cost of money borrowed from the bank is, let us assume, 12 per cent p.a. This gives a cost of 1 per cent for money owing for one month. A company selling on 'net monthly' or 'net 30 days' terms should therefore include in its price at least 1 per cent to cover the cost of credit. But this assumes that customers pay on time. If the average debtor period is three months, then this is costing 3 per cent.

The only way this can be recognised and properly accounted for is to charge interest for overdue payments — and conversely to give discount for cash-on-delivery. Exhibit 1.1 illustrates this, comparing Company A (giving no credit), Company B (receiving payments on time) and Company C (charging interest). The subject of payment terms, discounts and charges will be returned to in more detail later.

Exhibit 1.1

	Company A	Company B	Company C
Annual sales	600,000	600,000	600,000
Debtor level	Nil	50,000	150,000
		(1 month)	(3 months)
Net profit (5%) before credit cost	30,000	30,000	30,000
Less 1% discount for C.O.D payment	(6,000)		
Less 1% (cost of 1 month credit)		(6,000)	
Less 3% (cost of 3 months credit)			(18,000)
Plus interest @ 1% per month			12,000
REVISED NET PROFIT	24,000	24,000	24,000

Besides the cost of money, granting credit involves many other costs such as staff, space, equipment, stationery, credit information, debt recovery, etc. In most companies these costs should be readily obtainable but, unlike borrowing costs, they do not increase uniformly according to the length of credit taken. It is suggested, therefore, given the company is selling on credit terms, that these be regarded as part of the total administration cost built into the price structure. When a decision is taken to spend more money on credit management, care must be taken to relate the extra costs to the expected benefits.

A decision to recruit a credit manager at say £15,000 p.a., can only be justified if the likely result is to reduce bank interest by more than that through a reduction in level of debtors — as in Exhibit 1.2.

Exhibit 1.2

```
Before (Year 1)
Annual sales                            12,000,000
Debtors (90 days' sales)                 3,000,000
Cost of credit @ 12% p.a.                  360,000

After (Year 2)
Annual sales                            12,000,000
Debtors (75 days' sales)                 2,500,000
Cost of credit @ 12% p.a.                  300,000
```

```
INTEREST SAVED = £60,000 p.a.
```

The cost of credit in terms of bank borrowings can thus be measured fairly easily, but it goes further than this.

The effect of credit on profits

From Exhibit 1.1 it is clear that if Company C does *not* charge interest on its overdue accounts, the net profit of £24,000 (deducting the cost of one month's credit) will be reduced by a further £12,000. This might be counterbalanced by a reduction in stocks or delays in paying creditors but this is irrelevant. The effect of overdue accounts is a direct erosion of profit. Nonetheless, credit is sometimes used to promote sales more especially in export but also in the home market, usually in an endeavour to attract business from competitors. Long credit can have the opposite effect to that intended, however, since the cost of financing a higher level of debtors may outweigh the additional profit. This is illustrated in Exhibit 1.3. United Components Ltd is shown in Column A with a net profit of £5,400. A decision is made to give an extra 30 days' credit in the belief this will bring a 33.3 per cent increase in sales with a consequent increase of profit to £5,600 (Column B). In the event, sales only rise by 25 per cent and the increased profit is outweighed by higher credit costs (Column C). In desperation the

Exhibit 1.3

	A	B	C	D
Sales	120,000	160,000	150,000	180,000
Debtors	20,000	40,000	37,500	60,000
No.days credit	60	90	90	120
Net profit (6.5%)				
before credit cost	7,800	10,400	9,750	11,700
LESS				
Credit cost (12%)	(2,400)	(4,800)	(4,500)	(7,200)
REVISED NET PROFIT	5,400	5,600	5,250	4,500

company lengthens its terms by a further 30 days and turnover rises 50 per cent over the original level. The cost of financing 120-day credit, however, is so high that the end result is even worse (Column D).

The effect of credit on liquidity

Liquidity can be defined as the ease and speed with which current assets can be turned into cash sufficient to meet current liabilities. Stocks have to be turned into sales before they can generate cash and it is generally unprofitable to hold large cash balances. Debtors therefore hold the key to liquidity.

Exhibit 1.4 shows the working capital cycle.

In order to meet its regular commitments — wages and salaries, rent and rates, fuel and factory expenses, raw material and components, hire purchase and interest charges — a company depends on cash flowing through the system at a certain pace. If that pace slows down because debtors are out of control we have a 'cash flow' problem. In times of high inflation this problem is severely aggravated. This was vividly illustrated in the automotive industry in the mid-1970s. The near-monopoly suppliers of raw material imposed price increases and expected payment to terms from customers who could not recover the extra costs without protracted negotiations with the vehicle manufacturers.

If debtors are not being turned into cash fast enough, there can be only two reasons. Either credit terms are too long to support the business or there is an overdue situation. Credit terms have already been examined in the context of credit and profits. The problem of collecting — or avoiding — overdue

Exhibit 1.4

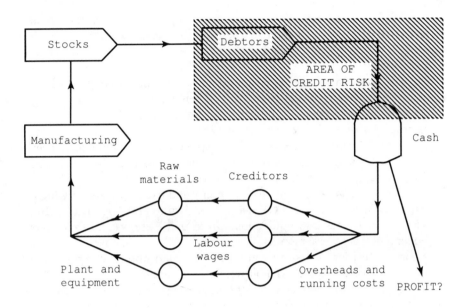

accounts is covered in Chapter 8. At this point it is interesting to examine the declining value of overdue accounts (see Exhibit 1.5). This table does not take inflation into account but merely expresses a realistic view of the problems a credit manager must cope with. It is not suggested that 70 per cent of debts over one year old will be 'bad debts' in the usual sense of the words. What is more likely is that the majority of such overdues are in dispute — probably with a large customer — and the end result will be a 'write-off' (hopefully shared) when neither party can prove the other's liability.

Exhibit 1.5

Current debts are worth	100%
30-day overdue debts are worth	90%
90-day overdue debts are worth	75%
180-day overdue debts are worth	50%
Debts over 12 months old are worth	30%

Bad debts

Bad debts are often regarded as the most important test of the credit manager's performance. Chapter 19 questions this view and deals with other ways of measuring performance. What needs to be examined here is the effect of bad debts on profits.

When a bad debt occurs it is important to consider what would have happened if that sale had not been made. There are two situations:

1 The factory is working at full capacity and has more orders than it can handle. An order is accepted from Company Y which later goes into liquidation owing 2–3 months' debts. Since business could have been accepted from alternative buyers, the eventual loss must be considered 100 per cent bad — with no mitigating circumstances.

2 The factory is working well below capacity and fixed costs are very high. An order is accepted from Company Z, known to be a 'high risk'. After six months it goes into liquidation. Given that there was no alternative buyer and that several months' sales were paid for, it could well have been a correct decision to take the business. The contribution to costs before insolvency occurs could even outweigh the bad debt.

This is a very difficult area for the credit manager. Correct decisions depend on a good knowledge of the company's costing system, and there may be other factors to consider such as the cost of redundancies if business is refused, or the need to build up a new market.

Exhibit 1.6

INDUSTRY	1995	1996	1997
Building & construction	704	762	741
Engineering & metals	522	498	511
Retail & wholesale dist.	780	777	782
Services	347	398	410
Textiles & clothing	252	312	395
Furniture & upholstery	206	153	72
Food & agriculture	236	248	197
Chemicals	68	68	101
Total	3115	3216	3209

Source: Number of business failures reported to Trade Indemnity Plc

The actual risks of incurring bad debts vary greatly from industry to industry. Engineering firms producing goods to individual customer specifications incur greater risks than distributors supplying 'off the shelf' as not only has the debt been lost but very probably the value of work-in-progress and even raw materials. Exhibit 1.6 shows the number of insolvencies notified to Trade Indemnity PLC in 1995–97, analysed into the major industries concerned. The question of bad debt reserves is considered in Chapter 19.

Exhibit 1.7

ADDITIONAL SALES REQUIRED TO RECOVER PROFIT LOST FROM BAD DEBTS

Value of bad debts (£)	Percentage pre-tax profit on sales		
	2%	5%	10%
500	25,000	10,000	5,000
1000	50,000	20,000	10,000
2000	100,000	40,000	20,000
5000	250,000	100,000	50,000
10000	500,000	200,000	100,000

Chapter 2

The role of credit management

The purpose of this chapter is to examine the role of the credit manager, to look at his relationships within the company, in particular the sales/credit relationship, and to consider the organisation of the credit department.

Over the last twenty years there have been many surveys of credit management in British industry, usually coinciding with periods of economic recession which bring to the fore the problems of costly overdues and insolvencies.

Delays in payment in the UK are contrasted with experience in the USA and the European Community. Whilst there are no reliable national statistics, surveys in recent years by the ICM, Dun and Bradstreet and Intrum Justitia indicate 'average' payment periods between 55 and 60 days. It seems safe to assume that, on average, invoices are paid during the third month after invoicing. Comparable statistics outside the UK are also hard to collect, but the consensus appears to be that UK payments are up to one month later than in the USA and the EC — even in France and Italy where delays are shorter on longer terms.

The cost of credit and its effects on profits and liquidity have been examined. It is clear that uncontrolled credit can rapidly bring disaster. Demands for statutory interest to be paid on overdue accounts ignore the real problem — which is the need for better credit management.

The credit manager

The status of the credit manager has undoubtedly improved in the last decade. Surveys conducted by CCN Business Information and published in 1989 and 1990 included the facts that out of 200 credit managers, approximately 42 per cent reported to a director and 77 per cent stated that they believed the status of credit management had increased. Regrettably there are still companies which have not yet woken up to the need for a specialist professional to take control of the sales ledger — and many that do employ a credit manager regard him (or her) primarily as a debt collector.

Exhibit 2.1 gives a brief job description which should fit most companies' requirements. Most of the other chapters in this book are an attempt to describe how these functions should be carried out and controlled.

Exhibit 2.1 The job of the credit manager

Basic function
Protection of the company's investment in debtors.
Principal tasks
(a) *Assessment of credit standing of both new and existing customers.*
(b) *Establishment of terms, having regard to the risk involved and the potential profit.*
(c) *Maintenance of the sales ledger.*
(d) *Monitoring and control of customer balances.*
(e) *Collection of payment as close to terms as possible without jeopardising future business.*

To return to the credit manager himself. Many arguments have been fought over his line of responsibility. The most usual arrangement is to report to the financial controller. Less frequently the credit manager is found within the sales/marketing area. This suggests a different view of the credit function, with the accent on granting credit rather than controlling it. There must be a real danger of inadequate control if the credit manager is subject to the immediate authority of the sales director.

There is a case for making the credit manager independent of both finance and marketing, i.e. reporting direct to the managing director.

This is unusual in the UK — more commonly found in the USA — and clearly demands a person of a very high calibre.

The best arrangement is perhaps for the credit department to be an independent unit under the finance director. The credit manager must have a fundamental grasp of and sympathy with both finance and marketing, but his ultimate responsibility must be to the head of finance.

Basis of credit policy

It is essential that a newly appointed credit manager be given clear guidance on company policy towards the granting of credit. A few companies provide a detailed written credit policy but the majority — whether deliberately or by neglect — do not do this, relying instead on the day-to-day relationships between the credit manager and his superior. This avoids the rigidity of a written policy but it can result in areas of doubt and uncertainty. Much will depend on the size of the firm. Generally speaking, the bigger the firm the greater the need for some form of written statement, if only to define the credit manager's authority and terms of reference. Guidelines of this kind are very desirable. There are two key points to be considered before the credit manager can operate effectively:

1   What level of receivables is regarded as acceptable? What is the nature of the market, i.e. steady or seasonal? The policy of the competition and the current marketing strategy will both have an influence but in most companies there will be a simple requirement — keep debtors as low as possible without losing business.

The credit manager must know what is expected of him and he must be prepared to argue his case if presented with a target which he feels can only be achieved by unduly stringent controls. This point will come up again when credit approval and collections are examined. It is very easy to set rigid standards, to accept only the demonstrably good risks and to demand payment to terms without exception. In the long run a policy of this nature is sure to restrict sales and lose goodwill.

2   Does the credit manager have authority to accept or reject new customers and new orders, to decide credit limits and terms of payment? Failure to clarify these issues lies at the root of many bad sales/credit relationships. Too often the credit manager assumes that he has authority when the sales manager has not been consulted and quite naturally resents interference with his customers. Responsibility for payment terms rests as frequently with sales as it does with credit control, although the questions of risk assessment and acceptance of new customers are more often decided by the credit department. This is hardly logical, since credit limits and payment terms are both different aspects of risk control and should not be determined in isolation from each other.

The best situation is where close liaison exists between credit and sales. Regular meetings between sales and credit departments can produce this. The sales manager will advise the credit manager of a new prospect who he

12

hopes will take a certain volume of goods. The credit manager's job is to check the financial condition of the prospect and try to set a credit limit which will accommodate the expected sales on normal terms. If the required limit cannot be justified, perhaps a solution can be found by shortening the terms or seeking some form of security. This theme will be returned to in Chapter 3, but whatever the answer it can only emerge from a close working relationship between sales and credit departments. The final decision should lie with the credit manager, since by training and experience he is better equipped to make a correct judgement. There must always be a 'court of appeal' to which a problem can be referred but this will rarely be used where a good relationship exists.

The sales/credit relationship

The need for this relationship to be positive and close cannot be overemphasised. It is very easy for the credit manager to be regarded as a negative figure whose purpose is to restrict sales, impose limits, demand money and stop deliveries. Such actions have to be taken — they will only be accepted and recognised as necessary if there exists between sales and credit a climate of confidence. Confidence is bred primarily by good personal relationships. The credit manager who rarely leaves his desk and bombards the marketing department with a stream of procedures, controls and blacklists, must not be surprised if his efforts are greeted by a lack of enthusiasm or even hostility. Written communication is certainly necessary, but how much better if it is preceded by a face-to-face chat or at least a 'phone-call to clear the way.

A more long-term route to confidence is education. The credit manager must ensure that his own staff have some basic product knowledge, as well as detailed information about customers. Of vital importance is the training of new sales staff, who must be taught at the outset the effect on profits of slow payments and insolvencies.

Regular meetings with sales management are another way to promote confidence. Items to be included in monthly credit meetings might be as shown in Exhibit 2.2. The wide range of topics given illustrates the need for a close working relationship with the sales team. Item 5 — 'Proposed blacklist' — is a particularly sensitive area over which friction can easily develop. The decision to suspend deliveries as a means of extracting payment and reducing the risk of a bad debt cannot be taken lightly in any company. Some form of early warning system is essential, to alert the sales manager to the situation and give him the opportunity of intervening. In large companies slow payment is often deliberate policy but the firm's buyer may not be aware that important supplies are being jeopardised. A telephone call from the creditor's

Exhibit 2.2

```
 1 Minutes of last month's meeting.
 2 Last month's collection results and debtor figures.
 3 Discussion on problem accounts.
 4 Review of outstanding queries.
 5 Proposed blacklist.
 6 Changes in distribution network.
 7 Marketing prospects.
 8 Cash discounts.
 9 Should we introduce a reservation of property
   clause?
10 Should we charge interest on overdue accounts?
11 Problems in controlling consignment stock.
12 Who should be responsible for export documentation?
13 Next month's sales conference.
14 Next month's programme of customer visits.
```

---

sales manager warning the buyer of the problem can sometimes accelerate a payment after all approaches to the accountant have failed.

The credit manager has to beware of handing responsibility over to the sales department. It is his job to obtain payment and to use every means at his disposal. This must include liaison with the sales department in the manner suggested above. At the end of the day payment has to be extracted before the profit is wiped out by extended credit.

Organisation of the credit department

In the early days of a firm's life the credit function either begins as part of the accountant's responsibilities or it remains under the personal control of the proprietor. Up to a certain point — determined by the pressures created by a growing business and by the nature of the business — this is perfectly adequate. As a firm grows, its list of buyers becomes longer and what began as an easily managed routine for the accountant develops into a full-time job. What often happens is that the accountant delegates the running of the sales ledger to one of his staff with no knowledge of or training in credit control. Sooner or later management realise that the cash is not flowing as fast as it should or maybe they are hit by a run of bad debts. Ultimately the need for proper credit management is recognised and a new person is appointed — often recruited from outside.

This type of development is typical of UK businesses. Even some of the biggest companies did not employ professional credit people until the 1960s or later. It is comparatively rare for a credit manager to be appointed from the start — although this often happens when American firms set up subsidiary companies in the UK.

A new credit manager is most often faced with the task of creating a credit department outside of the sales ledger organisation, unless he is established outside of the sales ledger with no responsibility for its operation. Opinions differ about which is the better arrangement. My own view is that good credit control is so dependent upon an up-to-date and efficient receivables system that it is essential for the credit manager to be in control. If he is not, then his own operation can be endangered by different priorities outside his control.

Given that the credit manager has the ledger responsibility, the key question to be answered is whether to employ separate people for credit and ledger work. The requirements of a good credit clerk are different from those of a good ledger clerk, and a separation of functions means that credit work is done by specialists whose time and energy is not diluted by ledger work. Ledger work does not demand the ability to talk fluently and persuasively over the telephone, the art of good correspondence or, above all, the capacity to detect problems and to make judgements. Credit work requires a higher level of skill and intelligence. There are nonetheless arguments for uniting the functions. Duplication of work (such as marking-up of payments prior to full reconciliation) is avoided. There is no danger of the credit person being let down because his section of the ledger has not been brought up to date. Against this there is the risk that ledger routines will expand to fill most of the day, leaving credit work to be fitted in later. Above all, good ledger clerks do not necessarily make good credit clerks.

A good solution is to organise the department in teams, where both credit clerks and ledger clerks work on the same accounts with either one capable in an emergency of doing the other's job.

This kind of organisation should not be regarded as applicable only to big companies with large credit departments. Many medium-sized companies could improve their cash-flow by employing, say two credit clerks and one ledger clerk instead of three ledger clerks who struggle to do the credit job after doing all the ledger routines. It is not unknown to find companies whose collection effort each month covers customers from A to P because time ran out.

The size of the credit operation must depend primarily on the number of active customers. The spread of business is also important. In many companies the 80–20 rule applies, i.e. 80 per cent of turnover goes to 20 per cent of customers. Where this applies, it is worth seeing whether that top layer of customers can be grouped together for special attention, rather than keeping to a straightforward alphabetical division. The following examples illustrate this, as well as giving an indication of total staff required (for both ledger and credit work):

Firm A   Turnover £500,000; 500 active accounts; business evenly spread. One or two clerks should suffice. There should be time for most overdue accounts to be telephoned, the biggest dozen or so being covered personally by the credit manager.

Firm B   Turnover £5,000,000; 1,000 active accounts; 70 per cent of sales going to 50 customers. One experienced clerk or supervisor is needed to deal with the top 50 names. The remainder can be handled by three clerks doing ledger work, administration and collections.

Every position in the credit department should be clearly defined and carry a written job description. The bigger a department becomes the more essential it is to have a clear reporting structure within which the responsibilities of clerks, supervisors and managers are positively defined. Exhibit 2.3 illustrates how the credit department of a medium-sized company (say 5,000 accounts, £50,000,000 turnover with 20 per cent export) might be arranged. The features to note in the structure are as follows:

1   Three teams report to the credit manager. One of the team members will be a supervisor or senior person.
2   The inclusion of a credit representative ensures that key accounts are properly controlled. Export customers also require specialist attention.
3   The administration section covers those routine activities vital to the whole department.

Credit training

The Institute of Credit Management regularly holds seminars, aimed either at different levels of credit people, at different aspects of credit management or at different parts of industry and commerce. A number of commercial firms are also active in this field. The quality varies considerably and it is recommended that the following points be checked in choosing a seminar:

a   Exactly what do you want? Specific advice on credit assessment or collection techniques or legal proceedings? Decide first what you are looking for.
b   Examine closely the subject-headings of the seminars in view. They should be broken down into enough detail for you to see whether your topics are being covered.
c   Who are the speakers? There are a fairly small number of practising credit managers involved regularly in seminars who have both the direct experience and the ability to communicate. There are also a number of academics who may be close enough to the action to speak convincingly.
d   How many speakers and sessions are there? More than four or five ses-

16

Exhibit 2.3

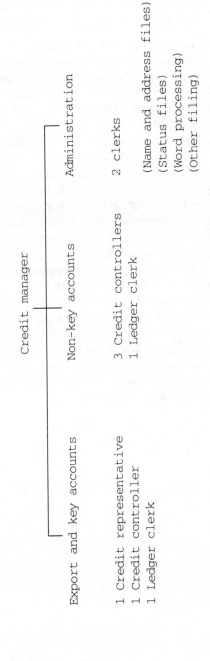

Credit manager

Export and key accounts   Non-key accounts   Administration

1 Credit representative
1 Credit controller
1 Ledger clerk

3 Credit controllers
1 Ledger clerk

2 clerks

(Name and address files)
(Status files)
(Word processing)
(Other filing)

sions in a day usually means that some of the topics can only be covered superficially. It is much better to have four speakers each talking for 45–60 minutes than seven 30-minute speakers.

e　There should be at least 45 minutes for questions from the floor.

f　There should be detailed notes provided from each speaker.

Membership of the Institute of Credit Management is essential for anyone intent on a career in credit. Study courses for ICM examinations are held by colleges of further education in many centres throughout the UK. Details may be obtained from the Institute of Credit Management, The Water Mill, Station Road, South Luffenham, Oakham, Leics. LE15 8NB.

Internal training should always be given to new starters in the credit department and, if possible, should also cater for existing staff. To be of any real value, internal training needs to be carefully planned and a timetable worked out, giving the new staff a logical progression through the various functions of the department at a reasonable pace. The credit manager or another senior person should regularly review progress — probably at weekly intervals. It is useful if brief sessions can be arranged with other departments so that the credit function can be put into context. Sales, shipping, data processing and accounts are all areas which inter-relate with credit. A period in the bought ledger is very useful in preparing someone for collection work — he can study the techniques employed by both sides.

There are some skills which have to be developed over a period of time and which can only be covered superficially in a training programme. Balance sheet analysis and credit assessment generally fall into this category. The development of sound credit judgement needs the pressure and conflicts of real situations. The credit manager must find time to sit with his staff and discuss current problems, explain why certain decisions were taken or why this customer should be considered a high risk.

Chapter 3

Payment terms and methods

Selection of the appropriate payment terms is a vital step in establishing the supplier/customer relationship, because this together with the credit limit decision will determine not only the required rate of cash-flow but also the volume of sales permissible. For example, a customer with a credit limit of £10,000 will only be able to purchase up to £60,000 annually if terms are net monthly, since the limit will be reached after two months' sales. A decision to give half-monthly terms in return for, say, 1 per cent discount would allow double that sales volume to be made within the same limit. This is illustrated in Exhibits 3.1 and 3.2 from which it is clear that shortening the terms has achieved the following results:

1 Turnover is doubled.
2 Cash flow is improved (83.3 per cent of sales paid within the sales period, compared to 66.6 per cent).
3 Credit risk is kept at £10,000.

Whilst net profit as a percentage of sales is down by 1 per cent (the cost of a reduction in the payment period), profits in total are substantially increased as a result of the extra sales.

This is a simple illustration of how the credit manager can make a positive contribution to profits through *flexibility* on terms. Most companies have standard terms of payment for home sales, but these should not be regarded as sacrosanct.

Exhibit 3.1 Company A: monthly terms

Month	Week of sale	Sales volume	Cash payment	Balance
1	1	1,250		1,250
	2	1,250		2,500
	3	1,250		3,750
	4	1,250		5,000
2	5	1,250		6,250
	6	1,250		7,500
	7	1,250		8,750
	8	1,250		10,000
		Payment due	5,000	5,000
3	9	1,250		6,250
	10	1,250		7,500
	11	1,250		8,750
	12	1,250		10,000
		Payment due	5,000	5,000

Sales in 3 months	= £15,000
Cash flow	= £10,000
Net profit at 5%	= £ 750

Factors influencing settlement terms

Before examining the different terms in use, it is worth listing the factors that influence the choice of terms. These are not given in any order of importance.
1 The normal practice of the trade. It is always very difficult to achieve sales if your terms do not at least match those offered by competitors.
2 The amount of working capital available to finance debtors. These costs have already been discussed.
3 The degree of credit risk. The higher the risk, the shorter the terms must be to achieve the required turnover.
4 The nature of the product. It is usual for quick-selling consumer products, especially perishable goods, to be sold on relatively short terms

Exhibit 3.2 Company B: half-monthly terrns

Month	Week of sale	Sales volume	Cash payment	Balance
1	1	2,500		2,500
	2	2,500		5,000
	3	2,500		7,500
	4	2,500		10,000
		Payment due	5,000	5,000
2	5	2,500		7,500
	6	2,500		10,000
		Payment due	5,000	5,000
	7	2,500		7,500
	8	2,500		10,000
		Payment due	5,000	5,000
3	9	2,500		7,500
	10	2,500		10,000
		Payment due	5,000	5,000
	11	2,500		7,500
	12	2,500		10,000
		Payment due	5,000	5,000

Sales in 3 months	= £30,000
Cash flow	= £25,000
Net profit	= £1,500
Less 1% discount for shorter terms	(£300)
Adjusted net profit	= £1,200

compared to single expensive items of equipment which may often require stage payments — both before and after delivery.

5   The size of order. Firms selling large quantities of 'off-the-shelf' goods frequently impose a minimum order value if credit terms are required, below which it is uneconomic to supply except on cash-with-order terms.

Credit terms in the UK

Whilst not an exhaustive list, this includes most terms commonly offered.

Net monthly This requires payment of one month's deliveries — or one month's invoices — to be made at the end of the following month. The chief difficulty here is that while many companies expect to purchase under these terms, all too frequently invoices for the last week's despatches are excluded from the bought ledger's listing on the grounds that the firm's computer has to cut-off by a certain date. The excuse that invoices were received after month-end or just too late for processing is well worn and very hard to counter.

Net 30 days Probably the most widely used term, this often ends up being seen as the same as net monthly. In many cases this is unavoidable since on a large account with invoices entered daily, it is unrealistic and impracticable to expect each daily batch of invoices to be covered by a separate payment. Nonetheless, terms of net 30 days are definitely more beneficial to the supplier since he has the right to request payment much sooner (an average of 15 days sooner) than under net monthly terms. High-risk accounts can therefore be controlled far more tightly and, indeed, a higher sales volume can be achieved, as we saw in Exhibit 3.2.

Net 14 days (or any number up to or above 30) The same principles apply here as for net 30 days. The shorter the period, the tighter the control. A long period, say 45, 60 or 90 days, is usually only found where there is a strong marketing reason. No matter how strong that reason may be, the credit manager has to be very sure that the risk is acceptable before agreeing.

Stage payments Where expensive plant or equipment is being sold, or where a long 'delivery' period is involved, e.g. in the building trade, it is normal to find stage or progress payments agreed. For machinery requiring a heavy capital outlay and a long manufacturing period, there is often a down payment, anything from 10 to 30 per cent, followed either by full payment on delivery or further stage payments at agreed intervals. In the building trade, if the contract is under RIBA rules, a supplier can claim payment at various stages providing he can submit the appropriate certificate.

Where tools are being manufactured, it is common practice for a down payment to be agreed, followed by a percentage on 'sample approval', followed by a final payment on delivery and acceptance. In any of these situations the buyer may require a retention, say 10 per cent of the purchase price, which is withheld for an agreed period or until an agreed event takes

22

place. For example, this could be the agreement of the main contractor's final account or the commissioning of a vessel or a factory.

It is vital for a supplier in these types of business to plan his cash-flow requirements and fix payment terms accordingly. It would be foolish to accept 20 per cent down-payment and the balance on completion in twelve months' time if the suppliers of raw material (which might amount to 50 per cent of the selling price) are going to demand 100 per cent payment by the time manufacture is only half completed.

All the above terms are related to time. There are others related to delivery, which may be used either because the credit risk is unacceptable or because the size of order does not justify the expense of maintaining a credit account.

Cash with order The most stringent terms. No work is commenced until payment.

Cash before shipment A little less harsh. Not recommended where goods are being produced to customer specification since non-payment will leave you with unsaleable goods. In any event, cheques should be cleared before goods are despatched. Note: 'pro-forma' terms may mean either cash with order or cash before shipment. To avoid confusion, it is best not to use the term 'pro-forma'.

Cash on delivery The driver is usually entrusted with obtaining payment before releasing the goods. As well as the danger noted above, there is the added possibility of a cheque being dishonoured.

Load over load Payment of this delivery has to be received before the next delivery is made. Normally only used in trades involving a regular weekly or monthly delivery.

Letter of Credit Normally found only in export transactions, Letter of Credit terms are occasionally used for domestic business. The buyer instructs his bank to open a Letter of Credit in favour of the supplier for the value of the order and payment is made by the bank on receipt of the supplier's invoice and/or signed delivery note. Unlike in the export trade, no documents of title are involved. It is merely a way of securing payment by a bank guarantee.

Cash discounts

A further group of settlement terms includes the granting of a cash discount in return for payment within an agreed period. In some businesses cash discounts are customary, as for example in the retail trade where such terms as '5% 7 days' ('2% 7 days' in the food trade) and '2½% 14 days' are often encountered.

Settlement terms of $2\frac{1}{2}$ per cent monthly were common in non-retail trades many years ago, but have now largely disappeared. Cash discounts are still prevalent in the USA and in many European countries, particularly terms of $\frac{1}{2}$ or 1 per cent for payment in 10 days with the alternative of paying net in 30 days.

There is considerable misunderstanding of the cost of cash discounts. A discount is a reward for prompt payment and its cost must, therefore, be related to the period of time gained by the supplier on his cash-flow. This presents an immediate difficulty in deciding when a customer would pay if no discount were offered. This will depend primarily on the ability of the customer to extract payment and on the liquidity of the customer. As an example, let us assume that 90 days' credit (from the end of month of invoicing) will be taken if no discount is offered. It is decided to offer 2½ per cent for payment by the end of the first month after the month of invoicing. The true annual cost of this is calculated in Exhibit 3.3.

Exhibit 3.3

Amount of time gained, i.e. 90 days less 30 days = 60 days, divided into 365 to produce the annual rate, multiplied by the rate of discount. Thus:

$$\frac{365}{90 - 30} \times 2.5 = 15\% \text{ approximately}$$

Unless the borrowing cost of the supplier exceeded 15 per cent p.a., the above would represent an uneconomic rate. Recent surveys indicate a decline in the use of discounts and it is difficult to justify their use (apart from where dictated by custom and practice) on an 'across-the-board' basis. Quite apart from the cost, a major problem is that customers will tend to take discounts even when their payments arrive outside the qualifying period. To allow X days' grace merely pushes the problem further ahead. The inevitable result is either regular 'write-offs' of unearned discounts or a prolonged and often fruitless follow-up procedure — or maybe even both of these.

Discounts can be valuable however if used selectively. A reduction of the payment period also reduces the risk and the use of discounts to increase sales volume on high-risk accounts is recommended.

At the beginning of this chapter there was an example of this (see Exhibit 3.2). A further illustration is where a customer with a very low credit standing is persuaded to buy on a 'cash before shipment' basis in return for a discount. The discount given should, if possible, equate to the actual cost of money, i.e. if normal bank lending rate is 12 per cent p.a., a discount of 1½ per cent would be fair. A higher discount still must also be regarded as worthwhile if the end result is to produce a substantial increase in sales and profits.

24

Whenever discount terms are agreed, they must be practicable. To offer a discount for payment in 7 or even 10 days is presuming no delays in delivery or postal transit. In practice such short terms are almost unworkable without the use of a personal delivery and cash-collection service.

Interest charges

In contrast to discounts, the practice of charging interest on overdue accounts appears to be on the increase. Periods of high interest rates, coupled with periods of strained liquidity, regularly cause many companies to consider interest-charging as a means of accelerating payments. Four main problems have to be faced.

1   Interest on overdue payments may only be charged if it is specifically permitted in the company's Conditions of Sale. If it is decided to amend these conditions to include an appropriate clause on interest, it is advisable for the company to tell its customers about the change, thereby running some slight risk of loss of goodwill or (far worse) retaliatory action from customers who are also suppliers. If the decision is taken, it is prudent to word the amendment in such a way as to leave the company with the *option* of charging interest. At the same time, care must be taken to avoid giving the customer the option of paying to terms or paying late with interest.

2   The effect on business must be considered. If competitors are not charging interest, there is a real danger that some business will be lost. In a very competitive market, a decision to 'go it alone' could be extremely harmful.

3   What rate of interest should be charged? Clearly it must be high enough to avoid being an attractive alternative to payment within terms. On the other hand, to be too high runs the risk of being considered extortionate. A reasonable compromise would be to charge somewhere between 4 and 6 per cent above the Bank of England minimum lending rate.

4   What happens if customers refuse to pay interest charges? This is similar to the problem of unearned discount. Unless the supplier is prepared to go to extreme lengths to enforce payment, there is little point in charging. Ultimately, the strength of the supplier in the market will determine this question.

A serious attempt to introduce and enforce the charging of interest could well be detrimental to customer goodwill, without having any appreciable effect on cash-flow. There is nonetheless some merit in *reserving the right* to charge interest, so that it can be exercised from time to time at the discretion of the credit manager.

In 1998 the U.K. government indicated its intention of phasing in, over several years, a statutory right to charge interest on late payment. Initially only small businesses would be allowed this right against large firms. The second phase would allow small businesses to charge all customers. In the final stage all businesses would have the right to charge all customers. It seems unlikely that such legislation will achieve its objectives of improving cash-flow generally and benefitting small firms in particular. The principal arguments against it are that it ignores the relative commercial strengths and weaknesses of large customers, and small suppliers and that it could result in undue reliance on the legal right to interest rather than the need for strong credit management.

Methods of payment

Having agreed terms with the buyer, the next step should be to determine the manner of payment. In practice this is rarely considered. Payment by cheque or bank transfer is regarded as normal, any other method being exceptional — unless peculiar to a certain trade or business. Nonetheless, the credit manager should be aware not only of the alternatives but also of the pros and cons of all payment methods.

1 *Cheque* Post-dated cheques should not be accepted, except in exceptional circumstances, since they are an obvious pointer to liquidity problems. The problem of dishonoured cheques will be dealt with in Chapter 9.

2 *Credit transfer, through BACS (bankers automated clearing system)* Some companies prefer to pay all their suppliers by credit transfer. A considerable amount of time is saved by not having to sign cheques but there is some loss of flexibility to the supplier. Nonetheless receipt of a bank transfer represents cleared funds, compared to a 2–3 day delay in cheque clearance plus the risk of dishonour. This benefit outweighs the possible drawbacks. A supplier should not however treat a remittance advice as proof of payment. This can only be obtained by verifying a credit entry on the bank statement.

3 *Direct debit* This is a system whereby a supplier's bank collects payment from the customer's bank under the terms of a direct debit mandate. A mandate can allow either fixed or variable amounts to be collected. This arrangement is particularly suitable for regular payments such as insurance premiums, rental charges, maintenance charges and annual subscriptions. Its use for variable payments is not so widespread since it requires a very high degree of trust between buyer and seller. The work needed to set up a customer is time-consuming, but the benefits are considerable, particularly where large numbers of small payments are involved.

4 *Bills of Exchange* In domestic trade there has been a revival of interest

in bills (sometimes referred to as 'trade bills'). A bill is an unconditional order to pay the amount stated on a given date. It has to be accepted for payment by the debtor and is payable to the creditor. Bills are normally drawn by the creditor — although they can be raised and accepted by the debtor and then passed to the creditor who signs as drawer. The benefits of using bills are as follows:

a   An accepted bill is better than a promise to send a cheque. No further initiative is required of the customer.

b   An accepted bill is normally presented for payment at the customer's bank. Failure to have sufficient funds to meet the bill will obviously embarrass the customer with his bank. Unless there are no funds at all, the holder of an accepted bill is in a better position than a supplier awaiting a cheque.

c   A supplier can sue on a dishonoured bill, no other evidence of debt being required.

d   An accepted bill can be discounted with a bank if the money is needed before maturity.

Bills are particularly useful to determine a series of payments under a special arrangement. A customer in temporary cash-flow trouble might agree to clear a debt in six installments. The supplier who holds six accepted bills is in a stronger position than one who depends on six cheques being sent.

When bills are discounted it is most important to keep their value on record against the customer's credit limit. If a discounted bill is dishonoured, the bank has recourse to the drawer, i.e. the supplier. For the same reason, it is illogical for longer credit terms to be extended because a customer is paying by bill rather than by cheque. Whilst the holder of accepted bills is in a better position, nonetheless insolvency will strike equally hard and the ultimate credit risk remains the same. Occasionally, accepted bills are endorsed by a third party, generally the buyer's parent company or possibly a main shareholder or the proprietor. Providing the financial standing of the guarantor is known to be good, this adds very considerably to the strength of a bill. It is seldom found that a UK public company is willing to endorse bills accepted by a subsidiary or associate company. Banks do so even less frequently. A risk-free method of using a bill of exchange is to have the bill endorsed by the customer's bank before the goods or services are supplied. The effect is to create security similar to that provided by a letter of credit, but with a far simpler procedure which is known as an aval.

5   *Contra accounts*   Where firms are both buying from and selling to one another, it is sensible to arrange a regular offset so that one party pays the net balance. Whilst apparently simple, this can be very difficult to run for a number of reasons:

a   Disputed items prevent a clean reconciliation and may even lead to both parties claiming a balance in their favour.

b   Differences in internal cut-off dates and payment dates can easily cause friction.

c   Unless both companies supply each other every month, there will be arguments about when the balance should be paid.

It is essential that any contra arrangement be set out in writing and signed by both parties; otherwise sooner or later problems of the kind indicated above will arise. Also, if one company becomes insolvent, the right of the other to set-off debts will only be admitted by a Receiver or Liquidator if there is clear evidence in writing.

6   *Electronic funds transfer*   As yet in its infancy, this method of payment is sure to become more widespread. Where supplier and customer have an established trading relationship using electronic data interchange (EDI), it is possible for EDI to be extended beyond the communication of quotations, orders and invoices to the transmission of payments and remittance details direct from the customer's bank to the supplier's bank. The initiative for such arrangements must come from the clearing banks, several of whom are now offering an EDI trade payment service to selected major customers. The advantage to the supplier is clear when compared to cheque payments since the time-scale between despatch of payment and receipt of cleared funds would be reduced to three days. When compared to payment by BACS credit transfer, however, the only benefit would appear to be receipt of remittance advice information by computer rather than by post. Where the amounts paid are capable of instant and infallible reconciliation, a bank tape or disc can be interfaced into the supplier's sales ledger thus eliminating the need for manual cash allocation. Such applications would be the exception rather than the rule.

7   *Credit card*   Payment by corporate credit card (as opposed to a personal card) is a growing method, especially useful for low-value, high-volume transactions such as office stationary. In return for complete certainty of payment, the supplier pays an agreed percentage of turnover to the credit card provider.

Reservation of property

Companies supplying goods which are readily identifiable and distinguishable one from another may obtain protection from a retention of title clause in their Conditions of Sale. Such a clause will prohibit the buyer from obtaining title until payment has been made and can give the supplier preferential status in a receivership, liquidation or bankruptcy.

There are, however, many pitfalls in the way of successful R.O.T. claims.

The principal ones a credit manager should be aware of are as follows:

a   The R.O.T. clause must be contained in the supplier's terms and conditions of sale which must be quoted on all order acknowledgements. If the inclusion represents a change in terms, there must be evidence that the buyer's attention was drawn to the change.

b   The goods must retain their original identity and not have been incorporated or processed into a different product.

c   The unpaid goods must be capable of being clearly identified and cross-referred to unpaid invoices.

d   The goods must still be in possession of the buyer. If they have been sold to a third party, recovery of their value may be possible, but only if the R.O.T. clause is worded in such a way that a *fiduciary relationship* is created. To achieve this requires expert legal advice.

A type of R.O.T. clause which has come into frequent use in recent years is the *all-monies clause*. A typical wording is as follows:

> Title in goods delivered shall not pass to the buyer until the seller is paid in full for all goods supplied to the buyer hereunder previously.

Such a clause has not yet been fully tested in the courts, so its effectiveness should not be relied upon. The most famous case concerned with the subject of reservation of property was Romalpa (1976) which opened the doors to a controversy which has endured ever since.

Two final words of advice are offered:

1   Do not supply goods to an uncreditworthy buyer in the belief that R.O.T. will give sufficient protection.

2   If a receiver or liquidator is appointed to a customer owing debts covered by R.O.T., it is essential to obtain immediate acceptance by the receiver, etc. that this situation exists. In many cases a personal visit to identify, and, if necessary, clearly label such goods will be very worthwhile. Perseverance is called for, since a receiver will fight to avoid the asset value being reduced and the smallest inconsistency or lack of evidence can prove fatal.

Chapter 4

Risk assessment — basic steps

The correct evaluation of credit risk is the most difficult part of the credit manager's job. It is often neglected and sometimes left to the judgement of the sales manager. This tends to happen in companies where the credit manager is regarded primarily (or solely) as a debt collector, with no interest or involvement in a sale until the goods have left the factory. This is 'credit control' as opposed to 'credit management', and it ignores the potential contribution to profits which a trained credit manager can bring.

To select only good risks or safe customers is relatively easy, but the company which follows this policy will not keep its factory busy for long or retain its share of the market. Maximising sales and profits can only be achieved by trading with the marginal accounts — and this demands good credit management.

The credit manager, therefore, has a very positive function. He must assess the degree of risk the company will be exposed to in trading with both existing and potential buyers. Payment terms and credit limits must be established in order to achieve the maximum turnover compatible with that risk. If this is done carefully and with good judgement, the other main part of the credit job — collecting the cash — will be performed that much more effectively. The nature and timing of follow-up procedures should be dictated by the level of risk. The degree of sympathy or consideration extended to a customer asking for extra time must be determined by knowledge of the financial strength and other resources at his disposal.

It is not only the so-called 'marginal' accounts which need careful assessment. Major buyers must also be kept under review. Where danger signals are spotted — perhaps by a steady increase in debt financing not accompanied by rising profits — the credit manager must consult with his sales and marketing colleagues so that a positive decision is taken to continue, to restrict or even to cease trading. When such problems arise with major customers, the credit viewpoint should form part of a general business decision, in which the risk of non-payment has to be balanced against other factors such as the stoppage of a production line and the laying-off of workers.

Risk assessment is based on information which is available from a variety of sources. These are covered both in this chapter and Chapter 5.

Customer identity

One of the key points in establishing customer identity is the type of business organization — in particular whether it is a limited company. Precise identity is crucial, principally to ensure that contractual relations are established with the correct legal entity. A clear distinction must be made between such names as J. Wilson & Sons, J. Wilson & Sons Ltd and J. Wilson Ltd. If legal action has to be taken to obtain payment, both time and money will be lost if proceedings are started against the wrong name. A further reason is to ensure that invoices are correctly addressed, particularly when the customer is part of a large group.

A business letter-head obtained by the sales person is very desirable, failing this a business card. When the prospect is part of a group, a phone-call may be useful to remove any uncertainty over the exact name, trading style or invoicing address.

Trade reference

The traditional method of credit checking — and sometimes the only one — is to ask for two trade references before an account is opened. If relied upon solely, this is a most unsatisfactory procedure, since it can be assumed that companies will not quote suppliers likely to give a bad report; some companies go even further and deliberately cultivate good references by selective prompt payment. Nonetheless, references can be helpful, particularly with small buyers who provide local referees.

The request for trade references should be made formally and should incorporate a request for credit terms. This is easily done by using a standard pre-printed form, as in Exhibit 4.1.

Exhibit 4.1 Specimen request for references

Attention: Credit Department

I/We request you to open a credit account in the
name of:

I/We give below the names and addresses of referees
of whom the customary enquiries may be made.

I/We note that payment terms are net 30 days from
date of invoice and agree to pay in accordance with
these terms.

Expected maximum amount of credit required: £
                                   total/monthly*
                              *(delete as appropriate)

    Signature_____

    Position_____

Trade referees

(1) Name: Address:

(2) Name: Address:

(NB: Referees should be able to speak for credit figures comparable with
that indicated above.)

Points to note are as follows:

1 The precise name, address and trading style of the buyer are established. A very common problem is to be asked to clear an order from a firm whose name is either misquoted or misspelt. It is essential to get the name absolutely correct when the account is first opened. To this end it is helpful to instruct the sales force to ask for a letterhead when visiting a prospect.

2 Attention is drawn to the standard conditions of payment. The buyer is required to sign his acceptance of these terms. (This document should be filed carefully, as it can prove invaluable to refute subsequent allegations that 'your sales representative said we needn't pay for three months'.)

3 The buyer is asked to indicate his expected level of business. This can be a useful guide to the credit limit decision (see Chapter 6) and may be balanced against the natural optimism of the sales representative who may be predicting a far higher figure!

4 It is made clear that the references supplied must be able to speak for a similar level of business to that envisaged. There is little point in receiving references which give good experience up to £500 monthly if you want to sell £5,000 per month.

5 It is also made clear to the customer that the account is going to be handled in a business-like manner. For a prospective customer to obtain the impression that anyone can obtain credit merely by placing an order is bad and will not improve the seller's reputation.

Having obtained a completed reference form, the credit manager must contact the referees. Here again, the use of a standard format is recommend, as in Exhibit 4.2.

The question asked are straightforward and as detailed as necessary to produce helpful answers. What is of equal importance is to whom they are addressed. Some guidelines are as follows. Are the referees reputable companies who can be relied upon to give honest answers? Or does closer examination reveal connections with the potential buyer — either through common directors or an actual legal/financial association? If the amount of credit in view is substantial it may be worth telephoning the credit manager of the referee company. This should certainly be done if the answers on the forms are contradictory (between two referees) or if any additional comment is given which needs following up. Much can be said over the telephone which is better not put on paper.

A final point on trade referees — always send a reply-paid envelope. Credit managers are busy people and small courtesies are appreciated.

Exhibit 4.2 Specimen reference letter

```
1 How long have you known          .......months
        this firm?                 ........years
                                   Many years

2 How much credit do you           £
    normally allow?

3 What are your payment terms?      Pro-forma
                                    Monthly
                                    ........days

4 Are payments generally made       To terms
    to your satisfaction?           Up to 1 month
                                       late
                                    More than 1 month
                                       month late
                                    Very slow/
                                       irregular

5 Any other relevant information will be appreciated:
```

```
The above information is given in strict confidence
and without responsibility on my/our part.
```

```
Date:_____       Signed:_____
```

Bank references

Anyone requiring a bank reference must obtain the written consent of the subject. A special form (issued by the banks) has to be used. This is reproduced in Exhibit 4.3. Once signed by the subject, the form is sent to the bank with the appropriate fee, which varies at around £10. The bank's reply will come directly to the enquirer.

Some skill is needed to interpret bank references correctly and the type of reply given to such an enquiry will fall under one of three headings:

a   An unqualified, positive assurance that the risk is good, such as the word 'undoubted'. Not given frequently and therefore of high value.

b   A general indication that the firm in question is operating normally — lacking the positive tenor of (*a*) above. Commonly used references under this heading are 'Respectably constituted private limited company, considered good for its normal engagements', or '... we do not think the company would undertake any engagements it could not fulfil'. Such references are of little value.

c   A rather guarded statement whose message lies in what is not said rather than in what is said. Examples of this type are: '... their capital appears to be rather fully employed', or (worse) '... we regret we are unable to speak for your figures'. Such replies must immediately put the credit manager on his guard.

This major change in the obtaining of bank references has had a significant effect. Whilst much criticised in the past, bank references were traditionally regarded as a prime source of information. The difficulty and cost of obtaining them have caused many credit managers to drop them altogether and have given a boost to credit reporting agencies; these are discussed later in this chapter.

A final point on bank references is that the bank is obliged to state the fact that 'charges are registered' when it is aware of this fact. This tells the enquirer that all or part of the assets of the prospective buyer are pledged as security for a loan. The significance of this will be examined in Chapter 5.

Agency registers

Probably the best known is the Dun & Bradstreet Credit Register, available only on CD — although some companies still have a microfiche version. It contains information on over 2 million UK limited and non-limited companies. Data includes name and address, trading style, date established, registration details (ltd cos.), issued capital, turnover, bank details, employees, date of last filed accounts, mortgage and charges indicator, county court judgement indicator, parent details, D & B rating and maximum credit recommendation. CDs are updated and replaced monthly. Users can store information from their enquiries on the data-base, thus giving them status files on selected businesses.

This register is an extremely valuable aid to credit assessment, but it should not be used as the sole criterion. Its main value lies in providing a fast reference from which the next step may be immediate order acceptance or further investigation. The fact that an order for £5,000 is outside the rating

Exhibit 4.3 Combined enquiry and consent form

Private and confidential

Bank name: Branch: Address: Sort code No:	**Enquiry to: The Manager**
Name: Address: Post code: Telephone No: Fax No: Date: Contact Name:	**Enquiry from:**
Name of customer Account No: Customer's address:	**Information requested on:** I/We request your opinion as to the means and standing of: and his/her/their trustworthiness in the way of business to the extent of £
To be completed by the person/company who is the subject of the enquiry. Subject's full name Subject's bank Full name and address of enquirer	**Consent** I/We consent to Bank plc providing a reference on me/us to: Signed Date

(of, say, £500) does not mean that the risk is unacceptably high. It is merely an indication that £5,000 is above the normal amount of credit given and that more facts must be obtained before making a decision.

36

Agency reports

There are in the UK a large number of reporting agencies, some offering a service related to specific trades or industries and others giving a general service. It is worth checking if there is a specialised agency for your particular industry, since these can frequently offer more detailed information.

The features that should be included in a credit report are as follows:

1 Full name and registered address. Also any trading styles used.
2 Names of proprietors, partners or directors.
3 Amount of authorised and issued capital.
4 Details of any associations with other companies, including associations through common directors. This section should clearly indicate the nature and extent of control exercised by other companies.
5 Brief particulars of the firm's operations, including whereabouts of factories and branches.
6 An extract from, if not the entire, latest Balance Sheet and Profit and Loss Account. The extract should include details of current assets and current liabilities.
7 A list of secured charges.
8 Details of any County Court judgements recorded within the last twelve months.
9 Name and address of bankers.
10 The recent payment experience of a number of other suppliers (including comments supplied).

Many agencies also indicate the amount of credit they regard as being 'within scope'. Generally any figures given are based on information obtained from other suppliers and are not the result of any attempt at balance sheet analysis. Where a comment is provided such as 'care recommended' or 'the account should be supervised closely', these again are frequently derived from suppliers' comments, often supplemented by the enquiry agent's own experience in collecting overdue debts.

As with the use of an agency register, a credit report is of most value when it indicates the proposed business to be well within the experience of other suppliers. Failing this, its chief use may be in the balance sheet details — provided these are of recent date.

On-line information

A number of the larger reporting agencies maintain computer databanks of credit information. These include Dun & Bradstreet Ltd, Experian Ltd, ICC Information Group Ltd, Equifax Europe (who also own Infocheck Ltd, another major provider) and Graydon UK Ltd. The information available usually takes the form of a credit report, starting with company registration details and progressing to extracts from the last three or four years' filed accounts. It should be noted that not all agencies carry the latest accounts for all limited companies. Payment behaviour records may also be included, together with county court judgements, balance sheet ratios and industry comparisons for those ratios, and winding-up orders. The cost of these on-line systems varies considerably and the prudent credit manager will check on several before committing his company. Apart from usage, costs should be confined to a modem and a telephone line. Many of these agencies have set up web-sites on the Internet.

The credit manager should also be aware of the difference between the type of agency described above, which assembles public record information and may add comparative statistics, standardised comments on financial strength and a credit limit, and other smaller agencies which provide some real added value in the form of an interpretation and commentary on the general condition of the subject company. Such agencies are not usually 'on-line', so the credit manager may have to choose between speed and added value.

A valuable facility offered by most of these agencies is a 'constant watch' service. The client either gives the agency his complete customer list or a list of those he regards as high risk or of critical importance. The agency undertakes to inform the client immediately of any significant events, such as the filing of annual accounts, the presentation of a winding-up petition, the entry of a county court judgement, or the registration of a debenture.

Trade and competitors' opinions and credit grapevine

By trade opinions is meant the opinions of suppliers *not* already quoted as referees. These may include competitors.

Sales staff should be trained to make a mental note of other suppliers' names when visiting the factory or the buyer's office. A telephone call between credit managers can be very informative and often leads to a fruitful exchange on other mutual customers.

Where possible this interchange should be developed with other firms in the industry, who may or may not be direct competitors. In a number of UK industries there are credit interchange groups, consisting of anything from 6 to 30 suppliers who meet regularly and exchange experience and information on common customers. Some go beyond this and co-operate on credit training for their staff. These groups can only succeed if the individual credit managers have complete faith in the integrity of all members. A credit manager who uses membership primarily as a means of obtaining 'inside' or 'advance' information to promote his own company's sales has no place there and will be swiftly found out. The real value is in providing an early warning system about bad payers, in safeguarding each other against potential bad debts and in helping one another on matters of fact, such as the appointment of a new finance director or a change in the internal accounting structure or the invoice passing procedure.

It is advisable for the credit manager to tell the finance director (if not the marketing director) of his intention to join such an interchange group.

Further References

Dun & Bradstreet are the leading providers of business information. Publications (either on CD-ROM, on disc or in book form) include Who Owns Whom, Key British Enterprises, Key Business Ratios and UK Executives Report. This last title includes directorships and private addresses and is accessible on-line via the D & B Access software.

The sales representative's report

Frequently this will be the only first-hand personal information available to the credit manager and potentially it is of high value. But its actual value depends almost entirely on the degree of credit education prevailing in the sales force. A sales representative trained in the importance of credit can help in risk-assessment in several different ways by reporting on:
1   The character and competence of the management.
2   The level of activity and the general impression obtained from factory and office
3   The names of other suppliers who may be useful contacts.
4   Details of the major customers of the client and an assessment of the product.
5   The anticipated level of business.

If the credit manager is able to influence the design and format of the sales representative's report, he should be able to stimulate answers to such questions. Regular contact with the sales staff will also help to dispel any impression that his object is merely to control and restrict sales. In all of this, however, the credit manager must never forget that the sales representative's primary job is to sell and that glowing opinions of new prospects may be the result of rose-tinted spectacles!

Summary

All the avenues of enquiry detailed in this chapter should be explored, since to rely on one or two sources alone carries the risk that they may be out of date or misinformed. A decision based on a credit report which is later found to be inaccurate will deal a severe blow to the credit manager's reputation.

Very often time is too short and a decision has to be made within the day. The credit manager must rely on his network of contacts, using phone, fax and e-mail, and upon his on-line information sources.

Many credit decisions can be made purely on the information available from the 'basic' sources covered in this chapter. Whenever this information is inadequate or contradictory, or the size of the credit decision demands fuller investigation, the credit manager must proceed to the 'depth' sources covered in the next chapter.

Chapter 5

Risk assessment — in-depth investigation

The most important source of detailed information is the annual accounts. It must be remembered however that a balance sheet is a statement of the company's finances on one day, different the previous day and different the day after. Even if the accounts were examined the day they were completed, this would usually be at least four to six months after the financial year-end. When you add to this the delays commonly experienced before accounts are lodged at the Companies Registry, the interval between the balance sheet date and the date of analysis is rarely under twelve months and often nearer two years.

The Companies Registry is at Cardiff but a reading room facility is maintained at Companies House in London where the last three years' accounts are recorded on microfilm. Many credit agencies offer a balance sheet service to enquirers not able to visit the Registry and some of the larger ones have set up computer databases containing the last three or four years' accounts and other information (see Chapter 4 under *Agency reports*). By law (*The Companies Act*, 1985) a public company has to file accounts within seven months of its financial year-end and a private company within ten months.

Over a million company records are held on the live register and over 100,000 are added every year. Enquiries can be made on line and documents are also available by post or fax.

Despite all these benefits from technology, the credit manager will still often be frustrated by the delayed filing of accounts. To counter this, the credit manager should not hesitate to ask the prospect direct for a sight of the

41

latest accounts. He has ample justification for such a request, considering that a bank or finance company would not contemplate an investment without a close examination of the accounts. The trade creditor is also being expected to invest money in the prospect — in the form of goods or services — and moreover he will lack the security commonly afforded to a banker. Another point worth remembering is the dependence customers have on their key suppliers. This gives weight to the request for information.

Whilst there are still companies who resent being asked for their accounts and who refuse on the grounds of privacy — or without giving any reason — there is a general tendency towards a positive response. Sometimes it is even possible to see management accounts made up to the previous month-end, which, although unaudited, are the nearest thing to a completely up-to-date financial picture. Whenever accounts are produced for examination, it is essential that confidence is respected. The credit manager must not, on his return to the office, promptly circulate, to all and sundry, copies of accounts supplied to him in confidence.

Before examining the various ratios found in the accounts, there are a number of precepts which the credit analyst should learn:

1 Never form an opinion on one year's figures. It is more important to identify trends, preferably over three years or more (or over several months if management accounts are involved).

2 Always be aware of distortions caused by inter-company transactions. More and more companies are linking together in groups for tax advantages, and it is often difficult to assess the financial position of any one company without surveying other members of the group.

3 Remember that it is just as easy for a profitable company to become insolvent as an unprofitable one. Paper profits are of no value unless the rate of cash-flow is enough to meet the needs of the business.

4 Try to relate a company's financial performance to the industry in which it operates. ICC Information Group Ltd regularly publish *Industrial Performance Analysis* which gives a three-year detailed comparison of the average performance of companies in 200 business sectors within 27 major industries under various headings including return on capital employed, liquidity, stock turnover and credit period. What one hopes to find is a better performance than the average, if the company is to be

regarded as successful. Similar comparisons are available from some on-line credit reporting systems including ICC themselves.

Analysis of balance sheets and profit and loss accounts

The following quotation from 'Business failures in England and Wales' [R. Brough, *Business Ratios*, No. 2 (1967)] is still valid.

'The very small commitment of proprietors' personal capital hardly seems to have prevented them from obtaining credit for an infinitely larger amount. Creditors seem to have been, in fact, the true entrepreneurs in many companies, so far as the risk-bearing function of entrepreneurship is concerned.'

It is interesting to note that approximately 50 per cent of all new companies fail within 2 years of starting.

The types of business most prone to failure during 1990–93, as a percentage of the total, were:

Building and construction	30%
Engineering and metals	22%
Retail and wholesale distribution	17%

There are many ways of reading a balance sheet, depending on the viewpoint of the reader. The credit manager is trying to assess the ability of the prospect to meet its commitments over a period, sometimes fairly short, i.e. under six months, but often in the context of a long-term relationship. There are three principal aspects of a company's financial standing on which a credit analyst should concentrate:
1 Solvency.
2 Profitability.
3 Capital strength.

Solvency

By solvency is meant the ability of a company to meet its current debts, i.e. those due within one year of balance sheet date, from its current assets (those capable of being turned into cash within one year). The obvious first test of solvency is to compare one with the other. This is known as the current ratio:

$$\frac{\text{Current assets}}{\text{Current liabilities}}$$

The traditional 'good' ratio is 2:1, as is seen in Exhibit 5.1. But examination of UK company balance sheets shows a steady decline in the average current ratio from around 2:1 in the early 1960s, to 1.5:1 in the mid-1970s, to nearer 1:1 in the late 1980s. The main danger in relying on this ratio as the key to solvency is the inclusion of stocks. A high stock figure may include slow-moving or obsolescent items that may never be sold. To overcome this problem, another ratio is calculated — the quick ratio or 'acid test':

$$\frac{\text{Current assets less stocks}}{\text{Current liabilities}}$$

A 1:1 ratio used to be regarded as a necessary sign of liquidity, but many companies have proved capable of surviving on far thinner ratios than this. One reason is that bank overdrafts, whilst often substantial and granted on a short-term basis, are commonly renewed from year to year. Nonetheless the credit analyst should be particularly wary of an adverse quick ratio since UK banks are not slow to safeguard their loans and overdrafts in times of financial strain.

The quality of debtors as a current asset should also be checked. Providing turnover figures are available, the collection period can be calculated to give an idea of the rate of cash-flow.

$$\text{Collection period in days} = \frac{\text{Debtors} \times 365}{\text{Sales}}$$

If receivables are being turned over only three or four times a year compared to an industry average of say 65–70 days, this points to a lack of credit control — which the company may try to compensate for by slow payment of its own suppliers.

In all these calculations, the actual ratios are less important than the trend over a period of years. If this can also be compared with the average for the industry, the analysis becomes more valuable.

To summarise, in examining solvency ratios the credit manager is seeking evidence as to whether or not the company is growing less or more capable of covering current debts with current assets and whether slow payment may be expected because of inadequate credit control.

Profitability

A company that does not make profits will ultimately cease trading since it is not fulfilling its *raison d'être*. In business a company cannot stand still, except

Exhibit 5.1   XYZ Co. Ltd

Current assets

Stocks	500
Debtors	620
Cash	50
TOTAL CURRENT ASSETS	1,170

Less **Current liabilities**

Creditors	380
Taxation	200
NET CURRENT ASSETS	590

for very short periods, and the credit analyst must look for signs of healthy growth or of decline. As in all ratios, trends are all-important and must be put into context to make sense. If company X has a falling profit record over a five-year period when most companies in that industry were increasing their profits, there is evidently something wrong.

The most widely used measure of profitability is:

$$\frac{\text{Profit before tax}}{\text{Net assets}}$$

which is derived from the following calculations:

$$\frac{\text{Profit before tax}}{\text{Sales}} \quad \text{X} \quad \frac{\text{Sales}}{\text{Net assets}} = \frac{\text{Profit before tax}}{\text{Net assets}}$$

The term 'net assets' in this context is interchangeable with 'capital employed' or 'net worth'. This profusion of terms does not make balance sheet interpretation any easier for the non-accountant, but the underlying concept is the real value of the company — expressed either as a source of funds (capital employed) or as the use of those funds (net assets). Comparing profit to net assets is therefore measuring how effectively the assets are being employed. Even more than liquidity ratios, profit ratios have very little meaning unless compared from year to year, within the industry in question. A refinement preferred by some analysts is to use net *tangible* assets which means excluding items such as goodwill, formation expenses, patent rights and any other intangibles.

Capital strength

This third aspect of a company's finances is concerned with the ratio of risk capital (equity) to loan capital. Many of the £100 companies being formed will have a very high debt ratio — also known as being highly geared. Directors' loans frequently appear in the accounts of these companies, far outweighing the equity capital. In this situation the credit manager must pose a number of questions before making a major credit decision.

Why do the owners not risk more of their own money?

Are the loans secured on the company's assets?

The danger to a highly-geared company running into a liquidity crisis is the appointment of a Receiver by a bank or some other debenture holder, whose primary object is to protect their investment. Trade creditors then find themselves receiving a fraction of their debts, after the holders of secure loans have obtained full restitution.

A critical factor in a highly-geared company is the amount of profit required to pay the interest on its loan capital. A high level of borrowings may appear sustainable when profits are on target but the situation will change swiftly when profits fall.

The above ratios have been selected as 'key ratios'. There are others, but detailed balance sheet analysis can be very time-consuming and the credit manager must keep a balance between the need for a quick decision and the desirability of a detailed analysis. He is trying to seek answers — from the evidence of historical trends — to three principal questions:

1   Does the prospect seem capable of paying for the goods or services the company wishes to supply?

2   Does the prospect appear likely to continue in business long enough to justify whatever costs have to be incurred in making a supply decision, e.g. tooling, distribution, or marketing?

3   In the event of a crisis, are the unsecured creditors reasonably well placed?

Exhibits 5.2 and 5.3 set out the basic facts needed for balance sheet analysis.

Exhibit 5.2 Balance sheet and profit and loss summary

```
NAME OF COMPANY
```

	Year ended	Year ended	Year ended
Net assets employed			
1 Fixed assets			
2 Investments	_____	_____	_____
	_____	_____	_____
3 Stocks and work-in-progress			
4 Debtors			
5 Other	_____	_____	_____
6 Total current assets	_____	_____	_____
7 Creditors			
8 Bank overdraft			
9 Other			
10 Total current liabilities	_____	_____	_____
	_____	_____	_____
11 Net current assets			
	_____	_____	_____
12 Net assets	_____	_____	_____
Sources of finance			
13 Issued capital			
14 Reserves	_____	_____	_____
15 Total shareholders' funds			
16 Loan capital			
17 Other	_____	_____	_____
18 Total capital employed	_____	_____	_____
Profit and loss account			
19 Sales			
20 Purchases			
21 Trading profit			
22 Interest paid			
23 Profit before tax			
24 Profit after tax			
25 Profit retained in the business			

Exhibit 5.3 Balance sheet analysis

NAME OF COMPANY				
Key ratio	Method of calculation*	Year ended	Year ended	Year ended
Current	6 ÷ 10			
Quick	(6 - 3) ÷ 10			
Coverage of current debt	10 as % of 12			
Profit on sales	23 as % of 19			
Asset turnover	19 ÷ 12			
Return on capital employed	23 as % of 18			
Collection period in days	(4 ÷ 19)/365			
Stock turnover in days	(3 ÷ 20)/365 or (3 ÷ 19)/365			
Working capital turnover	19 ÷ 11			
Debt ratio	16 as % of 15			

NOTES
1 Liquidity is good/bad and improving/steady/worsening.
2 Profitability is improving/steady/worsening.
3 Use of assets is vigorous/slow and improving/steady/worsening.
4 Debt ratio is rising/steady/dropping.

*The numbers in this column refer to the item numbers in Exhibit 5.2.

Small and medium-sized companies

The Companies Act 1985 (Section 247) permits the submission of modified accounts to the Registrar providing two of the following three criteria are met:
- Turnover does not exceed £4 million (small companies) or £8 million (medium)
- Balance sheet does not exceed £2 million (small) or £5.6 million (medium)
- Employees do not exceed 50 (small) or 250 (medium)

The modifications allowed are as follows:
1 Medium-sized companies may omit details of turnover and pre-tax profit by line of business and geographical area.
2 Small companies do not have to file a profit and loss account nor a Directors' report, nor any breakdown of balance-sheet items below the level of main headings such as stocks, debtors, investments, tangible assets, creditors, etc.

It will be clear that the unavailability of these details makes the interpretation of accounts extremely difficult — if only because the absence of a turnover figure prevents many of the principal ratios being calculated. Around 90 per cent of all registered companies qualify as small companies, but fortunately not all of these bother to prepare the modified accounts as well as the full set required by their shareholders.

Detailed analysis of modified accounts can only be attempted on the back of a number of estimates and assumptions. Major credit decisions should not of course be based on such foundations. The only way forward is a direct approach to the prospective customer, asking for his co-operation in establishing the required line of credit.

Companies Registry

As well as revealing the latest filed accounts, a search at the Companies Registry can produce two other pieces of information:
1 Details of all mortgages and other registered charges. The credit investigator is thus fully informed about the existence of secured loans, which must be paid out in full before the claims of unsecured creditors are considered.
2 The names of all directors and shareholders, plus details of other companies with which the directors may be associated.

Each company is identified in the Registry by a unique number. A company can, however, change its name by lodging full particulars with the Registry. A situation can occur (and one is known to the writer) where two companies controlled by the same directors and shareholders exchanged names and, in fact, appeared to be what they were not. Company A with issued capital of £2 can become Company B which has £10,000 share capital. Only the registered number cannot be altered and an unsuspecting creditor may be supplying to a 'straw' company, believing it to be one of substance.

A credit problem which can sometimes be created by a visit to the Companies Registry is that of 'agency' or 'management' companies. Many reputable organisations, within their group structure, have companies which, whilst appearing to trade, actually have no assets. Orders are placed, deliveries accepted and payments made, but in fact the supplier is dealing with a 'straw' company which is acting as an agent for another company within the group. It may be argued that it is better to be blissfully ignorant, since if a Registry search reveals this situation the prudent credit manager will be obliged to seek an undertaking or guarantee from the principal company actually utilising the product or service. It is standard practice for many public companies to refuse requests for guarantees. In that event the supplier is left having to decide whether to trust that the parent company would indeed back its subsidiary in the event of a crisis. This point is returned to later under the heading 'Guarantees'.

Press reports

Daily reading of the *Financial Times* is essential, not only to obtain the latest news of and comment on customers' final or half-year accounts, but also to keep abreast of trends and problems in the industry. Articles of this nature usually comment on the performance and standing of leading companies in the field in question, giving invaluable background data to the credit manager.

Most industries have a trade journal, weekly or monthly, which carries snippets of useful information not of sufficient news value to reach the national press.

After being read, all news items and articles should be cut out and filed on a customer status file which will include agency reports, accounts, references and reports of visits and interviews. The importance of keeping press information cannot be over-stressed, since it is often the only material available between annual reports.

Special reports

Most reporting agencies, in addition to producing the standard credit reports referred to in Chapter 4, also have a special reporting service. Assuming sufficient information is available on the subject company, a special report will usually contain detailed balance sheet analysis over several years, a narrative summary of the company's performance and standing, details of all connections with other companies and information on the current directors. The cost of such reports varies according to the volume and accessibility of information and can exceed £100.

Credit visits

There will be occasions — usually involving a major credit decision — when the credit manager needs to visit a prospect because the information available from his usual sources is either inadequate or out-of-date.

Quite apart from the possibility of obtaining very recent management accounts, a visit gives an opportunity to meet the management, to discuss the likely trading relationship and to look around and gain an overall impression. A joint visit with the sales manager is a good idea, because the buyer is at once made aware of the sales/credit relationship — the fact that the credit manager is an accepted part of the team helping to establish a mutually profitable association. The credit manager is looking for evidence of capable management which can be revealed in many ways. Does the accounting system operate efficiently? Are the directors or managers experienced people? Do they have properly thought-out-out marketing and production plans? How is the business financed? Is a cash-now forecast available? A chief executive (whether a sole proprietor or managing director) who holds the reins of power closely to himself, delegating only routine decisions and withholding information from his subordinates, can be a danger to his company and should put the credit manager on his guard.

In addition to good management, the credit manager should also be looking for the outward signs of a well-organised and healthy company. Is the product well-established and in demand? If a new product, what evidence is there of sufficient demand? Are the plant and equipment in good condition? Who are the principal customers?

In short, the purpose of a credit visit is to enable the credit manager to decide to what degree the company and its management inspire confidence. When added to all the other information, does this confidence point to a favourable credit decision? (Further notes on credit visits appear in Chapter 8.)

Guarantees

A mention has already been made of the refusal of many public companies to give guarantees for the payment of debts incurred by subsidiaries. It is important to remember that a parent company has no legal responsibility to the creditors of a subsidiary. The corollary of this is never to make credit decisions based on the strength of the parent company — but nonetheless the existence of a prosperous parent cannot be ignored and should increase confidence. Exhibit 5.4 gives two illustrations of undertakings given by parent companies which are frequently included in the notes to the accounts. Neither of these can be regarded as legally-binding guarantees and the credit manager should not see them as anything more than 'letters of comfort'. Their real value will depend upon the reputation of the parent company. If the parent company is for example a PLC with a full Stock Exchange listing, it would be reasonable to place a good measure of confidence in such an undertaking. In any situation where a financially weak subsidiary is seeking credit, it does not harm to ask for a guarantee. Sometimes the reply is favourable and Exhibit 5.5 shows a recommended format. A refusal can either indicate a lack of confidence coupled with a degree of self-protection, or it may be no more than a policy decision regardless of the particular facts in view.

Equally common is the situation where there is no parent company, but the director and principal shareholder is known to have substantial private means. This often arises when a limited company is recently formed, and the

Exhibit 5.4   Parent company undertakings

---

1. The ultimate holding company has agreed to
   continue to provide such financial support as the
   company requires for its continued operation.

2. The ultimate holding company has given an undertaking to provide financial and other assistance
   as may be necessary to enable the company to meet
   its liabilities as they fall due for payment.

Exhibit 5.5

Dear Sirs,

In consideration of your readiness to comply with
our desire that you should supply goods or services
to:

(hereinafter referred to as 'the Buyer'), we hereby
guarantee the due payment to you of all sums which
are now or may hereafter become owing to you by the
Buyer.

Our liability shall not in any way be diminished or
affected by your giving time or indulgence to the
Buyer, nor by any release, agreement not to sue,
composition or arrangement of any description granted
or entered into by you to or with the Buyer and we
shall be liable to you in respect of any obligation
accrued hereunder as if we were principal and not
surety.

This guarantee shall be a continuing guarantee,
subject to our right to give notice of revocation
thereof. Any such notice shall be in writing and
become effective upon its actual receipt by you
at............ but no revocation shall in any way
diminish or affect our liability to you in respect of
any indebtedness of the Buyer incurred under any
contract or obligation entered into between you and
the Buyer prior to your receipt of such notice.

Yours faithfully,

Witness to the signature ....
(Signed) ....
Address....................Date.....................

creditors suddenly lose the protection they enjoyed in selling to a sole trader or partnership. A request for the personal guarantee of the director in these circumstances is perfectly legitimate. Even better is to seek the joint and several guarantees of the director and his or her spouse, to avoid the danger that all the assets have been put in the spouse's name.

Success in obtaining personal guarantees depends in part upon goodwill between the guarantor and the credit manager, and to a greater degree upon the customer's dependence upon the seller. The bigger the company, the more difficult it is to obtain a guarantee because of the need to consult fellow directors and to pass a board resolution.

A guarantee should never be requested and obtained in the belief that it will be enforced. It represents the 'fall-back' position, enabling more credit to be extended than would otherwise be prudent. Further reference to guarantees is made later in this chapter under the heading 'Government-controlled companies'.

Sales ledger information

A prime source of information on a customer wishing to increase business should be the sales ledger. Providing it is organised efficiently it should give the credit manager immediate evidence of payment behaviour.

Whilst manual, ledger-card systems give a continuous historical record of payments received and invoices cleared, a simple computer programme can produce a far clearer record. An illustration is given in Chapter 7 (Exhibit 7.4).

A desirable feature in a computerised receivables system is a record of account follow-up activity to augment the bare outline of payment statistics.

Special situations

Most of the analysis techniques covered in this chapter relate to the granting of credit to companies limited by shares, which are the most common form of corporate body. Corporate bodies exist independently from their members and have a legal existence which enables them, *inter alia*, to sue and be sued.

The requirements of the Companies Acts apply also to companies limited by guarantee and to unlimited companies. Both these types of organisation are usually confined to non-trading bodies, although often subsidiaries within a group adopt the latter form for tax purposes. As far as credit analysis is concerned, members of a company limited by guarantee are liable up to the amount of their guarantee if the company cannot pay its debts and is declared insolvent. The liability of members of an unlimited company is unlimited.

Other kinds of corporate bodies include corporations created by Charter, such as the BBC, corporations created by Statute such as County Councils and British Coal and corporations sole such as a Bishop or the Queen. Credit problems encountered in dealing with some of these are examined later in this chapter.

Sole traders and partnerships

The most important aspect of these bodies for the credit manager is the absence of limited liability. An unpaid creditor looks to the personal assets of the partners, members of the proprietor. While this may sound safer than dealing with a limited company, other problems must be considered. Firstly it is difficult to establish even an approximate idea of the value of those personal assets. Secondly the assets will be open to recourse from other creditors — perhaps supplying other businesses controlled by the same proprietor or partners. Assessment of a partnership or sole trader must follow the same principles as for a company. The analyst is looking for evidence of a stable, profitable business with reasonable liquidity. A particular hazard in dealing with sole traders is, of course, the death of the proprietor which, unless succession plans have been made for competent people to take over, may mean the sudden collapse or gradual stagnation of the firm. The life-style of a sole trader can also be significant — a good life may be taking precedence over a good business.

Other unincorporated bodies

These include clubs, societies, charities, trade unions and friendly societies. Just because a body is non-profit-making, it does not mean there is no risk in allowing credit. Charities, for example, often depend upon voluntary help for their administration, and accounts are sometimes prepared with the primary objective of concealing operational and administrative costs. Very often, of course, the name and reputation is such that it would not be allowed to collapse and government money would probably be found. This would be small comfort to a supplier deprived of the use of his money for several months. In the case of clubs, societies, etc., if no funds are available to pay creditors, personal liability devolves upon the secretary or other officer placing the order with joint liability on the committee authorising the transaction — if this can be proved from the minutes.

Local Authority bodies — councils, schools, hospitals, etc.

While the risk of a bad debt may appear to be non-existent, the risk of delayed payment is high particularly in times of restricted public expenditure. Many suppliers of schools and, more particularly, of hospitals have traditionally taken a lenient attitude towards slow payment. If they were to stop doing so, our educational and health services would suffer severely. But suppliers must be aware of the danger and the effect on profits. Even the ultimate risk — complete insolvency — could become reality, witness the problems of New York City in the 1980's.

Government-controlled and government-backed companies

Despite the many privatisations carried out by Conservative governments up to 1995 there are still a few companies dependent upon government finance for their survival.

How should the credit analyst view these companies? It is tempting to assume that no risk exists because the government will always provide cash, but this is not a tenable argument. There have been instances of government-backed companies being allowed to crash, and trade creditors, who had given credit in the belief that government support was indefinite, were left with nothing. The classic case is Upper Clyde Shipbuilders Ltd, which was put into liquidation in 1971. Not only did the government hold 48 per cent of the share capital, but it was also a very substantial loan creditor. There is no doubt that suppliers were encouraged to grant credit by the continued close involvement of the government in the management of the company. Attempts to persuade the government to accept some responsibility towards the creditors, who were owed around £7½ million, came to an end in December 1977.

Another instance was Beagle Aircraft which had a Receiver appointed in December 1969. The company owed over £1.2 million to unsecured creditors who had to a large degree relied on government support; £6 million of public money was lost.

There are other companies whose government support comes from special bodies such as the Scottish and Welsh Development Agencies and the Northern Ireland Department of Commerce. The most well-known case of a company being allowed to collapse was that of De Lorean Motor Cars Ltd in 1982. Over £50 million of taxpayers' money was lost and many small suppliers came close to insolvency because they had given unsecured credit to a self-pronounced high-risk enterprise.

The message should be clear. Any supplier required to grant substantial credit to a company dependent upon government finance should seek and press vigorously for a guarantee.

Conclusion

This chapter ends with two case-studies, in which only the names have been removed to prevent identification. One illustrates success despite financial problems. The other warns of the danger of acting on insufficient information.

Case study 1 – an engineering group

This case study deals with an engineering group that was within a hair's breadth of failure on several occasions. Accounts are shown for six years in Exhibits 5.6–5.9. Key ratios have been calculated. What do they show?

1 Liquidity This was bad throughout the period. The apparent slight improvement in Year 2 was due to the massive increase in the collection period. Years 3 and 4 show a small upward trend, more pronounced in the current liabilities/net worth ratio. In a financially strong company, net worth should cover current liabilities several times, indicating that creditors would be reasonably well cushioned in the event of a break-up. In this instance net worth does not approach parity with current liabilities until Year 5. Apart from the peculiar upsurge in debtors in Year 2 (probably caused by a major contract being invoiced at year-end), neither debtors nor stocks show any significant trends.

2 Profitability The level of trading profit fluctuated violently, showing an upward trend in Years 4-6. The turnover of net assets declined, principally because the asset value at the outset was so very low. Return on net assets is extremely high in Years 4, 5 and 6 — but again this is a product of the low asset base coupled with a rising margin on sales.

3 Capital structure The relationship between loan capital and shareholders' funds points to the same conclusion as the other ratios. Year 3 was the nadir of the company's fortunes, when trading profit almost disappeared and loan capital exceeded the equity value. Bank overdraft also reached a maximum, as did interest payable.

The most significant feature of these accounts is what they do *not* show. This company survived, yet a prospective supplier looking at the results of Years 1, 2 and 3 could well assume that it was on the verge of collapse. It was. Survival was primarily due to non-financial factors, including dedicated and determined management, a good product and excellent public relations.

Case study 2 — an international commodity broker

In mid-April 1994 an order was received for printer consumables, value £4,900, from a new customer. Credit clearance was given on the basis of an

Exhibit 5.6	Balance sheet and profit and loss summary		

NAME OF COMPANY (Case study 1)			
	Year 1 ended £000s	Year 2 ended £000s	Year 3 ended £000s
Net assets employed			
1 Fixed assets	2,507	3,360	3,407
2 Investments	67	83	128
	2,674	3,443	3,535
3 Stocks and work-in-progress	4,555	6,320	7,802
4 Debtors	1,817	4,594	3,661
5 Other	44	76	66
6 Total current assets	6,416	10,990	11,529
7 Creditors	4,340	7,078	7,527
8 Bank overdraft	729	2,189	3,013
9 Other	1,915	1,293	1,253
10 Total current liabilities	6984	10,560	11,793
11 Net current assets	(568)	430	(264)
12 Net assets	2,006	3,873	3,271
Sources of finance			
13 Issued capital	204	205	205
14 Reserves	1,272	2,209	1,343
15 Total shareholders' funds	1,476	2,414	1,548
16 Loan capital	530	1,459	1,723
17 Other	—	—	—
18 Total capital employed	2,006	3,873	3,271
Profit and loss account			
19 Sales	13,657	16,466	21,610
20 Purchases	—	—	—
21 Trading profiit	(71)	1,224	407
22 Interest paid	448	658	1,239
23 Profit before tax	(519)	336	(832)
24 Profit after tax	(451)	307	(758)
25 Profit retained in the business	—	—	—

Exhibit 5.7 Balance sheet analysis

NAME OF COMPANY	(Case study 1)			
Key ratio	Method of calculation*	Year 1 ended	Year 2 ended	Year 3 ended
Current	6 ÷ 10	0.9:1	1:1	1:1
Quick	(6 − 3) ÷ 10	0.3:1	0.4:1	0.3:1
Coverage of current debt	12 ÷ 10	0.3	0.4	0.3
Profit on sales	23 as % of 19	(3.8)	2.0	(3.9)
Asset turnover	19 ÷ 12	6.8	4.3	6.6
Return on capital employed	23 as % of 18	(25.9)	8.7	(25.4)
Collection period in days	(4 ÷ 19)/365	48	102	62
Stock turnover in days	(3 ÷ 20)/365 or (3 ÷ 19)/365	122	140	132
Working capital turnover	19 ÷ 11	−	38.3	−
Debt ratio	16 as % of 15	36	60	111

NOTES
1 Liquidity is good/bad and improving/steady/worsening.
2 Profitability is improving/steady/worsening.
3 Use of assets is vigorous/slow and improving/steady/worsening.
4 Debt ratio is rising/steady/dropping.

* The numbers in this column refer to the item numbers in Exhibit 5.6.

on-line credit report which, whilst not containing any financial data, offered no adverse information. The account was opened as 'high risk' with a £5,000 limit.

Over the next three weeks further orders were received which, through negligence, were not referred to Credit Control. More goods were shipped and invoiced, totalling £35,000.

An on-line credit report from a well-known agency recommended maximum credit of £28,000, but within 24 hours revised the report downward to £10,000! After a further six weeks the rating was withdrawn completely. Contact with other suppliers of similar products established similar experience and feelings of unease.

The salesman pressed hard for ways and means to be found of accepting further business; £250,000 was mentioned. A cheque to clear the first two deliveries was promised, in exchange for another delivery of similar value. Draft accounts were faxed which appeared satisfactory, and the customer undertook to pay for all future deliveries by Letter of Credit (all goods were being exported against L/C payments). The other unpaid deliveries were to be paid by banker's draft within a week. This was agreed (early May).

The new delivery was made and the promised cheque obtained. The cheque was drawn on the personal account of a supposed director and it bounced.

The Credit Manager visited the customer the next day and received a very plausible explanation and a promise to pay all outstanding invoices (now around £52,000) plus advance payment for further deliveries once a satisfactory Letter of Credit was opened covering all existing and future debts. A pro-forma invoice for over £133,000 was requested. A letter was also provided giving permission for a bank reference to be sought.

The Letter of Credit never materialised. The bank said they had no knowledge of the company. The supplier took legal advice and the solicitor sent a letter threatening a winding-up petition if payment was not made within three days. In the event, another supplier got in first and the company was put into compulsory liquidation in September 1994. No assets were traced and the draft accounts (being unaudited) were clearly worthless. Many other suppliers also suffered, some for substantially more than this supplier. The fraud squad were notified and investigations continued into 1995.

This is a true, if abbreviated, story which illustrates how the lack of good management control, plus a single-minded determination to achieve sales at any cost can defeat credit control, particularly when faced with a deliberately fraudulent operation.

Z-scores and Pas-scores

Z-score analysis is a statistical method used to identify companies which display characteristics similar to those found in companies that later become insolvent.

It was originally developed in the USA in 1968 and modified and adapted for use in the UK in the 1970s. In the early 1980s a further refinement was

Exhibit 5.8 Balance sheet and profit and loss summary

NAME OF COMPANY (Case study 1)	Year 4 ended £000s	Year 5 ended £000s	Year 6 ended £000s
Net assets employed			
1 Fixed assets	3,197	3,319	5,013
2 Investments	117	104	
	3,314	3,423	5,013
3 Stocks and work-in-progress	6,136	8,989	10,608
4 Debtors	3,181	3,583	3,386
5 Other	110	78	534
6 Total current assets	9,427	12,650	14,528
7 Creditors	5,103	7,805	7,490
8 Bank overdraft	2,391	606	172
9 Other	1,438	273	257
10 Total current liabilities	8,832	8,684	7,919
11 Net current assets	595	3,966	6,609
12 Net assets	3,909	7,389	11,622
Sources of finance			
13 Issued capital	205	205	205
14 Reserves	2,179	4,613	8,023
15 Total shareholders' funds	2,385	4,818	8,228
16 Loan capital	1,325	2,318	2,011
17 Other	199	253	1,383
18 Total capital employed	3,909	7,389	11,622
Profit and loss account			
19 Sales	21,060	22,270	31,088
20 Purchases			
21 Trading profiit	1,724	2,894	4,378
22 Interest paid	941	637	437
23 Profit before tax	783	2,257	3,941
24 Profit after tax	799	2,318	2,902
25 Profit retained in the business	928	2,307	3,302

added to produce the Pas-score system. Four key ratios, relating to profitability, liquidity, solvency and financial risk, are combined in a formula which produces the Z-score. Companies with a negative Z-score resemble those companies which have previously failed. The Pas-score shows the relative risks of companies in the same industry on a scale of 1 to 100 which includes a solvency threshold (below which the Z-score is negative).

Exhibit 5.9   Balance sheet analysis

NAME OF COMPANY (Case study 1)				
Key ratio	Method of calculation*	Year 4 ended	Year 5 ended	Year 6 ended
Current	6 ÷ 10	1.1:1	1.5:1	1.8:1
Quick	(6 − 3) ÷ 10	0.4:1	0.4:1	0.5:1
Coverage of current debt	12 ÷ 10	0.4	0.9	1.5
Profit on sales	23 as % of 19	3.7	10.1	12.7
Asset turnover	19 ÷ 12	5.4	3.0	2.7
Return on capital employed	23 as % of 18	20.0	30.5	33.9
Collection period in days	(4 ÷ 19)/365	55	59	40
Stock turnover in days	(3 ÷ 20)/365 or (3 ÷ 19)/365	106	147	125
Working capital turnover	19 ÷ 11	35.4	5.6	4.7
Debt ratio	16 as % of 15	56	53	41

NOTES
1 Liquidity is good/bad and improving/steady/worsening.
2 Profitability is improving/steady/worsening.
3 Use of assets is vigorous/slow and improving/steady/ worsening.
4 Debt ratio is rising/steady/dropping.

* The numbers in this column refer to the item numbers in Exhibit 5.8.

Different formulae are used for manufacturing and distribution companies, quoted and unquoted.

The essence of the system is its claim to identify potential insolvencies which can only be avoided if appropriate management action is taken in time. The track record is impressive and it is claimed that 99 per cent of failed companies have been identified as potential insolvencies up to three years before the event.

There is an obvious application of Pas-scoring to credit management. A computer software programme is available, which includes the accounts of all quoted companies. Any company with a large number of high-value customer accounts could benefit from this system, since it not only identifies existing customers requiring special care and control, but it can also be invaluable in the initial assessment of a new customer.

The system is available from Syspas Ltd, 11–13 Dowgate Hill, London EC4R 2SU.

Chapter 6

Credit decisions, credit limits and controls

The true function of the credit manager is to contribute to company profits through positive assessment and control. It is not good enough to play safe, to follow a cautious conservative policy towards new business, to deny credit to all but those whose ability to pay is undoubted. There are times when such an approach is justified. If the order book is full, the factory working at full capacity and the demand for goods outstrips the supply, the credit manager can send the doubtful risks to the back of the queue, insist on cash-in-advance or demand security. Such boom periods have been rare and generally short-lived since the 1960s. Instead the credit manager today finds himself in a very different environment in which his ability to turn marginal accounts into good customers is becoming increasingly valuable.

From the information sources examined in Chapters 4 and 5, facts and indications emerge on which credit decisions have to be made. Sometimes the decisions are easy, as when the anticipated level of business is seen to be well within the normal scope of an established company. Others are more difficult and call for examination of balance sheets and perhaps a personal visit.

Other factors affecting credit decisions

There will also be occasions when the final decisions must take into account factors beyond the credit manager's sphere of knowledge or jurisdiction. Examples of this are as follows:

1   Is there an alternative, more creditworthy buyer for the product? (This is applicable only for standard goods.)
2   If the goods have already been made to customer specifications and there is only scrap value, does this justify a high risk?
3   Are the goods obsolete stock with a very small book value? If so, a higher risk can be undertaken.
4   Does rejection of the order mean the closing of a production line?
5   Does it mean losing a vital opportunity to gain a foothold in a new market?

The credit manager is not usually in a position to answer these questions, but he must be aware of such implications — which is only possible if he is an accepted member of company management. His job is then to produce an information file which will pass to sales or production for their observations before the final decision is cast at board level.

The time factor

In an ideal world the credit analyst is given lengthy advance notice of new business and has ample time to obtain and evaluate all available data. This does happen — sometimes — depending on how well he has educated the sales manager! More usually, the request for credit clearance comes within days (or even hours) of the despatch or collection date, and there is no time to do anything except check the on-line credit enquiry system and use the telephone. Despite the wealth of information available through the computer, all credit managers fall victim to the seemingly inexorable law which dictates that when you most need it, the information required is either not there at all, is not up to date, or the system is down.

In these situations three or four telephone calls will, given a little luck, produce enough to either refuse or approve an initial order. In order of priority these calls should be made:

a   To one or more credit contacts likely to know of the new buyer. Up-to-date experience from a trusted colleague is worth several credit reports.
b   To the buyer himself, to ask approval to phone his banker and to ask as much as he will allow about the company.
c   To the buyer's banker — if the buyer has authorised his banker to disclose helpful information.
d   To a credit agency to see whether there is an up-to-date report on file.

From time to time attempts have been made to reduce the credit decision process to a formula. These vary from the simple rule of not giving more credit than X per cent of the issued capital or the net worth of the buyer, to a complex system of credit scoring calling for detailed information data to be analysed or fed into a computer. Such methods are aimed at removing the guesswork from credit sanctioning and making it more scientific. Their efficiency is very doubtful, because they seek to delete what is often the most important element — human judgement of a total array of facts, impressions and opinions. For example, not many suppliers would have continued giving credit to the company in Case Study I (see Chapter 5) had their decisions been based entirely on the financial facts. In actual fact, many suppliers continued in blissful ignorance of these facts, which was probably fortunate for the company.

The basic questions to be considered in any credit decision are 'How much?' and 'For how long?'. The importance of flexible payment terms has been examined in Chapter 3 but the principle bears repeating. If monthly purchases of £5,000 result in an exposure that looks too high — on net monthly terms — the same turnover may be achieved without that degree of risk by reducing the credit period. Apart from the question of terms, a credit decision may be affected by the period of the contract. On the one hand, the credit manager may be encouraged on a doubtful case by the fact that deliveries will be completed within, say, two months, and the chances of the buyer collapsing that quickly should be a lot less than if supplies are to be made over a long period. Against this, however, is the danger that once deliveries are completed, he loses the deterrent of stopping supplies.

In some companies, depending on the average order value, it may be worth operating a 'discretionary limit' or blanket approval system for initial orders. Thus new customers' orders up to, say, £100 could be approved automatically. This policy is clearly beneficial to the marketing department since delays on first orders may mean lost business. Problems can easily occur, however, if careful control is not exercised. Suppose, for example, an initial order for £70 is accepted, an account is opened and an account number is allocated. Unless that account is clearly tagged 'first order only approved' or given some kind of identification, further orders of increasing value may be accepted without question, and within a few months a £500 balance is showing on an account that has had no credit clearance at all.

To avoid this sort of problem — which can rapidly get out of hand — it is suggested that as soon as the initial order is accepted, a letter of the form shown in Exhibit 6.1 is sent by the credit department.

Risk categories

The use of risk categories provides a valuable framework both for credit limits and for determining credit management priorities.

Every customer is placed in a risk category according to the perceived level of risk. Categories are then used to decide the degree of order-entry control and overdue follow-up. They are also helpful in the credit limit decision. Exhibit 6.2 shows a basic risk-category structure, with three categories: A, B and C. It is possible to use only two categories — but this reduces the systems

Exhibit 6.1

Dear Sir,

We thank you for your recent order, number ....
value ....

To avoid any unnecessary delay, this order is being processed
immediately on our standard terms of:

So that we can handle future orders on credit terms we ask you
to complete the attached form and return it to us.

Our Conditions of Sale are printed on the reverse of this letter.
Would you please note that all cheques should be made payable to
.... and sent to the following
address:

....

....

Thank you for your co-operation.
                    Yours faithfully,

Exhibit 6.2

Risk category	Type of customer	Order referral	Purpose of credit limit
A	Government and public bodies, hospitals, schools, and large, strong public companies	None	To indicate a change in payment or buying behaviour
B	All others	Over £X	
C	Customers of doubtful standing and/or persistent bad payment behaviour	All orders	To indicate maximum balance allowable

flexibility. On the other hand, the number of categories can be increased at will, depending on the complexity of the business and the level of sophistication required.

The system illustrated in Exhibit 6.2 operates as follows:

Category A should be reserved for customers with zero or extremely low credit risk. This will include central and local government bodies, hospitals, schools and universities, nationalised undertakings and national or international companies of the highest standing. Since inclusion in this top category means the absence of any form of order-entry control — apart from restrictions imposed because of non-payment — it is essential that a regular check be made on the fortunes of admitted companies. By definition most of these will be public companies whose annual reports are obtainable free and on whom frequent press comment and information appears. The credit limits on Category A customers will all be guidelines, related to the expected maximum balance assuming that sales do not exceed forecast and that payments are arriving within one month of due date. No order referral is necessary since these customers can increase their purchases without giving rise to a significant credit risk.

At the other end of the scale is *Category C* which is used for all customers whose credit limit is a barrier. It should also include any buyers whose payment behaviour demands strict control — whether or not there is a credit limit problem. Order-referral will be 100 per cent for Category C customers, to ensure that credit limits are not exceeded.

Having covered buyers at both ends of the risk scale, we are left with the middle range, neither 'blue-chip' nor high-risk, which are placed in *Category B*. For nearly all companies, this is where the majority of customers will be grouped. Credit limits in this category will be guidelines, as in Category A, but a measure of order-entry control is necessary because these companies are not of the highest standing and an unexpected increase in purchasing could push a balance beyond the theoretical maximum. The degree of order-entry control will depend on the type of business and the average order value, but it makes sense to try to relate the referral level to the credit limit. For example, a customer with a £5,000 credit line might require referral of all orders over £2,000 since that figure is more than one month's average purchases. It might be safer — but more difficult to operate — to have all orders in any month referred once a cumulative total of £2,000 has been reached.

Risk categories must be used flexibly, i.e. customers should be moved from category to category according to changes in their risk status or as a result of significant changes in payment performance. It is vital that credit status information files are kept up-to-date and the following system is recommended.

Category A Annual reports of public companies (obtainable free), plus regular flow of press cuttings and articles. For private companies an annual search if the volume of business warrants it, also press reports, etc. Common sense must be used. If ICI are buying £100 per month, it is not worth the trouble of sending for their annual report.

Category B As above, plus annual status reports on all private companies.

Category C As for Category B, with six-monthly up-dating of status information on any companies running high balances ('high' balances might mean over £2,000 for some suppliers and over £20,000 for others. Again, common sense must prevail).

The use of credit contacts to give and receive information should be a continuous process, especially for Category C accounts.

Finally, good use should be made of sales ledger information — as indicated in Chapter 5 — to ensure that trends in sales volume and payment behaviour are easily detected.

Another advantage of a risk-category system is that it facilitates variable follow-up procedures. Thus, where collection letters are used, the timing and frequency can be accelerated for Category C customers, where it is important that overdues are chased immediately, and action to stop shipment be taken sooner than for customers in Categories A and B.

Credit limits

Having placed a customer into a risk category, the next step is to set a credit limit. This should reflect the credit manager's assessment of both the customer's capacity and intentions to pay for a given volume of business.

Assessment should always be undertaken with a credit limit in mind, and the credit decision should aim at setting a limit high enough to accommodate the expected level of business, having regard also to the terms of payment. For example, an enquiry forecast at £1,000 per month on monthly terms indicates a credit limit requirement of £3,000. This allows for payment to be up to one month late without the credit limit being exceeded. A new buyer predicted to take £500,000 per annum on net 30-day terms will need a limit of, say, £150,000 — on the same principle of covering three month's sales plus an element of 'rounding-up' to allow for queries.

It follows that credit decisions formed on this basis will result in two distinct types of credit limit:

1 The credit limit which is merely a signpost or guideline to account performance. This would be appropriate for risk categories A or B. It may also be called a credit line.

2   The credit limit which is a barrier. This would be relevant to a risk category C customer.

Credit limits as guidelines occur when the limit needed to accommodate sales volume is well inside the 'maximum risk' figure. Thus a supplier approached by ICI plc on the basis of £10,000 a month can easily establish a credit line of £30,000. It may be argued that there is no point in having a limit at all in this kind of situation, or that the limit should be set at some astronomic figure (perhaps £1 million). The prime reasons for operating guideline limits on 'blue-chip' accounts are that they introduce a discipline into the credit department's routine. Every account which transgresses its limit must be looked at. Maybe sales are increasing — in which case the limit may need increasing. Perhaps payments are slowing down — corrective action is needed. Changing trends in account performance are highlighted, whether they relate to sales volume or payment performance. The next Rolls Royce disaster will never be anticipated if all the 'blue-chip' accounts are ignored or given £1 million limits.

The other type of credit limit is more readily understood but is hopefully used less frequently. If the 'three-month sales' limit requirement is £10,000, but all the available evidence points to £5,000 as being the absolute maximum, then the credit limit of £5,000 is a real limit. Similarly, if £10,000 can be agreed but any more seems dangerous, the limit has to be used as a barrier.

There are, of course, other ways of using credit limits. The limit chosen for each account can represent the maximum amount deemed to be an acceptable risk — regardless of the expected sales volume. In the case of companies of the highest standing, this tends to result in the £1 million limit situation, which has already been discussed. One method of calculating a maximum limit is to use a percentage of net worth or net current assets. The percentage chosen can be varied according to the risk category, e.g. a category A customer would be allowed a higher percentage than one in a lower category. There are two disadvantages to this system. First, the calculated limit has no relationship to the expected buying level — unless it is used solely as a barrier to any calculation based on expected purchases. Secondly, it relies upon the availability of up-to-date accounts — but of course these are necessary to any form of assessment.

The question that no book can answer is under what circumstances do you decide to fix a limit of £5,000 on a buyer who needs £10,000? The experience of other suppliers (apart from referees), the evidence of trends in the accounts, the comments of reporting agencies, the length of time in business, the hazards of the particular industry, the reputation of the company, the impression obtained of the management — all these factors contribute to the decision. The judgement of a credit manager should develop with experience, and not be too easily swayed by the arguments or pressures from the sales department.

It is a good principle to tell customers of their credit limits. This avoids any subsequent embarrassment or misunderstanding if order-acceptance is delayed because of a limit problem. Where the limit is a maximum figure, this must be stated, and conversely where it is no more than a reflection of the customer's needs, this should also be made clear. Problems can arise if an unfavourable credit decision is notified to the customer by the sales office, since the sales staff may not be aware of the reasons for refusal. If it can be arranged, it is better if credit staff have the responsibility for this since it provides an opportunity to explain and discuss the problem. Very often the goodwill of the buyer can be retained if he is persuaded that the reason for the order being refused is the failure of his accountant to pay!

Operating the controls

(a) The basic approach

It is important to use limits and categories in a positive manner. The easy way is to adopt an inflexible attitude, to play safe and always reject orders which would breach the limit. While this may be the right decision on some occasions, the credit manager should always be trying to find ways of accepting marginal business.

Credit limits must not remain static. Most of the problems will arise with Category C customers on a restrictive, maximum credit limit. Even here, however, a reasonable period (say, six months) of trading with good payments should provide sufficient confidence to increase the limit and gradually introduce a more liberal attitude.

Other ways of tackling limit problems include switching to a shorter credit period or even offering a cash discount. Discounts that are uneconomic in the strict context of money may be justifiable if they open the door to an increased sales volume not acceptable on ordinary credit terms.

(b) The welcome letter

Once an account has been opened it is good practice to write to the customer as in Exhibit 6.3

(c) Order entry

A prerequisite of order-entry is that the credit department has absolute authority over the opening of new accounts, the issuing of account numbers and the maintenance of name and address records.

The first essential is that the correct name and address are recorded when an account is opened. To this end, sales representatives and sales office staff

Exhibit 6.3

For the attention of the Purchase Ledger Manager

Dear Sirs

We are pleased to confirm that a credit account has been opened for you under the above name and address. If any of these details are incorrect — for either invoices or statements — please tell us quoting Account No. ....

An initial credit facility of £x has been allocated which we hope you will find satisfactory. The contact number for any query on this or anything relating to your account is given above.

Finally we would remind you that our terms of payment are net 30 days from date of invoice. To avoid any possible misunderstanding, would you please sign your acceptance of this on the tear-off slip below and return it in the free-post envelope provided.

Yours faithfully

---

should be asked to provide letterheads of new customers and to supply copies of orders where these include instructions to deliver and invoice to different locations. No account should be opened until credit clearance has been given, which will involve the allocation of a credit limit and risk category — unless a discretionary limit is used for initial orders. Credit approval should be in writing, along the lines indicated in Exhibit 6.4.

Preferably, the request for a new account should also be in writing. Exhibit 6.5 illustrates this.

A more detailed examination of customer name and address records is deferred to Chapter 7.

Once an account is opened and a credit limit and category allocated, order referral should be on an exception basis. Thus there is no point in checking orders from Category A customers or from Category B unless the referral limit is exceeded. A sophisticated computer system can very easily cope with this requirement, provided all orders are processed through a central control before being accepted. Such a system can be developed to include checks against the credit limit and even against the payment situation on the ledger. A total order-referral system is illustrated in Exhibit 6.6, each stage either culminating in referral to the credit department or being continued through the computer.

Stage I Customer order details are keyed into the system, the first check being against the risk category. Category A status allows the order to move straight to Stage III, whilst B and C proceed to:

72

Exhibit 6.4

To: From: Credit Dept
                                       Date:

   Re:

Enquiry/Order No._____ dated _____ Value _____

Existing buyer

1 Order can be accepted	☐
2 Order can be shipped	☐
3 Please refer again before shipment	☐
4 Order cannot be accepted/shipped because customer is overdue and/or over limit	☐

1 Information obtained, details attached	☐
2 Business may be accepted	☐
3 Payment terms to be established	☐
4 No information available yet	☐
5 Initial order may be supplied up to	☐
on payment terms of	☐
6 Risk category is	☐
7 Temporary credit limit is	☐
8 Other comment	☐

A customer code must be applied for in the normal
manner. If a code is not requested within six
months, the above decisions are null and void.

Exhibit 6.5

```
To: Credit Dept                           Date:
From:
                  ADVICE OF NEW CUSTOMER
The following firm is expected to place/has placed an
enquiry/order with us:

Trade and bank references obtained:

1
2
3

Likely monthly level of purchases - £_____

Existing suppliers:

Payment terms sought (if different from net 30 days):

Other information
```

Stage II There is no need for an order-referral level in a computer system. All orders are added to the outstanding balance on the account, to which is added the total value of previously accepted orders not yet shipped. A further adjustment would be to *exclude* that part of the new order (or of existing orders) which is not scheduled for delivery for a further month. The grand total is then compared to the credit limit. Orders which would breach the limit are referred direct to the credit department, otherwise they move into Stage III.

Stage III For Categories A and B, a check is made whether the account is more than one month overdue. For Category C the ageing check looks for an account being more than 10 days overdue. Negative answers will allow the order to be accepted. Positive answers will lead to Stage IV.

Stage IV The final decision is made — not by the computer but by the credit manager or his trained staff. An additional control which could be built into a computer system and which should take place automatically in any event is to check how long since the credit limit was last reviewed. The above example is most suited to a company selling standard off-the-shelf products to a high volume of customers. Different problems arise where goods are specially made to customer specification, which are looked at below under the heading 'Marginal accounts'.

(d) High credit requests

Requests for credit substantially above the normal buying level usually involve special marketing or production considerations.

Exhibit 6.6

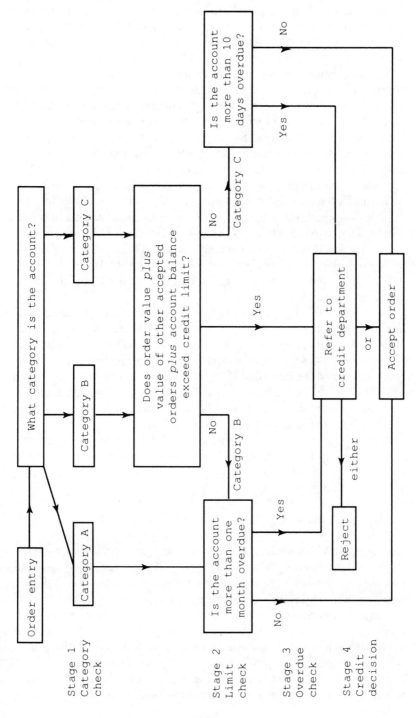

Order entry

Stage 1
Category
check

What category is the account?

Category A   Category B   Category C

Stage 2
Limit
check

Does order value *plus* value of other accepted orders *plus* account balance exceed credit limit?

No
Category B

Is the account more than one month overdue?

No
Category C

Is the account more than 10 days overdue?

Stage 3
Overdue
check

Yes

Yes

No

Stage 4
Credit
decision

Refer to credit department

either   or

Reject

Accept order

75

Opportunities to make significant increases in sales and profits do not arise every day and invariably there is a price in the shape of a greater credit risk. The credit manager must take care to investigate thoroughly, looking all the while for a way of justifying the additional credit.

The most important step is to determine the reason for the extra volume. Is the customer working on a special contract? If so, with whom and how will it affect his cash-flow? If the end product is going overseas, does he have ECGD cover? If he is looking for extended credit, is this because of the demands of his overseas buyer? Is the rise in purchasing a seasonal event, as when a brewery builds up its stock of kegs ready for the summer? If the increased demand is based on no more than a decision to build up stocks hoping for an up-turn in the market, the credit manager will be a little cautious. In the period 1977–8 many companies anticipated a boom — especially in consumer durables — which did not take place. A common occurrence was for such companies to request extended credit — or just take it — from their suppliers when they found themselves in a cash squeeze. This type of problem is likely to be seen more often, since the cost of reducing the labour force and the difficulties of so doing continue to increase and firms are pushed towards the alternative of making for stock.

To return to the more usual situation, where the customer has obtained an important contract, it may be possible to secure payment by taking advantage of his own security. For example, a customer is selling an end-product to a buyer in the Middle East on Letter of Credit terms and he needs an exceptional increase in credit. If the risk appears too high, payment may be secured by a back-to-back credit or a transferable credit arrangement. This is examined in more detail in Chapter 12 but in essence it is the establishment of a lien on the customer's payment from his buyer.

Refusal by a customer to give information about his need for higher credit or to supply up-to-date financial information to justify an increased line of credit must inevitably put the credit manager on his guard.

(e) Marginal accounts

All Category C customers should be listed and circulated to sales and shipping departments. Where orders are fulfilled from stock and standard products are involved, the vital control point is the despatch area. The credit manager must make sure the shipping manager and staff not only operate the controls but understand why. If each order is a special production job, there must be two control points, firstly, in the sales office before manufacture is commenced and, secondly, in despatch. If the production period is lengthy, it is possible that a despatch may have to be withheld because the position on the account has altered since the order was accepted. Where goods to customer specification have been made, there will always be arguments that they may as well be despatched since they are of no value or interest to any other buyer and if they are not shipped they only have scrap value. This proposition should be resisted, principally because if the customer is overdue, to permit further deliveries will be seen as a sign of weakness. Also, any leverage on the customer to pay is given up. A different situation arises where production orders arrive and the customer is over-limit or overdue or both. The sales manager must decide whether to allow production, knowing that despatch will be delayed or prohibited unless the position is put to rights in the meantime.

(f) Stopping supplies

If an effective order-referral system is used, as described above, it may seem superfluous to issue a separate blacklist. This is necessary, however, for the following reasons:

1 A blacklist may include customers from Categories A and B, as well as C.
2 Sales must be told of customers whose orders or despatches are being held — as opposed to merely being referred for approval.
3 A blacklist should be used in a different way from a referral list. Customers on 'stop' remain so until released by the credit department — whereas all orders from referral customers must be put forward for approval. The *effectiveness* of stopping deliveries is examined in Chapter 8.

Chapter 7

The sales ledger and computer systems

Sales ledger management and organisation will be examined under the following headings:
1   Purpose and nature of the sales ledger.
2   Input to the ledger.
3   The name and address file.
4   Statements.
5   Computer aids to credit control.
6   Debit notes.
7   Filing.

The purpose and nature of the sales ledger

The basic purpose of a sales ledger is to record the company's sales to and payments from customers and any adjusting entries in such a manner that each individual transaction can be traced and verified from date of despatch to receipt of payment.

Some companies record cash sales on the ledger; others restrict entries to credit sales — although this might include sales on pro-forma or COD terms. A consequence of this basic function is the need to balance the ledger every month in the following manner:

Balance at last month-end
Plus   Net invoiced sales this month

Less   Cash received

Equals New balance plus/minus sundry adjustments.

A failure to balance resulting from duplicate entries, a missing batch of invoices or merely incorrect arithmetic should be of great concern to the credit manager whether or not he is responsible for the ledger. If the difference is substantial, a decision must be made whether to delay the despatch of statements. To do this would be exceptional, since the effect of a small number of statements having to be corrected later is normally less than the risk of customers delaying payments because of late statements.

Ledgers are either 'open-item' or historical. The open-item format is generally associated with a computer system. A new ledger is produced at the end of each month including only those items which are still outstanding or unreconciled. The advantage of this is that the position on each customer's account can be seen at a glance. The historical or 'brought-forward' method involves a continuous ledger to which new items are added each month. For the purpose of statements, it is normal to carry forward the total owing from the previous month and to show individually only the new month's transactions. The drawback of this system is the need for constant manual reconciliations of the previous month's balance. The only benefit of the historical method is that account history, i.e. sales and payment performance, can be obtained immediately from the ledger, whereas an open-item system requires this information to be stored for reference elsewhere. Ways of doing this will be looked at later in this chapter.

Input to the ledger

(a) *Internal input* The essential requirements of all internally produced entries — invoices, credit notes, contra items and journal items — are that they are given the correct customer account or code number and that their reference numbers are easily identifiable and distinctive. This means taking care that all departments responsible for raising such documents have an up-to-date list of account numbers cross-referenced to names and addresses. The allocation of series of invoice numbers to different divisions or branches must be planned to avoid the possibility of the same numbers being used twice. A simple way to ensure this is to give each division or branch its own alpha-betical or numerical prefix to invoice numbers.

As well as being entered on the ledger, invoices have to be sent out. Good credit control starts here, because customers who do not receive their invoices within a few days of the dates thereon will use this as a reason to delay payment. This is a particular problem at month-end, when in many companies invoicing rises to a peak. All customers impose 'cut-off' dates, denoting the latest date invoices will be accepted in the period. There are two things the credit manager should do. First, he should constantly try to ensure that all invoices are produced and maïled within two to three days of period-end. Secondly, where many invoices are raised for a small number of very large customers, he may find it worthwhile collecting all these together and making personal delivery of them to the appropriate person.

Invoice design and layout are also of interest to the credit manager. There should be a designated space for the customer's order number. The address to which payment is to be sent should be prominently indicated. The terms of payment must be clearly stated. The invoice number, date and customer's account number must be easily identified, not buried amidst a welter of information about job numbers and part numbers. Credit notes should always carry a clear reference to the original invoice and/or customer's debit note.

(b) *External input*   This means customer payments in the form of cheques, bank transfers, direct debits, postal orders or cash.

Responsibility for listing, totalling and banking lies with the cashier, but the way each day's receipts are presented to the sales ledger should be dictated by the credit manager. Speed and ease of identification are the key points. A straight alphabetical list is normal, but if this goes beyond, say, 100 items, it will often not be available until midday or later. Meanwhile orders are being held and decisions are in suspense. Is it worth having all payments over a certain minimum — £100 or £500 or £5,000 for example — listed separately and given to the credit manager ahead of the main list? In a busy department handling hundreds of remittances daily, this could mean several hours' prior knowledge of all important payments. If cash-allocation is divided alphabetically amongst several clerks, it is sensible to ask the cashier to have the cash-lists typed on separate sheets so that each clerk can have his own. Another responsibility of the cashier is to inform the credit manager *immediately* of any dishonoured cheques — taking care to distinguish between those which are returned by the bank marked 'refer to drawer' and those which are merely marked 'please represent'.

If possible, payments should be reconciled within 24 hours of receipt. Correct allocation of cash is very important, and strict controls should operate to prevent an accumulation of unreconciled payments. This demands discipline in the ledger clerk's job, and the credit manager must not tolerate cash remaining unallocated beyond, say, one month after receipt. 'On account' payments often cannot be avoided and, indeed, are sometimes the only way of maintaining satisfactory cash-flow. A clear distinction must be made between 'on account' payments from major buyers who are temporarily behind in the clearance of invoices through their purchase ledger and 'on account' payments from customers unable to make full settlement. The problem with the former is that if no effort is made to obtain regular reconciliations, the list of potential invoice queries grows ever longer. By the time they come to light, these queries are several months old and more difficult to resolve.

Receipt of an 'on account' payment in place of the full amount requested should sound a warning bell. It is almost invariably a sign of cash shortage and must be followed up immediately.

The name and address file

Control of this should rest with the credit manager and involve the following precautions:
1 Input of new or amended information to be restricted to the credit department.
2 Issue of account numbers to be in the hands of the credit department.

Other departments will need access to the file for shipping addresses, invoicing addresses, account numbers, etc., but only the credit department should be allowed to alter or add to the file. In addition to account number, name, shipping and invoicing addresses, the following information should also be kept on file:
a Statement address.
b Credit limit.
c Risk category.
d Payments terms.
e Product code.
f Regional or branch-office code.

These are merely the principal items that most operations will need to have on file; numerous others can be added to suit individual conditions.

In a manual system, this data is usually kept on a card-index file which, because it is needed by different users, has to be reproduced several times, with great risk of error and lack of control. If it can be put on to computer tape or disk storage, these problems virtually disappear since complete tabulations — either in card form or as a print-out — can be provided to all users simultaneously and control over additions and amendments is easily centralised.

A comprehensive, up-to-date name and address file is an essential basis for operating the sales ledger by computer. The principal ways in which the computer can be used to aid credit management will now be examined.

Statements

Most, if not all, trading companies send statements to their customers, usually monthly. The purpose is to draw attention to unpaid items and to induce payment. So engrained is this practice that payment will often be refused — or at least delayed — on the grounds that the supplier's statement has not arrived or that it is not agreed. Some companies who pay on their own remittance advices also attach the statement giving a reconciliation, and many more use statements as a control over their own bought ledger. Demands for payment of old invoices are much easier to verify or challenge if a regular statement reconciliation takes place.

The two key features of statements are, first, timing and, secondly, clarity. Statements should be ready for despatch within as few days as possible after month-end. On a manual system where they have to be typed or photocopied, long delays are difficult to avoid compared to a computer operation. In practice the statement run-date will probably be determined by other demands on computer time, since most companies impose a cut-off system for input at month-end.

Clarity of statements demands considerable thought and planning if the end result is to help the customer identify unpaid items and reduce queries to a minimum. Exhibit 7.1 is an example of a computer statement having most of the features and headings normally required. The main points to note are as follows:

a   The statement is 'open-item' — only uncleared items are shown.
b   Each type of transaction is clearly identified — by an abbreviation rather than a code.
c   Only one value column is used, with 'CR' to denote credit items. This saves valuable space.
d   The use of an item number — generated by the computer — means that the entire line can be identified by that number. This is useful in cash reconciliation.
e   There is a running balance.
f   Customer's order number is shown against each item.
g   An aged analysis of the balance is given.

Many companies produce a statement with a tear-off portion on the right, headed 'Remittance Advice'. It is hoped that customers will return this with their cheque, thus assisting with cash reconciliation. In practice the percentage who use this slip is very small, and there is a case for using this part of the statement to give more information — customer order number and due date for payment, for example.

It is generally desirable to show on the statement all items up to the end of the calendar month. This often conflicts with internal cost periods finishing on different dates. If possible, statements should be held over to include calendar month entries falling into the subsequent cost period. This may mean disturbing the arrangements for computer time and requires careful planning with the computer manager.

With a computer system, it is easy to arrange for the statement to be produced in two or more copies — the top copy to go to the customer and the others for internal use. One copy would act as the ledger for the month — the

82

Exhibit 7.1

XYZ CO. LTD
5 New Road, Anytown, Wessex

STATEMENT

Telephone: _____
Telegrams: _____
Telex: _____

Account No.

| Customer's name and address | Document codes | Terms – Net 30 days | Page Period end |

Document codes

INV – Invoice
C/N – Credit note
D/N – Debit note
CSH – Cash
O/P – Overpayment
U/P – Underpayment
JNL – Journal
CTR – Contra

Cheques to be sent to cashiers dept at heading address. BACS payments to Barclays Bank Ltd, Anytown, A/C No. 1234567

Document date	Document code	Product	Document number	Order number	Item number	Due date	Value	CR	Balance

Current

1-30 days overdue

31-60 days overdue

Over 60 days overdue

Debit notes

Unreconciled cash

Total outstanding _____

working documents on which incoming payments and reconciliations are recorded.

Computer aids to credit control

Aged analysis

For any credit operation, unless the number of live accounts is below, say, 100, a properly designed aged analysis of the sales ledger is *vital*. Generally produced monthly — but more often if needed — this will provide information on the age of each customer's account, the total balance compared to the credit limit and the amount of cash required to keep it within terms. Exhibit 7.2 shows a typical analysis. Points to note are as follows:

a Payment terms, credit limit, risk category and area office are all clearly visible.

b Debit notes and unreconciled cash are not aged but shown in separate columns. This is important since debit notes cannot be regarded as 'collectable' items and should be controlled separately (see below under *Debit notes*).

c Customers who have exceeded their limit are highlighted by an asterisk. A better way of identifying over-limit accounts, especially in a large operation, is to have a separate tabulation.

Where different product groups are involved, the analysis can be programmed to print in the required sequence, similarly if analysis under regional offices is desired. Another useful sequence is to have an analysis by risk category.

Major account collection (MAC) schedule

In a company with many thousands of accounts, even the aged analysis can become a bulky document which because of its size is not good enough to give the credit manager immediate access to those customers needing priority attention. A further refinement is to have a Major Account Collection (MAC) schedule such as that illustrated in Exhibit 7.3. The MAC schedule only includes customers owing above a certain predetermined figure, chosen to fit the cash collection procedures. Broken down alphabetically, it forms an immediate working collection document for credit clerks. Space is available for cash targets and cash received. Debit notes are excluded altogether.

Exhibit 7.2

CUSTOMER AGE ANALYSIS		DATE 31.3.91										
A/C NO.	NAME	RISK CAT.	CREDIT LIMIT	TERMS	AREA	TOTAL BALANCE	CURRENT	1-30	31-60	61-90	OVER 90	UNALL'D CASH	D/NOTES
A1153	ABC LTD	B	100000	30	N	82546	43881	35923	37520	143		-35000	79

Exhibit 7.3

MAJOR A/C COLLECTION SCHEDULE		31.3.91								
A/C NO.	NAME	RISK CAT.	CREDIT LIMIT	TERMS	TOTAL AREA	BALANCE	CURRENT	OVERDUE	DATE PHONED	RESULT
A1153	ABC LTD	B	100000	30	N	82546	43881	38665		

Payment history

We have already noted the need for access to ledger history, so that trends in payment performance and sales volume can be detected. No visit should be made to a customer — whether the purpose is to collect money or discuss terms — without a prior look at the account history. In an open-item system this information has to be made available on a separate tabulation, as in Exhibit 7.4.

The account history is built up line by line, a month at a time. If desired it can be done on a selective basis, e.g. only category B and C customers, or only customers whose total balance has exceeded a certain minimum. A drawback to this type of payment history is that payments received at the end of the month have the same effect as those arriving at the beginning, and any deterioration in payment behaviour is only identified when the payment is delayed into the next month.

Exhibit 7.5 shows a different type of account history, in which the number of days credit taken is recorded. Payment terms have to be net monthly for this analysis to be of value, since the credit period is measured from the end of the month of invoicing. Sales volume can also be incorporated.

Reminder letters

In the next chapter, reminder letters will be examined in detail. If there are enough small accounts to necessitate reminders, the computer can be programmed to produce them on the required dates during the month based on the age and size of the debt, with further selection possible through the use of risk categories.

The merits of computer reminders are speed and economy. While the standard of computer printing has improved over the years, computer letters are usually identified as such and given the familiar treatment — into the waste-bin. If the purpose of sending a reminder, however, is primarily to start a collection cycle which only finishes when the customer has paid or is sued, computer reminders are worth using.

If it is decided to use pre-printed letters, typing in the variable details, or to type complete letters, the computer can still give assistance. A program can be set to identify all customers due to receive a first or second reminder, but instead of printing complete letters, a list of names and addresses is produced. Thus all the tedious and lengthy work of finding the relevant accounts is eliminated.

The key to success in all these operations is to write the program so that the number of letters produced but not sent is reduced to a minimum. Some points to include in the program are as follows:

Exhibit 7.4

ACCOUNT HISTORY 31.3.91

A/C NO.	NAME	RISK CAT.	CREDIT LIMIT	TERMS	AREA	TOTAL BALANCE	CURRENT	1-30	31-60	61-90	OVER 90	UNALL'D CASH	D/NOTES	SALES TO-DATE
A1153	ABC LTD	B	100000	30	N									
		PERIOD END	9-90											
			10-90											
			11-90											
			12-90											
			01-91			66355	37520	28365	22873		518	-23000	79	37520
			02-91			69887	35923	37520	28365			-32000	79	73443
			03-91			82546	43881	35923	37520	143		-35000	79	117324

Exhibit 7.5

ACCOUNT HISTORY - DAYS CREDIT TAKEN 31.3.91

A/C NO.	NAME	RISK CAT.	CREDIT LIMIT	TERMS	AREA	MONTH	SALES VALUE	DAYS CREDIT TAKEN	SALES TO-DATE
A1153	ABC LTD	B	100000	30	N				
						9-90			
						10-90			
						11-90			
						12-90			
						01-91	37520	69	37520
						02-91	35923	75	73443
						03-91	43881		117324

a Do not add in the value of debit notes to the overdue total.

b Do not print a first reminder if a second reminder was sent last month for an account which is still unpaid.

c Do not print letters for overdue accounts if unreconciled cash or credit notes have been entered on the account after the date of overdues.

Order-entry

A computer order-entry program was described in Chapter 6. The advantage and indeed the *raison d'être* of such systems is to allow management by exception. Time is precious and, whenever possible, routine checking should be delegated to a machine, leaving the credit manager free to concentrate on the problems which demand judgement.

Real-time systems

A big step forward in recent years has been the development of direct access to computer records through terminals, eliminating the need for written instructions followed by punching. The main advantages are as follows:

1 Up-dating of master file This involves the facility to add or change information held on the name and address file (see above). The new data would be fed in through a keyboard with a display screen showing the amended record.

2 Entry and reconciliation of cash This can be achieved in either one or two stages. If two stages are needed, the first action is to credit the account with the value received. This might be done by the cashier's department, but payments which have to be split between two or more accounts, and payments which require intimate knowledge of the ledger before being correctly identified, can cause problems. It is probably better to leave the job to the credit department. The second stage involves reconciling the new credit entry with the appropriate debits (and credits). Where large and detailed remittances are involved — especially if debit notes and under- and over-payments have to be put on the account — a certain amount of preparatory paperwork will be necessary before the allocation can proceed. Entry to the account can either be through a keyboard alongside the display or directly on to the screen by using a cursor.

3 Interrogation Unlike up-dating and cash reconciliation, interrogation can be available to a much wider range of users. Sales offices can interrogate the master file to check a name and address with an account number. Shipping offices can check despatch addresses. The credit manager can telephone a customer and have his account on the screen whilst talking. Controls are necessary to avoid the possibility of the sales manager making his own credit decisions through being able to call up a customer's account on his display terminal. A print facility should be available so that hard copies can be obtained immediately.

The information actually displayed for an account should be a replica of the ledger plus details of credit limit, risk category and, if possible, details of the last payment received and recent payment history.

4 Follow-up systems Many real-time systems now provide excellent aids to collection work, enabling the credit controller to select his priorities through a terminal on the basis of criteria such as age of debt, size of debt, range of account numbers, accounts exceeding credit limit, etc.

Some also have a credit diary facility, whereby when the diary is 'opened', all those accounts previously noted for follow-up on that day are displayed on the screen, and the credit controller keys in the details and results of his phone calls and the next follow-up date.

It is easy to enthuse over computer systems and to aim constantly for improvements and extensions. What has to be borne in mind is whether the costs of enhancements are justified by the benefits. Generally speaking, benefits resulting from computerised credit/ledger systems come under two headings:
a Efficiency and overall credit performance.
b Staff savings.
The first of these is always difficult to prove, particularly when a basic computer system is already operating and the improvements sought involve expensive equipment. A far more convincing case is to indicate a reduction in headcount. In a large department this should certainly be possible where the introduction of real-time systems eliminates a great deal of manual data preparation.

Debit notes

Most manufacturing companies have debit note problems, and these are usually given low priority amongst the routines and procedures of the sales ledger/credit department.

The inevitable consequence of neglect is a gradual build-up of debit notes on the ledger which have to be excluded from cash collections and which are actually a fictitious asset. The credit manager must not ignore the problem but establish controls.

A debit note is defined as a claim for credit made by a customer on a supplier, arising for one of three principal reasons:
1   Goods or services not received (either wholly or in part).

2 Goods or services believed to be incorrectly priced or invoiced.
3 Goods returned.

Clearance of debit notes, either by the issue of credit or proof of customer liability, depends upon action by other departments — production, engineering, quality control, sales, despatch, invoicing — none of whom are ever particularly interested in spending time on these queries. More often than not, the onus will be on the credit manager to activate people outside his control. Controls come under two headings: records and investigation.

Records

Proper records of all debit notes must be kept, preferably within the credit department, in whatever sequence is the most useful — by customer or by product group are common. Customers should be asked to send their debit notes to the person in charge of these files and internal instructions given to ensure that all debit notes are forwarded to the credit department. If the value of debit notes warrants it, it may be necessary to have a separate section within the credit department doing nothing but debit note control.

For large accounts which have a constant high volume of debit notes, it is worthwhile keeping a record card with space to show the history and status of each item. Exhibit 7.6 gives an example of this.

An alternative for a computerised ledger is to have a monthly tabulation of debit notes on each account. Since notes about follow-up and clearance constantly have to be added, a card system may still be preferred.

Investigation

A copy of every incoming debit note should be sent to the appropriate person/department with a request for clearance. This must be followed up regularly. If the complaint is not accepted, a letter of explanation must be written to the customer with a copy to the credit department. Similarly, the issue of part credit should also be covered by a letter.

A common evasion of controls which should be resisted strongly is the practice of free-of-charge replacements. This may seem a quick and inexpensive way of clearing debit notes, but all too often the action needed to cancel the debit note through the customer's purchase ledger is not taken. The apparently unnecessary costs of crediting and re-invoicing are invariably outweighed by the fact that the accounts of both parties are straight.

If, despite these controls, the problem continues to grow, the credit manager should highlight it in his reports to management. Different aspects which can be featured include:

Exhibit 7.6

DEBIT NOTE RECORD

Date	Debit note	Product code	Value	Covered by provision	Copy sent to	Date	Liability accepted Credit note issued			Liability denied		Customer pays	Remarks
							No.	Date	Value	Letter to customer	Customer accepts		

a　The effect on cash-flow. Calculate how many days' sales are accounted for by debit notes.

b　The impact on profits resulting from the need to carry provisions against debit notes.

c　The detrimental effect of uncleared debit notes on customer relations.

One final point on debit notes. Customers who do *not* raise them will cost the company far more than those who do, since it is better to be paid 100 per cent less 5 per cent debit notes than for the whole 100 per cent to be withheld for the sake of 5 per cent credit.

Filing

A well run filing system, while never in the limelight, is nonetheless essential for an efficient credit operation. It is only when filing gets out of hand that its importance is recognised.

Certain documents by their nature can only be filed one way, i.e. correspondence and status files (alphabetically) and invoices (numerically). Other papers, such as remittance advices, need a little thought. Many companies keep all the remittance advices for one month together in date sequence. This may be satisfactory, until something is taken out. A much better system is to file the advices by customer. Big customers will have individual files and others will merely run alphabetically.

A major problem with computer tabulations is space. Microfilm is the answer, providing money is available, but the credit manager must decide which tabulations need to be kept and for how long — apart from the sales ledger print-out which has to be kept for six years.

Chapter 8

Collecting the cash

Effective collections do not just happen. They are the result of planning.

Organisation

The traditional method of follow-up is to start at 'A' and plod through hoping to reach 'Z' before the month has finished. Even where the number of accounts is small or there are sufficient people to ensure 100 per cent coverage, this is a very inefficient system.

Most companies will find that the pattern of their sales ledger follows to a greater or lesser degree the Pareto principle. This means that 20 per cent of customers account for 80 per cent of sales. Frequently the proportion of high-volume accounts is even smaller. Exhibit 8.1 illustrates this. Given the spread of debt in Exhibit 8.1, it is immediately apparent that priority attention to the 300 largest customers will be more rewarding than an A–Z routine.

This fundamental step of determining how the debt is spread should be the first action of the credit manager in organising collection operations. The advantage of a computer system over a manual ledger is evident in this situation, as a simple program can identify or tabulate the large balances. Depending on the size of the ledger, the number of staff and the degree of sophistication required, other priorities in the collection routine can also be set. Examples of these are as follows:

1 All accounts with items aged over 90 days overdue.

Exhibit 8.1   The Pareto principle in the sales ledger

Group	Number of accounts	Range of balances	Total value, £	Percentage of total number	Percentage of total value
A	1000	Under £100	50,000	33.3	} 10
B	1,700	£100–£500	425,000	56.7	
C	190	£500–£5,000	860,000 ⎤		
D	100	£5,000–£50,000	2,295,000 ⎬ 10	} 90	
E	10	Over £50,000	1,120,000 ⎦		
TOTAL	3,000		£4,750,000		

2   All accounts in risk category C exceeding £500.

3   All accounts in risk categories B and C which have exceeded their credit limit.

These suggested priorities lead to another basic principle. To collect regularly current or near-current debts, ignoring long overdue items, is a short-sighted policy that will ultimately bring disaster. Study of the monthly age analysis will reveal areas where debts are stagnating. When these are found they must be brought into the open and reported on until cleared. Most age analyses have an end column on the right-hand side representing the oldest age bracket — perhaps over 90 or 120 days overdue. Neglected overdues fall into this column. A sure sign of bad credit control is a steady increase in this figure — which may go hand-in-hand with collections regularly on target because they are based solely on current sales.

There should be two objectives of a collection programme:

1   To collect sufficient cash to meet the target for the period.

2   To reduce overdues to a minimum, with particular reference to high-risk accounts.

The type of collection procedure will be dictated to a certain extent by the resources, i.e. staff available, but it is normal and good practice for the credit manager and any supervisors or section heads to assume personal responsibility for as many 'special' or problem accounts as can be managed, leaving the others to be followed up by the credit clerks — subject to whatever priorities are laid down.

There are three methods of follow-up, the techniques of which will be examined in detail later in this chapter. These are:

a   Visit.

b   Telephone.

c   Letter.

Even in the smallest company, the manager responsible for credit (whatever his job-title may be) should find time for an occasional visit to large customers. When the proprietor of a company does his own credit control, personal contact with his major buyers is a basic part of his routine, and this should not be neglected as the firm grows in size.

Some companies employ credit representatives who spend most of their time visiting customers. But the bulk of follow-up has to be done by telephone or by letter, and the credit manager must decide how much customer chasing can be done by telephone.

A good credit clerk not involved in ledger work will do well to average 30 telephone calls per day. On the basis of 20 working days per month and an average of 2 calls per customer, this indicates a coverage of 300 customers. Looking back to the example in Exhibit 8.1, telephone follow-up on the 300 accounts constituting 90 per cent of the debt should be possible with one credit clerk, given that some of the biggest or most difficult accounts will be under the personal control of the credit manager. Thus the lower limit for telephone follow-up might be fixed at £500. By definition all accounts below £500 balance will require follow-up by letter.

Targets

There is always a big difference between the results of someone 'doing his best' and someone striving to achieve a target. In the credit department every person engaged in collection work needs a personal target, not only to be measured against but more importantly as a self-discipline. Individual targets may be grouped together to give sectional targets which in turn will comprise the departmental target. Fixing the cash target should be a regular monthly routine, and it should be derived from the target or budget level of receivables at which the credit manager is aiming. Thus a receivables budget set in the autumn of Year 1 will set the required debtor level in terms of days', weeks' or months' sales outstanding for the whole of Year 2. This may be a constant objective — 70 days' sales for instance — or a different target may be established for each month-end. This will be looked at again in Chapter 19.

To express a target in cash terms, the following procedure is recommended. At the end of December, a cash target has to be issued which will produce a debtor level of 70 days at the end of January. Total debtors are £5,000,000, December sales £2,400,000 and November sales £2,000,000. The cash target is calculated as shown in Exhibit 8.2.

As soon as the total cash target is fixed it must be broken down as far as possible. Ideally, as already stated, every individual should have a target. When this smallest unit is reached, the individual or section should consider what has to be done to achieve the target. This will involve some form of listing of major accounts, an example of which is illustrated in Exhibit 8.3.

The use of targets and collection schedules can be further extended to include graphs and charts, so that each section or individual can watch his

Exhibit 8.2

```
Stage I
                                       Target 70 days
LESS number of calendar days in January        (31)
LESS number of calendar days in December       (31)
                                               ----
                                       Balance  8 days
                       = 27% of November calendar days

Stage II

Cash required is therefore the total
debtors at the end of December              5,000,000
LESS (a) All December sales                 2,400,000
     (b) 27% of November sales                540,000

Therefore the amount required is £2,060,000
```

---

progress through the month, as actual cash received is plotted alongside the 'cash required' line. While these have great visual impact and can promote a degree of competition, the credit manager should be wary. Some of the time spent in preparing and up-dating such displays might be better used in actually collecting cash, and a row of out-of-date or uncompleted charts is always a dismal sight.

Considerable care is required in the fixing of sectional targets. For example, the export section will almost certainly be running at a higher debtor level than domestic sections. A section of Ministry accounts, where payment depends on accurate and timely documentation, might be expected to operate at a lower debtor level than a section of local government accounts.

When the month is over and the results against targets are known, not much time should be spent on 'post-mortems'. The actual cash shortfall, if any, will automatically be carried forward into the next month's target and the collectors will know which customers have let them down or are proving difficult to move. In practice, there is often a week or so at the beginning of the month before the new target is fixed. During this early period every effort should be made to collect the late arrivals. This underlines another common-sense point which is often forgotten — the collection cycle is continuous and does not start with a blank sheet each month.

Preparation

Collection begins with the invoice, followed by the statement. The importance of both invoices and statements being rendered promptly and clearly has been looked at in Chapter 7. The credit manager should pay special attention to invoices. Is the order number quoted? Most companies have an absolute rule that no invoice can be approved unless it has a valid order number. It would prevent a lot of frustration and wasted effort if the supplier had an equally rigid policy about the despatch of goods and the raising of invoices. Another vital aspect is the name and address on the invoice. Large organisations often have complex procedures for the routing of invoices, often dependent upon which order-number prefix is shown. If these requirements are ignored, there will inevitably be delays before the invoice is passed for payment. A further complication that arises sometimes is that the customer may need to match the invoice with his own goods-received note in order to move the invoice into the 'authorised' file. If the credit department does not normally see customer orders, the sales office will be relied upon to interpret the buyer's instructions for invoicing. In dealing with large customers likely to have special requirements, the credit manager should ensure there is good liaison with the sales office. Exhibit 8.4 provides a check-list for good invoicing.

A further 'pre-follow-up' point concerns proof of delivery. If goods are delivered by road or rail, there will be a signed delivery note which should find its way back to the transport manager. This person may be first class at organising transport and arranging despatch of documents, but he may not

Exhibit 8.3 Cash planning form

MAJOR CUSTOMERS RECEIVED	RISK CATEGORY & CREDIT LIMIT	TOTAL OVERDUE	CURRENT	PROMISED
AAA & CO.LTD	A 150000	1381	73772	
ABC LTD	B 100000	38665	43881	
ALSO RAN LTD	C 25000	17889	6544	
—	—	—	—	
—	—	—	—	
—	—	—	—	
ZED LTD	B 5000	1459	2663	
TOTAL MAJOR CUSTOMERS		453766	244797	
TOTAL OTHER CUSTOMERS		8776	14006	
TOTAL ALL CUSTOMERS		462542	258803	
TARGET FOR THIS MONTH		641944	(TO ACHIEVE 45 DAYS CREDIT)	

be aware of the potential trouble if a careful check is not made that every delivery note is returned, signed and dated, with the receiving company's stamp also shown and, finally, filed in sequence. It is up to the credit manager to prevent problems of this kind. Similarly when customers return goods, the goods receiving procedure should be in good order. If possible, the credit department should be told automatically about goods returned so that the relevant invoice can be tagged and the follow-up routine adjusted. This principle also applies to queries of any kind which are received by the sales office. Education on the need to keep the credit department informed will pay dividends. The lack of good communications will undoubtedly result in customer goodwill being lost. Proper records must be kept of all customer follow-up. The best computer systems now have the facility to record and display on the screen not only the relatively permanent data on each customer — telephone, telex and fax numbers, and contact names — but also the action taken by credit control in a notepad/diary format. If such a system is not in use, a record card must be kept.

A card is needed for every account — big enough to last at least 12 months. Large customers may warrant a correspondence file of their own and the same principle applies — every call must be recorded. Not only is this a record to check back on before the next follow-up, it also provides a continuous record of relations with each customer. The best on-line computer systems offer a credit diary facility which makes record cards unnecessary.

The final point before we examine the actual collection techniques is the approach to the customer. It is a regrettable fact that in many UK industries it is common practice to ignore payment terms and to take at least an extra month's credit. The golden rule is — do *not* apologise for requesting payment. The customer has ordered and you have supplied goods on certain agreed terms. The contract is not complete until payment is made, and you are entitled to expect payment to be made to terms.

Credit visits

Credit visits other than for assessment purposes may be undertaken for many reasons, principally as follows —
1 To establish and develop personal relationships with key contacts.
2 To understand the invoice approval and payment systems so that invoicing and follow-up procedures can be aimed at the right people at the right time.
3 To resolve queries that are delaying payment.
4 To collect cheques.
5 To offer counselling, i.e. advice on improving credit control.

Exhibit 8.4   Good invoicing check-list

1 Check the customer name and address on the order. The existing name and address file may be out of date.

2 If there is a separate delivery address, show this on the invoice.

3 Quote the customer's order number

4 Check that the invoice detail matches the order detail.

5 Check that invoice and order prices agree.

6 Quote the final value clearly, also your payment terms.

7 Show the VAT rate, and quote your VAT number.

8 Check if the invoice should be sent to a specific person. If not, address it to the Purchase Ledger.

9 Ensure that credit notes quote both the original invoice number and the customer debit note number (if any).

10 Raise and despatch invoices as quickly as possible after delivery or service date.

Some companies employ credit representatives to visit major customers regularly with all of the above objectives in view.

Successful credit visiting requires a skilled approach. The manager or representative must be friendly and sociable and equally at ease whether over a pint with the bought ledger supervisor or entertaining the finance director to a four-star lunch. He requires considerable tact and diplomacy to move between accounts payable and purchasing, helping to lift his company's queries out of the log-jam in the buying office and bringing the cheque to the top of the pile. Apart from these requirements, he needs endless patience and determination, and the ability to realise when a fresh approach is needed and to recognise when a particular contact is proving valueless.

Successful credit visits also need proper back-up from the office. Frustration will soon set in if, when the time comes for a return visit, none of the queries brought back last time have been answered.

There are two problems likely to occur with credit representatives. First, because he is constantly dealing with queries and has also to remain on friendly terms with his contacts, he may gradually develop the attitude that his company is always wrong and always be ready to support the customer in his claims for credit and his arguments against having to pay. The second problem is simply that in developing such friendly relationships, the main objective — to be paid — is lost sight of. One partial solution (assuming more than one representative is employed) is to switch them around occasionally. This has the disadvantage that contacts have to be built up again and continuity is lost. The only real solution is for the credit manager to step in before the problems develop and to guide the representative on to the right path.

There is no satisfactory alternative method of controlling large accounts. 'Large' means accounts with several hundred open items. Telephone follow-up is not very practicable — apart from chasing a cheque — because of the large number of items that may have to be discussed. Letters are no better, since although these can run to great lengths in detailing outstanding problems, there is no way of ensuring that they are handled within a reasonable period. Long and complicated letters from suppliers tend to remain at the bottom of the pile while the short, easy ones are dealt with. If the company cannot afford a credit representative, then the credit manager must go out himself to do these visits. Indeed it is desirable that he makes visits whether or not representatives are on hand. The credit manager who remains behind his desk every day will rapidly lose touch with both his customers and his staff.

The second kind of customer visit needs a rather different approach. Whilst the basic aim is always the same — how to extract payment quickly and painlessly — the emphasis shifts from a battle with administrative problems to the narrower questions of when will the account be paid and what are the risks of continuing to supply. The decision to visit rather than continue to telephone or write usually depends on the size (or the potential size) of the business. Thus an account of £100 will rarely justify a journey, even though the circumstances, if known, might be as equally deserving as a £10,000 account. Time does not permit many visits in a month, however, and selection has to be on the basis of value to the company, whether the value is seen in terms of a possible bad debt or as profitable sales.

The following procedure is recommended:

1 Make an appointment at the highest level appropriate to the size of the customer. This can range from the proprietor of a small firm through the finance director of a medium-sized concern to the chief accountant of a large company. Very often it is helpful to make the arrangements through your sales manager, in which case the buyer may be the first contact. He can prove a useful ally against his own financial people!

2 Prepare the facts thoroughly before going. A clear summary of the last six months' payments is essential to demonstrate the justice of your case. Details of all orders on hand plus an estimate of future business will be useful. Finally a review should be made of the latest available status information.

3 On arriving at the premises, contrive to see as much as possible of the factory and offices to gain an impression of the level of activity, the amount of stock or finished goods and the general appearance of the firm. If a tour round is offered after talks have finished, always accept and never hesitate to ask questions — even though they may reveal your ignorance!

4 The actual approach when discussions begin will depend on the precise reason for the call. If it is simply to obtain immediate payment, having already decided that no more business will be accepted, there is little to do beyond being polite but insistent. Give the impression you are prepared to wait all day, but make it clear that the next step will be to instruct solicitors. Never refer to legal action unless you are ready to proceed accordingly and without delay.

If the ability to pay is not in question, it is necessary to find out why the account is outstanding. Reasons generally come under one of four headings:

a   Inefficiency.
b   Dissatisfaction.
c   Deliberate policy.
d   Misunderstanding or uncertainty over terms of payment.

A brief discussion should reveal which one.

Inefficiency

Causes of inefficiency are legion: 'we are going on to computer', 'we are short of staff', 'we are centralising/decentralising', are common excuses. Sometimes the real reason is not known until persistent probing from a supplier unearths a fault in the system no one had noticed.

It is always worth asking how the invoice-approval procedure works. (This should also be done on the 'administrative visits' described earlier in this chapter.) If there is time, meet the person responsible for handling goods received notes, the clerk who checks the price and order number and the clerk who is finally responsible for moving invoices on to the approved for payment list.

If there really is inefficiency on a big scale, the credit manager has to decide whether to live with it — albeit hoping for some improvement to result from getting himself known to the key people — or to take a tough line and demand that payments be made to terms. Ultimately, a tough line must be taken, but it may be better to accept a transition period and thereby retain goodwill than to insist on immediate action.

Dissatisfaction

There may be a legitimate complaint which has already been voiced but left unresolved. The best answer is to settle the query, which may require a joint visit with the salesman, but if this is impossible the next best thing is to identify and isolate the amount in dispute and to persuade the customer to pay everything else. Thus if a £5,000 invoice is withheld because of a price increase or an alleged shortage, it is reasonable to seek payment less a deduction. Indeed, if the value in query is a very small proportion of the total, it is highly unreasonable of the customer to refuse the whole invoice (or all the month's invoices if a price increase is involved). Nonetheless this is a very common strategem, frequently backed up by an assertion that it is 'company policy' or that 'our system does not allow part payment'. The credit manager's skills of persuasion are at a premium in this situation.

Another fairly common problem is that of 'contra accounts'. If the customer is also supplying goods, it is only natural he will not pay any sooner than he receives payment. The most satisfactory arrangement is either for both parties to exchange cheques at month-end (assuming similar payment terms) or for one side to pay the net difference. This sounds easy, but in practice it often goes wrong because one company or the other receives invoices outside the cost period, or problems of price, delivery, etc., mean that the expected payment or off-set does not work out. Even worse problems develop when the customer is supplying goods not to your company, but to another part of your Group, or when another part of the customer's group is supplying your company. Whether different companies are involved or the buying and selling is between the same two firms, there is no legal right of off-set unless agreed by both parties in writing or evidenced by regular practice. 'Contra' disputes demand a great deal of common sense and goodwill on both sides. Without these ingredients, success can only go to the company in the stronger supply position.

Occasionally a problem comes to light because of the credit visit. An example known to the author concerned a visit to a slow-paying customer, during which it was discovered that the supplier had been delivering ahead of schedule. The customer was content to store the goods until required, but the accounts department was instructed not to pay until the due date assuming correct delivery. The result of that visit was to improve control in the despatch area of the supplier.

Deliberate policy

There are a minority of companies which set out to take as much credit as they can get away with. Very often such companies neglect their own credit control. This policy is sometimes open and avowed, but at other times it is cloaked by pretexts such as 'all our cheques have to go to head office for counter signature' or 'if you give us a discount we could pay you much quicker'. The credit manager must be able to see through these attempts to hide the fact that his company is being used to provide free working capital. Even when there is no pretence, an attempt may be made to put the credit manager in the wrong — 'all our suppliers give us 90 days' is a common ploy. If this is checked with known suppliers, it usually transpires that 90 days is being taken — but not given.

Absolute refusal to accept such treatment is the correct attitude, but it must sometimes be tempered by the commercial circumstances. The market strength of a customer can result in his being able to dictate terms, especially if orders are scarce and the factory is operating at less than full capacity. The credit manager will only tolerate this after close discussion with sales management, and he should always try to put a time limit on the arrangement. The use of sanctions is examined later in this chapter. The question of customers who *request* extended credit is deferred to Chapter 9.

Misunderstanding or uncertainty over payment terms

This may be caused by terms not being properly established at quotation or order acknowledgement stage, or possibly the customer's purchase order quoted different terms which were not noticed or challenged. Another possibility is that the salesperson told the buyer or inferred that 'it would be OK to take 60 days'. Whatever the reason, payment for the order in question will have to be received on the customer's terms. The salesperson (or Sales Manager if it is an office error) must ensure that terms for future business are clearly agreed.

A visit report must always be made. It should include full details of discussions and actions agreed, plus a review date.

No visit is complete without a report. The credit manager should insist on a written report within seven days of the visit. The report should clearly state:

a   The names and positions of everyone seen.
b   The purpose of the call.
c   Any relevant background information.
d   Details of any queries discussed.
e   Action to be taken.
f   Recommended follow-up or review date.

Telephone follow-up

The advantage of the telephone over a letter is that of personal contact. A letter can be ignored but a phone call has to be dealt with. The best possible use should therefore be made of this technique. The human voice is capable of immense variation, and the effect produced on the listener depends very much on the tone and the attitude of the caller. The object is to achieve co-operation, to persuade someone to do something he might otherwise defer or not do at all. Too much aggression can easily cause resentment, just as an apologetic half-hearted approach will fail to stimulate any response. The caller must be crisp and business-like, yet ready to pick up a hint of humour or give a sympathetic ear.

There is a good deal of skill in telephone follow-up. Some points to consider are:

1   *Preparation*   Most calls are aimed solely at obtaining this month's payment, as opposed to the wider scope of a visit. Nonetheless the caller must know something about the customer. If the call is to a bought-ledger clerk of supervisor in a big company, the approach will not be the same if it were to the proprietor of a small company. With the former it is 'the company's money' under discussion, and there is little possibility of personal feelings being involved, as can easily happen when the person at the end of the phone is having to part with his own money! Other necessary preparation includes having the record card on the desk giving details of the last call made and the name and position of the contact, as well as having the up-to-date ledger. If properly kept, the record card will also show the names of other contacts — preferably in ascending order — and some indication of the customer's paying routine. If an on-line system is used, such information will of course be displayed on the screen during the conversation.

2   *Contact*   If there is no established contract, it may take more than one call to determine which person to ask for. In some companies the key person is the purchase ledger clerk, without whose co-operation the monthly cheque never exceeds 50 per cent of the required amount. In other firms the bought ledger

manager has to be cultivated, to ensure that your cheque is in the first batch for signing and despatch. In any event it is essential to learn the invoice approval and payment release system.

3 Approach   Having determined who is the best contact, the object is now to obtain agreement to pay the total amount due. Many companies do not phone until after the account becomes overdue. Unless time does not allow, the first call should be *before* the account is due. In this situation the caller has to be more cautious in his attitude, to avoid giving the impression that debts are being chased before they are due. A useful gambit is — 'Could you please confirm the balance on our account? We are doing our monthly cash-flow forecast, and we want to be sure there are no problems. When will you be sending the cheque?' This kind of approach can be suitably modified if the balance is partly or wholly overdue. The important point is to find out how much is approved. If it is well below the required figure, express surprise and try to check through invoice by invoice. Very often the difference is caused by the customer being 'behind with the ledger', and the caller has to decide whether to accept this or to ask to speak to someone with greater authority. If queries are mentioned, it may be worth trying to settle them over the phone, but more usually this is not feasible. Payment less the amount disputed should then be requested. A common delaying tactic is the request for copy invoices. This is very frustrating, especially when it occurs regularly with the same customers, but copies must always be sent. Send them if possible the same day, marked for the attention of the contact — having first asked him to arrange a special payment as soon as they are authorised.

4 Closing the call   Always strive for a firm promise of both date and amount. Only experience will develop judgement whether promises are genuine or just an attempt to fob off. Payments that do not arrive by the date promised — allowing an extra day for postal delays — must be followed up again. Often one is told that 'all the figures are in the computer' and that 'no indication can be given until later in the month'. Find out when the figures will be available and made a point of phoning on that day. Finally, when the payment arrives, if it is less than the amount promised or expected, a return call must be made requesting an immediate further payment to make up the difference. It is not good enough to leave it until next month. The customer must recognise that he is dealing with an efficient supplier who will not be satisfied with less than full settlement.

5 Danger signals   There are a number of signs of trouble or potential trouble which telephone collectors should be taught to identify:

a   The customer insists he is buying on extended terms or is entitled to a discount.

b   The customer says he is unable to pay.

c   The customer offers to pay part now and part next month.

d   The customer offers or sends an 'open account' payment.

e   Payment is made later and later each month.

f   Promises are persistently broken.

g   The volume of unsolved queries is having a serious effect on payments.

h   Contra claims are made.

Some of the problems have already been examined, such as queries and contras. The others all indicate an inability or, at best, a determination not to pay within a reasonable period (say within one month of due date at the latest). The credit manager must decide how much responsibility is to be given to the phone collectors in pursuing these customers. Lack of time will certainly mean that some at least of these will have to be passed to the supervisor or manager to deal with, but where possible collectors should be encouraged to follow through. Training of future managers depends a great deal on the experience gained in this way.

Collection letters

Letters are not an efficient means of stimulating payments. Any company whose customers are numbered in thousands rather than hundreds has to use them, however, and they must be used as effectively as possible.

A reminder letter system should be considered under a number of headings — purpose, number, content, design and further action.

1   Purpose   Letters are sent to provoke a response, preferably payment, but failing that a promise, a plea for time, a prevarication or a reason for non-payment. The 'first reminder' should also set the machinery in motion to ensure that within a reasonable time the account is either paid or credited or under special care of some kind, e.g. legal action or extended credit.

2   Number   Having established the purpose as described above, there is little merit in a procedure which involves a long series of letters, each one couched in stronger terms than the last. Two letters should be adequate , a first reminder and a final demand.

3   Frequency and timing   Assuming payments are net monthly, the first letter ought to go around the tenth of the first month after due date. This allows for the arrival of payments that just failed to come by month-end and should also give sufficient time for the supplier to have produced his new ledger. It is usual to allow 10–14 days before the second reminder — which should also be the final demand, so that if payment is provoked, there is a reasonable chance it will arrive before the end of the month.

If payment terms are net 30 days, first reminders should really be going out continually through the month depending on invoice dates. This evens out the work-flow but creates other problems. If a customer has one invoice per week, should he be sent four reminders at weekly intervals? A high level of organisation is required to ensure that final letters and first reminders are not sent to the same customer in the same month for different invoice. Whilst a computer program can be written to cope with these difficulties, the amount of effort required to prevent errors and absurdities is probably not justified by the end result. The majority of companies have a monthly work-cycle — regardless of suppliers' terms — and in most cases the sensible course will be to treat all invoices as falling due at month-end. This does not mean that 30-day terms might as well be monthly account. The benefit of 30-day terms is the additional control given over high-risk accounts, or any accounts running near their credit limit. While no action will normally be taken until after the end of the month following invoicing, customers needing close supervision can be singled out and followed-up as soon as the 30 days have passed.

4 Content Both first and final letters should be brief, polite and to the point. Examples are given in Exhibits 8.5 and 8.6. The first reminder is addressed to the accounts payable manager, since in most companies he will be the person who decides what response (if any) to make. By contrast the second reminder is addressed to the chief accountant or company secretary, drawing his attention to the prospect of some drastic action. The words 'placed in other hands for collection' are most suitable when both collection agencies and solicitors are used. If only solicitors are used, the wording is better changed to 'put in the hands of our solicitors'.

There is no point in including such phrases as: 'please let us know if you have a query'. If there are problems, the customer will state them without being prompted. Some letters include a disclaimer about payments sent in the last few days. This is a reasonable safeguard worth having if only because of the uncertainty of the postal service.

5 Design There are two opposing schools of thought on the design of reminder letters. The one argues that they should look like individually produced letters because this increases their chances of being answered. The logical extreme of this viewpoint is to have all letters individually typed. The other theory is that since 99 per cent of all reminders go straight into the waste-paper basket, there is no point in spending time and money on them. The object is to produce them quickly and start the conveyor-belt moving. The right answer will depend on several factors:

a How many typing staff are employed (or could *fewer* be employed)?
b What is the average volume of reminders?
c Can a computer be used either to print the letters or to print a name and address list?

In a situation where several thousand reminders are sent each month, the emphasis must be on speed. Some computer systems will produce letters. The alternative is a word-processor on which letter formats are stored, so that only name, address and account details have to be entered. If practicable, all final letters should be faxed.

Exhibit 8.5   Specimen first reminder

---

10 June 19..

Attention: <u>Accounts Payable Manager</u>

Dear Sirs,

We have not received payment for your April
account, value £75.63, which was due at the end of May.

Your prompt attention to this will be appreciated.

Yours faithfully,

Exhibit 8.6   Specimen final letter

Attention: <u>The Chief Accountant</u>

Dear Sirs,

<u>FINAL NOTICE - £75.63</u>

We cannot trace any response to our previous
reminders about this account.

We are not aware of any reason why it should not
be paid and we must now ask you to arrange full
settlement within seven days.

Failure to pay will result in the account being
placed in other hands for collection without further
reference to you.

Yours faithfully,

---

6 *Further action* It is a cardinal principle that action threatened must always be carried out. If seven days is the time limit then on day 8 the 'further action' must be taken, whether it be to instruct solicitors, put the account out for collection, stop supplies or just a phone call in a final attempt to avert a crisis. Legal action and the use of collection agents are dealt with in the next chapter. Stopping supplies is examined later in this chapter.

Payments that only clear part of the overdue account must be followed up immediately and brought back into the collection cycle on a revised time-scale. Exhibit 8.7 shows a letter of the type required.

Exhibit 8.7 Specimen part-payment reminder

```
Attention: Accounts Payable Manager

Dear Sirs,

Thank you for your payment of £34.27.

This clears part of the overdue account referred to
in our recent letter, leaving a balance of £41.36.

Your attention to this will be appreciated and we
look forward to receiving a further cheque from you.

                    Yours faithfully,
```

Other collection aids

Under this heading there are three different methods which may be used alone or in conjunction with letters or telephone follow-up:

1 Statements stickers These are brightly coloured, eye-catching, gummed labels carrying all manner of messages intended to incite payment. They are usually stuck on the monthly statement and try to give the basic message a humorous or snappy approach. Opinions vary on their effectiveness, but they are cheap enough to run a few month's trial. To make a proper test, all accounts should be sent the usual reminder letter, some with and some without stickers on the statement sent prior to the first reminder.

2 *Fax* Not only can copy invoices be sent and received within minutes, but also complete collection letters, with the certainty of immediate receipt.

3 *E-mail* Electronic mail now offers an alternative means of communication, even more person-to-person than a fax.

4 *Sales staff* Some companies make cash collection an integral part of the sales representative's job. Others take pains not to involve the sales force. The main argument in favour is the sales representative's personal contact with customers, especially with buyers who are often very influential in the payment of suppliers. Against this has to be set the fact that the sales representative's primary responsibility is to sell and that he should not be expected to risk damaging his relationships by asking for money.

While both these arguments are strong, the most satisfactory arrangement is for the credit manager to have sufficient resources within his department to do the job. If he knows that he can enlist the aid of sales staff or the sales manager when necessary, so much the better. Credit and sales departments should give each other their itineraries for each month so that the best use can be made of customer visits.

Stopping supplies

It is sometimes said that if the credit manager has to stop supplies in order to obtain payment he has failed. This is incorrect. The primary duty of the credit manager is to protect the company's investment, which may occasionally necessitate suspending delivery to minimise a possible bad debt, or more frequently to extract payment from a recalcitrant customer.

Earlier in this chapter the reasons for non-payment were discussed under five basic headings:

1 Inability.
2 Inefficiency.
3 Dissatisfaction.
4 Deliberate policy.
5 Misunderstanding or uncertainty over terms of payment.

If the customer is unable to pay, stopping further supplies is an obvious step to avoid increasing the problem. There are occasions when a customer pleads for a continuation of deliveries on the grounds that the product is essential to the life of the company. Whether this is true or not, the credit manager must be sure not to increase the size of the risk — unless he is convinced that with his company's support the debtor company will survive. This is always very difficult to assess and will be examined in more detail in Chapter 9.

Where inefficiency is delaying payment, stopping supplies should be a last resort, invoked only when it is apparent that no real effort is being made to put matters right.

Non-payment because of dissatisfaction should never result in a stoppage, unless the customer is being totally unreasonable, e.g. withholding £1,000 when only £5 is in dispute.

Customers who do not pay as deliberate policy should be cut off as soon as the condition is recognised. There is often great reluctance by small firms to withhold delivery to large companies because they fear the possibility of losing business. In practice this is unlikely to happen since the small supplier is usually chosen for the ability to supply a particular — often specialist — item which is not readily available from another source. Problems do arise with the supply of a standard off-the-shelf product for which there are always a number of alternative sources. In these situations a delicate balance must be held between losing too much profit on overdue accounts and risking the loss of business through too strict credit control. The advantages of credit interchange are at their greatest at such times. The names of habitual bad-payers who move from one supplier to another become well known. Sensible policies by members of the interchange group can curtail these activities to the benefit of all.

When a decision is made to stop delivery, the first step should be to check whether there are any outstanding orders on hand. If there are, the buyer should be told at once, quoting his order number and other particulars. If there are no orders outstanding, no action should be taken until the next order arrives. To advise a customer that supplies are stopped when no supplies are wanted is an invitation not to pay until the next delivery is required. All communication about stopped orders should be with the buyer. He probably does not know the account is overdue and can be very influential in obtaining payment.

It is not possible to say exactly when supplies should be stopped. Clearly it should be not too quickly after due date, and equally clearly it should not be so late as to give the company a reputation for lax and feeble control. For most companies the right moment will be somewhere between the middle of the first and second overdue months. Exceptions to this should be 'high-risk' accounts (Category C on the system recommended in Chapter 6), which demand very tight control because of the credit risk or because of their persistent bad payment record — or both.

Records need to be kept of the dates customers are put on and taken off the stoplist or blacklist. Any customers who have to be stopped so frequently that they are more often on than off the blacklist should be considered for pro-forma terms.

Close liaison with sales is vital in the operation of a blacklist. Prior notice of stop action should be given, either by a list of names or through the sending of a copy of the first or final reminder (depending at what point supplies are to be stopped). If large customers are involved, a briefing with the sales manager is desirable. A phone call to the buyer may be sufficient to avert a crisis.

Overdue accounts

Whilst the above review of collection methods may be said to cover the problem of overdue accounts, it is worth stepping back for a moment to distinguish the wood from the trees.

In Chapter 1 the declining value of overdues was examined in the context of the cost of credit. Sooner or later most companies wake up to an 'overdue problem'. How should this be tackled?

Planning is necessary, if the operation is not to degenerate into an uncoordinated series of panic measures.

Stage I   Identify the problem, both in terms of value, number and age.

Stage II Break it down into controllable units, defining each individual's responsibility.

Stage III Set targets for each person. These should be achievable — just. It may be worthwhile to introduce incentives such as cash bonuses or holidays, but these cannot be maintained forever, and the possibility of a slump in later results must be weighed against the prospects of high achievement early on.

Stage IV Action plan. Draw up guidelines on the use of different techniques — visits, phone calls, reminders.

Stage V   Monitor results. On a monthly basis, giving more points for a reduction in, say, over-90-day overdues than for more current items. Accounts which cannot be collected because of sales or service queries must be highlighted and brought to the notice of the appropriate managers every month until action is taken.

Chapter 9

Debtors in distress, collection agencies, legal action and insolvency

Debtors in distress

Customers who ask for extended credit as opposed to those who take it deserve more sympathetic consideration. Decisions must be based on the merits of each case, subject to the observance of three cardinal principles:
1   How is the credit risk affected?
2   Will the customer pay the cost of extra credit?
3   What is the impact on cash-flow?
   The most important of these criteria is the effect on credit risk. The credit manager relies here on his judgement, having first made sure he has all the available facts. A customer on 30-day terms with a good record of payment, who is well regarded by sales, requests an additional 30 or 60 days' credit for a temporary period of, say, six months. Typical of the reasons advanced for such requests are:

'Rather than reduce production and cut our labour force, we have decided to make for stock in anticipation of an upturn in the market later this year. To help finance this we are asking our major suppliers to give us extended credit for the period. . . .'

'A major export contract has fallen through, giving us a temporary cash-flow problem.'

'We are going to raise additional capital shortly and ask you to bear with us in the meantime.'

'We are reorganising our company/group of companies/capital structure and hope you can. . . .'

'If you want to keep our business you must give longer terms as our other suppliers do.'

All such approaches should be examined carefully and sceptically. A number of questions have to be asked, either directly of the customer or during the analysis.

1 Why are suppliers being asked to help, rather than the bank and/or the parent company?
2 From the latest available accounts, does the company seem to be basically sound and profitable? (Ask for last month's accounts.)
3 What are other companies doing in the same industry? Is this a common problem?
4 What is the attitude of other major suppliers? (Phone them and find out.)
5 How much will the credit limit need to be increased by to accommodate the extra time?

If the risk category system described in Chapter 6 is operating, a customer in Category A or B stands a reasonable chance of a favourable reply — given that the reasons and motive are accepted — whereas a Category C risk by definition will be very hard to approve.

Payment of the cost of extended credit is usually offered by the buyer. If not, it should be requested so that any illusions of free finance are immediately quashed. If business is to be retained (or even increased), the profit level must not be eroded by extra credit costs.

The final point to consider is the effect on cash-flow. If a major customer is involved, there will be a noticeable shortfall during the period before payments are resumed. Can the company stand this? Will it mean a slowing of payments to suppliers? Will discounts be lost?

Behind every request for extended credit there are two possibilities which cause the credit manager sleepless nights. If help is refused and the buyer nonetheless survives (thanks to other suppliers' assistance), will there be an adverse effect? Will the company lose future sales? Clearly consultation with the sales department is important, but fear of a possible sales loss must never be allowed to upset a credit risk decision where the facts indicate an unacceptable risk. The other nagging doubt is whether refusal of help may precipitate insolvency. The only answer to this is that if insolvency is that near, the risk is almost certainly too great, and the duty of the credit manager is to minimise the bad debt loss, not increase it.

If the decision is to give assistance, the arrangement should be put in writing. There must be a clear finishing date. It is worth insisting on payment by Bill of Exchange because:
a Bills can be drawn for the face value of the supplier's statement, thus avoiding the usual shortfall problem.

b   An accepted Bill can be discounted if required.
c   An accepted Bill at the bank is better than waiting for a cheque on the due date.
d   The agreed interest charge can be included in the Bill.

Collection agencies

The intervention of a third party between supplier and customer is generally recognised to be undesirable but effective.

There are two alternative forms of outside help (disregarding factoring which is examined later in this chapter), and many companies use both a collection agency and a solicitor. Since lack of success by the former is usually followed by legal action initiated by the agency, collection agencies may be regarded as no more than an intermediate stage on the road to the Courts. There are also companies who refuse to employ agencies, preferring to go direct to a solicitor or to the Courts. It is worth examining the arguments for and against collection agencies. Before doing this, some definitions are required.

Types of collection agency

In the UK there are hundreds of firms offering to collect debts, some local or restricted to particular trades and others operating on a national basis. Three principal types can be distinguished:
a   Mercantile agencies or trade associations.
b   Voucher agencies.
c   Commercial agencies.
Mercantile agencies are non-profit-making bodies, charging an annual membership fee and a percentage of monies recovered. Voucher agencies sell books of collection vouchers to client companies who are entitled to complete a voucher for any outstanding debt and send it to the agency. A series of collection letters is then started aimed at having the debt paid direct to the supplier. If this is not successful, some voucher agencies offer to continue collection action for a further fee — usually a percentage of the debt.

The most widely used type of agency is the commercial agency which offers to try and collect a debt on the basis of 'no collection — no charge'. The best of these firms follow up by phone after one letter and may even make personal visits. In practice a client company with a reasonable level of regular business to offer can usually negotiate a special arrangement with an agency, designed to dovetail the firm's own follow-up procedures with the agency system.

115

The case for collection agencies

1 Time otherwise spent in pursuing relatively small amounts is available for other work — such as phoning large customers. In a credit department with strained resources, it makes sense to use the time available to best effect.
2 A good agency is well equipped to trace absconded debtors and verify registered offices. A credit information service is often available, plus the services of solicitors specialising in debt recovery.
3 The alternatives are more expensive:
   a Employing sufficient staff to do all collection work — whereas an agency is only paid if it collects.
   b Passing accounts direct to a solicitor at an early stage may well be as effective but at a considerably higher cost than an agency.

The case against agencies

1 Why pay an agency for doing the job of a credit department? Sufficient staff should be employed to do all collection work, and if they do not have time, they should be better trained and organised.
2 The intervention of a third party is bound to upset customer relations. The agency has no long-term interest in maintaining goodwill.

Every credit manager must decide whether to use an agency. In general, a company with a high volume of small accounts can probably benefit.

Tips on choosing an agency

1 Check that the agency is licensed for debt collection under *The Consumer Credit Act, 1974*.
2 Ensure that the agency is financially sound. Run a credit check as if it were a new customer.
3 Obtain the names of several client companies and speak to their credit managers about the agency's performance.
4 Ensure that the agency uses an audited client trust account with its bank.
5 Check that all directors and senior staff are fully bonded.
6 Check that the agency either employs or works very closely with solicitors experienced in debt recovery.
7 Ensure that all cheques received are either passed straight over on receipt or are covered by a monthly (or more frequent) payment, whichever is preferred.

8 Check that the collection procedure will be tailored to form a proper extension to one's own follow-up system. There is no point in sending a further series of letters which merely repeat requests for payment.

9 Check that a regular report is given on all accounts passed over, to avoid the possibility of 'difficult' debts being overlooked or shelved.

10 Ensure that the interest rate charged is competitive. The higher the volume of accounts, the lower the rate should be. Depending on the volume of business offered and the quality of the debts, rates can vary from as low as 1 per cent to as high as 10 per cent. Rates over 10 per cent should be resisted, but are nonetheless quite common. Many agencies have scale fees reducing in size as the debt value increases.

A final point is that it pays to experiment with several agencies, monitoring their success rate over a period of several months before deciding which offer the best service. A good agency should show a success rate of 70–80 per cent within a month of receiving instructions.

It is important to decide at what stage an account should be passed to an agency. Too early is equivalent to giving money away, since a good proportion of customers are still paying without the need of more drastic efforts. Too late and the agency is given an impossible task. The 'right time' will vary from company to company, but with the majority it should be between the end of the second and the third overdue month.

Dishonoured cheques and bills

A cheque that is returned by the bank to the supplier — often marked 'refer to drawer' — can be taken as a sure indication that the customer is close to insolvency. Immediate action should be taken, generally a demand for cash (*not* another cheque) within seven days. Under no circumstances should the cheque be returned to the customer. The same applies to a Bill of Exchange not honoured at maturity.

By contrast, a cheque may be dishonoured and returned marked 'please represent'. This means that the customer's bank believes that funds will be available and the cheque may be represented over and over again until it is either met or 'referred to drawer'. It is good practice to advise the customer that his cheque has bounced, that it will be represented on a certain future date (not beyond seven days) and that failure to have it met will result in legal action being taken.

Cheques can also be dishonoured for other reasons, including being post-dated, out-of-date (i.e. over 6 months old), if the account is closed, if counter-manded by drawer, if the account-holder is deceased or if a receiver/liquidator has been appointed. Other generally less serious problems include the lack of a signature or second signature and words and figures differing.

In every case the supplier should telephone the customer immediately to determine the appropriate action.

Legal action

A number of points need checking before legal proceedings are started:

1   Is it certain that the debt is not disputed? Check thoroughly with the sales office that there are no unanswered queries on price, delivery, etc.

2   Is the name and trading style of the customer verified? The importance of careful checking when an account is first opened now becomes apparent.

3   Is it reasonably certain that the customer has sufficient assets to pay the debt? This is generally more difficult to establish with a sole trader or partnership than with a limited company, but personal assets are available to creditors in the former cases.

4   Is there documentary evidence of the debt?

As regards a minimum figure which is worth suing for, this depends upon whether or not an outside solicitor is being used and, if not, on how management time is valued. Below £50, say, the cost benefit becomes steadily more slender. Some companies however are willing to sue for any amount to demonstrate they are not a 'soft touch', or on principle in order to stop debtors 'getting away with it' and moving on to abuse other firms.

Legal action can be taken in one of four different ways:

a   Through the company's own legal department (restricted by definition to large firms).

b   By the solicitor employed by a collection agency.

c   By the credit manager or senior member of his staff working direct with the County Court.

d   Through a solicitor. This is by far the most common method, and care should be taken in the choice of solicitor. There are firms of solicitors specialising in debt collection, but for the majority of solicitors, debt collection and insolvency work is not regarded as a major activity. While the work may not be refused, it will probably not be carried out with the same expertise a specialist firm would apply.

The detailed procedures of legal action are not covered in this book. Exhibits 9.1 and 9.2 illustrate in simple form the various stages and alternative courses which are reached in both County Court and High Court actions.

A County Court summons can be issued for any amount. There is a general rule, however, that the County Court will only deal with debts up to £25,000. All County Court judgements over £5,000 have to be executed by the High

Court sheriff rather than the County Court bailiff. Any County Court judgement exceeding £1,000 may also be transferred to the High Court. Interest can be recovered on all High Court judgements. Costs are higher in the High Court but the service is generally faster and more efficient. Approximately 80 per cent of debts placed with the sheriff are recovered either fully or in part. There are different procedures in Scotland, Northern Ireland, the Isle of Man, the Channel Islands and the Republic of Ireland.

Statutory Demand

A supplier owed at least £750 can issue a Statutory Demand for payment. A special form has to be completed, obtainable from a law stationery supplier. It is a threat to petition the court for a winding-up or bankruptcy order if payment is not received within 21 days. It must be served on limited companies at the registered office, and on non-limited businesses at the principal place of business.

Its benefit is principally against customers who have the ability to pay and who would be severely embarrassed by a winding-up petition, which is advertised in the *London Gazette*. Such public notice will generally prompt the bank to withdraw its support and freeze the debtor's account. If the debtor does not respond, the supplier must decide whether to proceed with the winding-up, in which case all suppliers will rank equally for the distribution of any available assets. The total costs and expenses of serving a winding-up petition are around £1,000.

Enforcement procedures

As indicated in Exhibits 9.1 and 9.2 there are a number of ways in which judgement may be enforced, depending on the circumstances. Before any execution costs are incurred, however, the creditor should try to find out whether there are any assets. Obtaining judgement is of no value if the debtor is insolvent.

1 Seizure of goods by the bailiff (County Court) or sheriff's officer (High Court) This is usually more effective against companies or partnerships where items of value can be found in any office, e.g. typewriters, copying machines and furniture, as compared to a private house in which the spouse of the debtor can claim to own all the furniture. In both situations there is the danger that goods are under a hire-purchase agreement. Nonetheless, the threat of seizure often brings results.

119

Exhibit 9.1 High Court procedure

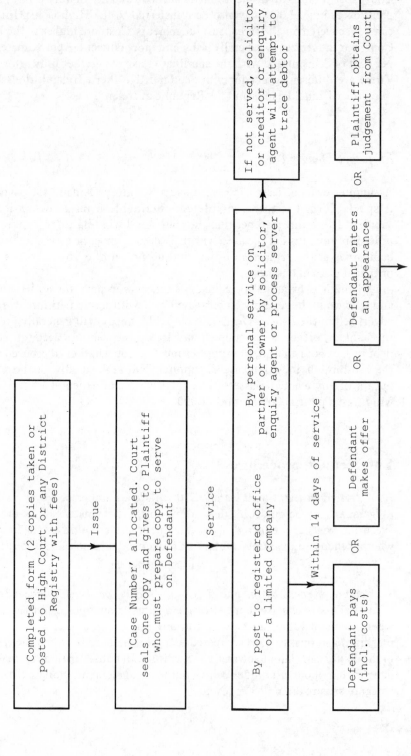

HIGH COURT WRIT

Completed form (2 copies taken or posted to High Court or any District Registry with fees)

Issue

'Case Number' allocated. Court seals one copy and gives to Plaintiff who must prepare copy to serve on Defendant

Service

By personal service on partner or owner by solicitor, enquiry agent or process server

By post to registered office of a limited company

If not served, solicitor or creditor or enquiry agent will attempt to trace debtor

Within 14 days of service

Defendant pays (incl. costs)

OR

Defendant makes offer

OR

Defendant enters an appearance

OR

Plaintiff obtains judgement from Court

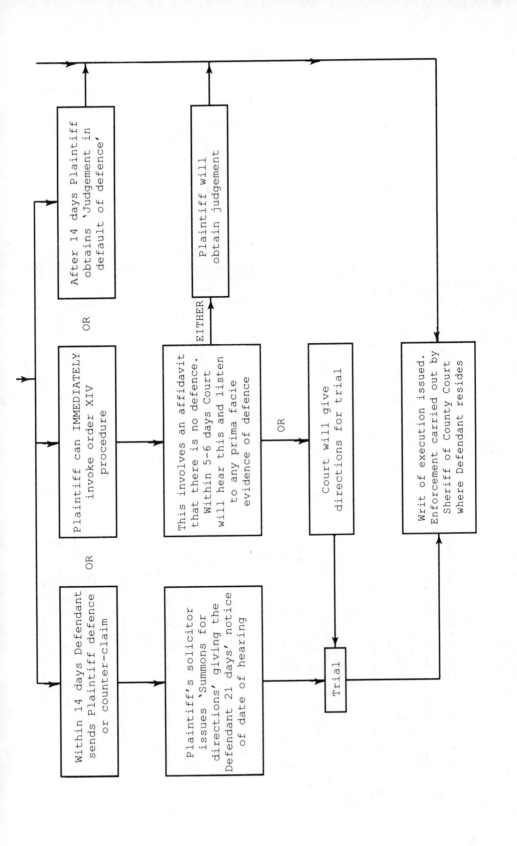

Exhibit 9.2 County Court procedure

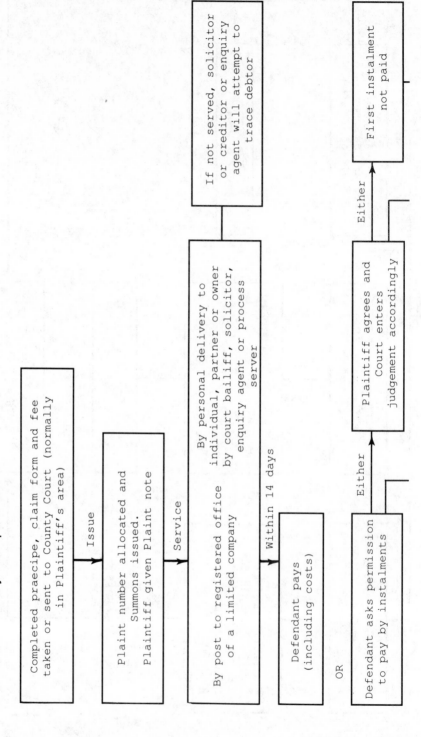

Completed praecipe, claim form and fee taken or sent to County Court (normally in Plaintiff's area)

Issue

Plaint number allocated and Summons issued. Plaintiff given Plaint note

Service

By personal delivery to individual, partner or owner by court bailiff, solicitor, enquiry agent or process server

By post to registered office of a limited company

If not served, solicitor or creditor or enquiry agent will attempt to trace debtor

Within 14 days

Defendant pays (including costs)

OR

Defendant asks permission to pay by instalments

Plaintiff agrees and Court enters judgement accordingly

Either

Either

First instalment not paid

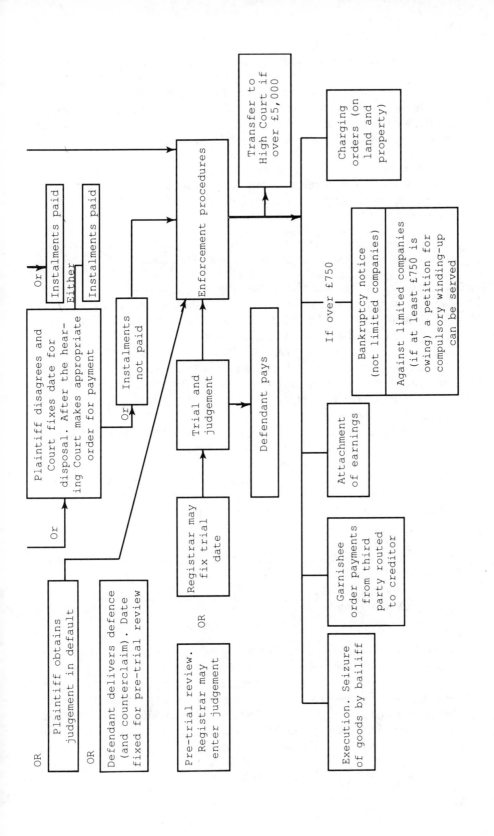

2 *Attachment of earnings* This is generally unsuccessful, depending in the first instance on the Court deciding how much 'protected earnings' should be and, secondly, on the debtor's employer co-operating fully. Since debtors are not normally in stable employment, the problems of tracing them and enforcing fresh attachment orders are immense. This remedy is only available in the County Court and against individuals in employment.

3 *Garnishee order* If the creditor can establish that a third party owes money to the debtor, application can be made for a garnishee order which requires the third party to pay the amount direct to the creditor. The most common method is to garnishee a debtor's bank account.

4 *Charging orders* A rarely used method, giving the creditor a charge on land, property or stocks and shares owned by the debtor.

5 *Bankruptcy notice (against partnerships or individuals)* The threat of bankruptcy can be very effective, providing the creditor is sure sufficient assets are available and he is confident the debtor will prefer to pay rather than go out of business. However, if the business is near to collapse anyway, there is little advantage in giving the final push since all creditors will be treated equally by the Official Receiver. It is more skilful to find a way of extracting payment without causing bankruptcy. The procedure is as follows:
a A creditor, alone or jointly owed at least £750, petitions the court for a bankruptcy order.
b Providing three weeks have elapsed since a statutory demand was made and the debtor is not able to show a reasonable prospect of paying, the court issues a bankruptcy order.
c The affairs of the debtor then come under the control of the Official Receiver, whose function is to distribute any assets between all creditors in accordance with the following order of precedence:
   (*i*)   Secured creditors.
   (*ii*) Bankruptcy costs.
   (*iii*) Preferential claims, principally rates, taxes, national insurance and a limited amount of wages and salaries.
   (*iv*) Unsecured creditors.
   (*v*)   Deferred creditors.
   (*vi*) The bankrupt.

6 *Winding-up petition (against limited companies)* Providing the debt is not below £750, a creditor with an unsatisfied judgement debt may present a winding-up petition to the High Court. The Court hears the petition — and any opposition to it — and decides whether to issue a winding-up order. Several creditors may join in the petition. If a winding-up order is made, the Official Receiver takes charge of all assets as provisional liquidator. His initial duty is to assess the financial condition of the company including the

causes of failure and make recommendations about further enquiries. Having prepared a statement to this effect, the Official receiver then must call a first meeting of creditors. This meeting decides whether to appoint an outside liquidator in place of the Official Receiver and whether to appoint a Committee of Inspection.

The liquidator's task is to realise the assets of the company and distribute them in accordance with the following order of precedence:
1 Secured creditors — *excluding* holders of floating charges.
2 Liquidation costs.
3 Preferential claims (principally rates, taxes, national insurance and a limited amount of wages and salaries).
4 Holders of floating charges.
5 Unsecured creditors.
6 Shareholders.
It is important to note that compulsory winding-up can be initiated in other ways than to enforce a judgement debt notably through use of a Statutory Demand (see page 118).

Other causes of compulsory liquidation include default in delivering the statutory report to the Registrar of Companies or in holding the statutory meeting, failure to commence its business within one year of its incorporation or suspension of business for a whole year, reduction of members below two (private companies) or seven (others), if the Court is of the opinion that winding-up is just and equitable, and, finally, if the company itself passes a special resolution to be compulsorily wound-up.

Other forms of winding-up A declaration of solvency by a company's directors enables a winding-up to be classed as a Members' voluntary winding-up. The absence of such a declaration produces a Creditors' voluntary winding-up.

A liquidator is appointed by the members in a members' winding-up. In a creditors' winding-up, both creditors and members may nominate a liquidator with the choice of the creditors taking precedence in the event of a disagreement. A liquidation committee to assist the liquidator may be appointed, but it only has statutory powers in a creditors' winding-up. In a members' winding-up, if the liquidator decides that the company is insolvent — despite the declaration of solvency — he must call a meeting of creditors and present them with a statement of affairs.

The detailed proceedings of voluntary liquidations are beyond the scope of this book.

Administrative receiverships

Under the *1986 Insolvency Act* functions previously performed by a Receiver are carried out by an Administrative Receiver. He is appointed by a debenture-holder having a floating or fixed and floating charge (usually a bank). His appointment must be notified to all creditors within 28 days. He must call a meeting of creditors within three months and present a formal report. Creditors are entitled to establish a creditor's committee which can require the administrative receiver to attend its meetings and answer questions.

The duty of an administrative receiver is primarily to protect the rights of the debenture-holder which will often result in the sale of the assets of the company and its ultimate liquidation. He has the right to sell property subject to a prior fixed charge other than the one by which he was appointed, providing the court agrees. He is deemed to be the agent of the company until liquidation commences but he is also personally liable for all contracts made in carrying out his duties. Only qualified insolvency practitioners may be appointed as administrative receivers.

The main changes effected by the *1986 Insolvency Act* are the benefits afforded to unsecured creditors who previously had no legal right to be informed about the progress of a receivership.

Administrators

The *1986 Insolvency Act* introduced a new concept for the possible rescue of companies in financial distress. The company itself, its directors, one or more creditors or any combination of these can petition the court for the appointment of an administrator. The powers of an administrator are very similar to those of an administrative receiver, including the right to sell property subject to fixed or floating charges, hire purchase agreements or retention of title clauses.

The administrator must call a meeting of creditors within three months of his appointment and submit his proposals on the future of the company. The meeting decides whether or not to approve the proposals or it may modify them with the assent of the administrator.

This procedure was intended to provide a constructive alternative to liquidation. Its main drawback is that the appointment of an administrator can be frustrated by a debenture-holder appointing an administrative receiver. In 1990 administrations accounted for less than 1 per cent of all company failures.

Corporate voluntary arrangements

A company which believes that a rescheduling of debt will be more beneficial to creditors than a liquidation and which will enable it to continue trading, can put forward proposals to both creditors and shareholders. Approval requires the consent of 75% of creditors by value and by number. It is binding on all creditors.

There have not been many successful CVAs since their introduction under the Insolvency Act of 1986. Not surprisingly creditors tend to be doubtful of the ability of an insolvent customer to trade itself out of trouble.

Conclusions A detailed description of insolvency procedures has deliberately been avoided in this book. Excellent references\ booklets on insolvency proceedings are available from the leading accountancy firms, including Cork Gully (Coopers & Lybrand), KPMG and Touche Ross.

Chapter 10

Credit insurance and factoring

The purpose of credit insurance is to guard against unexpected failures. It is not a substitute for credit management, and it does not provide a licence to sell to any willing buyer. Any company whose sales are unevenly spread among its buyers to such an extent that the failure of one or two major customers would have a serious impact on profits and cash-flow, would be well advised to consider the merits of its policy.

The leading credit insurer of domestic trade in the UK is Euler Trade Indemnity Plc. Other major underwriters include NCM, Coface LBF and Gerling Namur.

The credit insurance industry

The market consists of underwriters and brokers. A broker has two main functions. Firstly, he obtains business by selling the idea of credit insurance. Secondly, he liaises between the insurer and the insured, both in the establishment of policy terms and subsequently in the operation of the policy. It is quite possible for the policy holder to work directly with his underwriter. A valuable relationship can develop which brings benefits to both parties, but in practice it is more usual for the broker to act as middleman. This is partly because brokers see this as their job and partly because a close relationship between underwriter and policy holder is only feasible when the latter employs a credit manager of high professional standing.

The broker is paid a commission by the insurer which is part of the premium charged to the policy holder. A good broker's most valuable service is given at policy renewal, when his knowledge of the insurance business should be used to negotiate the most favourable premium for next year. Depending on the policy holder's degree of professionalism and on the time available, the broker may also handle the day-to-day running of the policy, i.e. the obtaining of limits and the submission of claims.

Since 1990 the UK credit insurance market has been open to insurers based in other EU countries, one of the stages towards the establishment of a free financial market by 1992. Companies contemplating credit insurance have a wide choice of underwriters, nearly all foreign-owned. The distinction between domestic and export business has become blurred and single policies covering both are widely available.

Types of credit insurance

The different forms of protection now available can be divided into four groups.

1   Whole turnover.

2   Datum line.

3   Catastrophe.

4   Specific account.

Certain broad principles apply in each type of policy. Since Euler Trade Indemnity is the leading company, there follow some details of how their policies operate.

1   Initial review and policy choice   Careful assessment is made of the client's credit procedures, and suggestions made where necessary to improve controls. Analysis of sales and receivables reveal the type of risk and generally determine what type of policy is most suitable. Thus a company with 5,000 customers, 1,000 of whom account for 80 per cent of turnover and receivables, may well choose a specific account or 'datum line' policy. The client decides to insure all buyers whose indebtedness exceeds an agreed figure, these buyers are identified and approved before the policy begins and new names are added as needed. This system is growing in popularity at the expense of whole-turnover policies, since many companies are happy not to pay premium on a percentage of their turnover where the individual risks are by definition very small.

The whole-turnover alternative will involve the use of a discretionary limit, which is equally, if not more, demanding on the policy holder's time and money, at a total cost equal to if not higher than that under a datum line arrangement. Trade Indemnity also benefit since they cut down on the volume of small claims. At the other end of the scale, a policy holder may wish to exclude from cover sales to some of his biggest customers on the grounds that the possibility of failure is too remote and why pay premium for nothing? Trade Indemnity will always consider such requests and, on occasions, may be quite happy to exclude certain names because they are already covering a high volume of debt and they are having difficulty in reinsuring or 'laying off the risk'. Very great care and thought needs to be exercised by the policy holder in this situation.

Since the collapse of Rolls Royce in 1971 there have been many major insolvencies, the most recent in 1995 being Union International and Dillons. No company can be regarded as a perpetual 'blue chip' credit risk.

Certain kinds of sale are automatically excluded from cover. These are:

a Sales to central or local government bodies, nationalised industries, hospitals, schools, etc.
b Sales to subsidiary or associate companies.
c Sales on pro-forma terms.
d Sales to individuals.

These definitions are not always as watertight as they may appear. In the case of companies controlled by the government, for example, Trade Indemnity may allow clients to choose whether or not to exclude them from cover.

Trade Indemnity also offer a 'multi-market' policy, giving protection against commercial risk in all EU and EFTA countries, USA, Canada, Australia, New Zealand and Japan.

2 *Policy terms* Certain terms are standard, such as the definition of insolvency. 'Protracted default' takes place when payment has not been made within 90 days of the due date. The level of indemnity, i.e. the proportion of a sale which is insured, is negotiable but rarely outside the range 75 to 90 per cent. Assuming an indemnity level of 80 per cent and a credit limit of £100,000, if insolvency occurs with £100,000 owing, the policy holder will recover £80,000.

If the balance owing is £150,000 he will still only recover £80,000, because the additional £50,000 sales have been made at his own risk and are outside the policy.

3 Premiums The rate is negotiable, depending very much on the industry record of business failures, the client's own bad debt experience, the mix of business offered and the effectiveness of the client's credit management. Rates have tended to rise over the years. For a new policy, a rate below 0.25 per cent is unusual and rates up to 1 per cent are sometimes encountered.

4 Credit limits The real test of a policy is whether the policy holder can obtain — over a period — a consistently high proportion (at least 90 per cent) of the limits requested. There will inevitably be refusals, either in the form of a maximum limit below that asked for or a complete rejection. It is here that a close relationship with the underwriter pays dividends. Confidence in the policy holder will result in better limits. The underwriter is able to tap sources of information unavailable to the policy holder, and the more he can learn about his client's business and the performance of the client's customers, the better able he is to make a correct judgement.

In requesting a credit limit, the policy holder (assuming terms are net monthly or 30 days) should calculate a figure representing around three months' sales. This allows for payment to be one month late before the limit is exceeded. To ask for less is imprudent. To ask for more should be unnecessary.

The experience of most policy holders is that Trade Indemnity is reasonably generous on limits. It has to be, since its purpose is not to restrict trade but to encourage it through protection against the unexpected failure. No policy holder should be surprised if a request for £10,000 credit on a company with equity of £100 and net worth of £500 is turned down. On the other hand, if a policy is worth anything it should enable more business to be done with the 'middle range' of buyers, because the limits given will be higher than the policy holder would care to risk on his own account.

Most policy holders have come across the situation where a maximum limit is applied on a customer. This may be because the underwriter is unable to agree a higher figure on the information available, or it may be because the underwriter has reached a 'ceiling' of cover available on that buyer in the reinsurance market. It is important that the policy holder finds out which reason is applicable, because if it is the latter he may well decide to trade beyond the maximum limit. This option is, of course, always available, but if a policy holder repeatedly chooses to exceed his credit limits, doubt must be thrown on the value of the policy.

Payment terms will naturally affect credit limits. Any extension beyond the agreed normal terms must be approved by the underwriter, even if no increase in credit limit is required. The reason is that the insurer may see such a request as part of a general approach to other suppliers, with implications that are hidden from individual clients.

Trade Indemnity will take into consideration the ledger history of a customer. If there is evidence of sound and consistent buying and paying, this can help to justify a limit which is difficult because of a lack of up-to-date information.

5 *Controls* Details of unpaid accounts must be declared when three months overdue, and even at this late stage the policy holder may, if he so wishes, put forward a case for continuing to deliver. The underwriter will be aware of overdue reports from other clients. If there is an active relationship with the underwriter, this kind of information is valuable in guiding the supplier to a good decision.

6 *Claims* Claims arising from insolvency are paid within 30 days of the client's debt being accepted against the insolvent estate. Any money eventually recovered by the policy holder after a claim has been paid must be shared between client and insurer in proportion to the insured and uninsured parts of the original debt.

In cases of protracted default, claims are not paid until six months after the date of default. Since legal action would normally have been taken within this period or the debtor declared insolvent, this type of claim has little real value apart from cases of disappearing debtors.

Trade Indemnity offer a debt collection service to policy holders.

Pre-shipment risk

Protection against losses on work-in-progress or finished goods is sometimes available from Trade Indemnity. It is more difficult to measure and evaluate but can be just as damaging as the loss of the book debt. The insolvency of a buyer just before delivery of a specially made piece of equipment can leave the manufacturer with no alternative customer and the prospect of obtaining only scrap value.

Catastrophe policies

These are available from Euler Trade Indemnity and other underwriters. The main features are as follows:

a   The client agrees to bear an aggregate first loss or 'deductible', the value of which is based upon the client's bad debt experience in recent years.

131

b Losses occurring above the level up to an agreed maximum are paid at 90 per cent or even 100 per cent.

c The approval of the insurer is only required for credit limits above an agreed (high) level.

d Premium may be calculated not on insured sales but on insured *balances*.

e Because great reliance is placed upon the competence of the insured's credit management, this is investigated thoroughly before a policy is issued.

This type of policy is only of interest to big companies, since all the insurers require a high minimum annual premium or a minimum insurable turnover (e.g. £30 million for Trade Indemnity).

Specific account policies

Some insurers (mainly Trade Indemnity and Credit and Guarantee) will offer protection against the failure of one or more named buyers.

Clearly no insurer will cover a 'high risk' name unless it is counter-balanced by a spread of 'good' risks, so the only way to use a specific account to protect against one high risk buyer is to take out a policy before that buyer comes to be regarded as a high risk. In fact, Trade Indemnity are known to have written a specific account policy against the failure of De Lorean Motor Cars Limited — and to have paid out when the Receiver was appointed one and a half years later.

Multi-market policies

Increasing trade with Europe, coupled with the single-market concept of the EU, has led many UK companies to look for single credit insurance policies covering commercial risk both in the UK and overseas. This demand has been recognised by the major insurers, all of which now offer this type of policy. Export credit insurance is dealt with specifically in Chapter 15.

Credit insurance services

Underwriters seek to attract clients by offering a more positive and interactive product than a policy which only comes to life when claims are made. The principal service offered is debt collection, which can often be more effective than a collection agency since the debtor is immediately aware that continued non-payment will affect his credit reputation. Other services include credit management advice, credit information and insolvency management.

Protection is against both the effect of bad debt losses on profit and against the temporary loss of cash-flow. Thus, creditors of Rolls Royce Limited were ultimately repaid in full, but they were denied the use of their money for years. Credit insurance bridges the gap.

Used properly, credit insurance is also a sales aid. Credit limits on many accounts will be higher than the credit manager could agree to without a safety net. When a customer runs into difficulties, the underwriter is usually very reluctant to 'come off cover' until the last possible moment, but policy holders are enabled to continue trading for longer than they would risk if unprotected.

Nonetheless credit insurance costs have to be justified in a tangible way. If premiums are paid over a number of years and the claims experience is very small, management must decide whether the cumulative outlay is still outweighed by the potential losses or whether to put next year's premium into a bad debt reserve. Very few, if any, companies build up bad debt reserves big enough to cover the sort of unexpected losses that credit insurance is aimed at. It would be unrealistic to expect them to do so, except in very high-risk industries such as construction, which demand a high degree of protection.

No kind of insurance policy is taken out with the intention of making a profit from it. Yet, unlike fire or motor insurance, credit insurance is often deemed to be a mistake unless, over a reasonable period, the value of claims paid somewhere near balances the total premium paid. One way of recognising this fact is the operation of a non-claims bonus on premium rates. Trade Indemnity do not like such schemes but occasionally can be persuaded to agree as the alternative to losing a policy. The services of a good broker are invaluable in such negotiations.

Factoring and invoicing discounting

The factoring business has grown steadily in recent years. Turnover of members of the Factors and Discounters Association was about £40 billion in 1997 from around 10,000 clients.

The biggest factoring companies are controlled by the clearing banks, which give both respectability and strength to the industry.

The services of a factor fall under three headings:

1   *Administration of the sales ledger and credit control functions from credit approval to collecting the cash*   The only functions left to the client are the

rendering of invoices and the clearance of disputes. The benefits of this include the elimination of credit enquiry and cash collection costs and the use of a sophisticated computerised sales ledger system. The cost of this diminishes as turnover rises and normally ranges between 0.5 and 3 per cent turnover.

2 *Credit insurance* Most factors cover against bad debts, although there are exceptions. The cost is included in the administration charge.

3 *Finance* Up to 80 or 85 per cent of the value of outstanding debts can be paid ahead of maturity if required. The cost will usually be slightly higher than the client's normal bank borrowing rate. If cash advances are not required, the factor will agree a cash-flow arrangement with the client, usually based on the average credit period experienced. This in itself is very advantageous since cash-flow is predetermined.

Factoring should not be regarded as an alternative to credit management, but as a service that can be of value to companies at a particular stage of development. To be eligible a turnover of at least £75,000 is normally required. As a company grows in size, its own accounting systems and staff increase, and a point will be reached where the cost of factoring (based on turnover) outweighs the benefits.

There is no doubt that the professional services provided by a factor in both ledger administration and credit control are of immense value, if only in releasing management time.

Factoring of export turnover can be arranged, either in addition to a domestic service or on its own. This latter course can be attractive to large companies operating their own domestic sales ledger, since they can use the factor's expertise to avoid currency risks, payment difficulties, and language and communication problems.

Some factoring companies offer a variation on the full factoring service — agency or bulk factoring. Under this system the client continues to operate his own sales ledger and collection function, except that customers are asked to remit to the factor. The factor provides 100 per cent bad debt protection (if required) and up to 80 per cent immediate payment against invoices.

Confidential invoice discounting involves the sale of invoices (100 per cent or on an agreed selective basis) to the factor, usually without bad debt protection and without the knowledge of the client's customers. The cost of this form of factoring is normally between 0.2 and 0.5 per cent, plus the cost of cash advances (usually at or just below the prevailing rate for bank overdrafts).

These variations on traditional factoring have enabled the factoring companies to widen their appeal and to attract clients with turnover considerably in excess of £1 million.

The decision to use a factor should be determined primarily by cost — the cost of administration and bad debt protection and the cost of finance.

Presuming the factoring service to be first-class, judgement must be made on such questions as:

1   Do we need the accelerated cash-flow?

2   How does the cost of finance compare to our normal sources (i.e. bank overdraft)?

3   Do we need bad debt protection? If we do, what would a credit insurance policy cost?

4   If the full factoring service is being considered, how do the costs compare with having our own sales ledger/credit control operation?

5   Are we prepared for credit decisions on our customers and prospective customers to be made by the factoring company?

Part Two
Export Credit
Management

The principles of credit management apply equally to export as to domestic business, but there are a number of significant differences which make export credit both more complex and more interesting.

The supply of goods or services to an overseas buyer introduces a range of factors unknown to the domestic credit manager. These arise from differences in the language, customs, currency, the regulations and the degree of industrial/commercial development found in export markets.

Over 90 per cent of all UK exports are made on 'short-term' credit, which means up to 180 days. The chapters which follow on payment terms, letters of credit and cash-flow are written primarily for this majority. Those on risk-assessment, credit insurance and foreign exchange should be of interest to all exporters. The chapters on export finance and bonds are specifically aimed at those exporters giving longer than six months' credit.

The management of trade credit in the UK has generally been under financial control, even to the extent of making it the accountant's responsibility, but control of export credit is more frequently found in the hands of sales and marketing people. Sometimes this is by design, but more often by default because the credit controller or accountant does not possess the knowledge necessary to handle export credit problems. Either way the results for the company can be disastrous. While the export sales ledger remains an accounting responsibility, the export sales office is expected to cope with documentation, credit insurance and currency. Many companies are realising that the division of functions is not sensible and that the consequences of weak control in export credit are worse than in the home market.

The professional credit manager has a major role to play in exporting. He should be the vital link between sales and finance, providing advice and guidance on payment terms, currency invoicing and smooth cash-flow. He should obtain full value from a credit insurance policy.

Chapter 11

Export risk assessment

Export risk assessment is divided into two parts — the market or political/ exchange risk and the buyer or commercial risk. In any evaluation, the market risk should be considered first, because if it proves unacceptable and unavoidable there is no point in moving on to examine the buyer risk.

Market risk

Several questions need to be asked in assessing market risk:

1   Is there any likelihood that trade between the UK and the buyer's country may be interrupted by war, revolution or some other political factor? Recent examples of this kind of problem include the former Yugoslavia and Iraq. Problems of this nature are very difficult to foresee, but caution must always be exercised in dealing with countries whose governments are either unstable or hostile to the UK, or both.

2   Will there be any difficulty in bringing payment into the UK? Shortage of foreign exchange has been a severe problem with a number of countries in recent years. Many Third World countries suffered severe economic difficulties in the 1980s. The former communist countries of Eastern Europe and the new nations created by the break-up of the Soviet empire, keen to develop trading links with the West, are also difficult markets because their imbalance of trade results in a lack of hard currency. There is also of course considerable political instability in some of them.
A country's ability to obtain foreign currency depends on its trading

position with other nations and on the way its own economy is performing. A continuous, heavy excess of imports over exports causes higher and higher borrowing from richer nations. Unless steps are taken to control this — which may be political, financial or both — confidence in the country's ability to repay borrowing diminishes. Monetary aid slows down and the government is forced to introduce even more severe controls and restraints.

The most frustrating aspect of the problem — from the point of view of both the exporter and the importer — is that the buyer may be a prosperous company which has obtained possession of the goods by paying in local currency. The fact that his bank is unable to buy sterling or whatever currency is needed means that the exporter may cease to supply and the importer suffers through no fault of his own.

Advice on possible exchange problems should always be sought from one's own bank.

3 *Are there any regulations or restrictions imposed either by the UK or by the buyer's country which may make trading difficult or virtually impossible?* Under this heading come a variety of different situations, including Nigeria which operates very tight import controls and pre-delivery inspection requirements.

These various market risks have firstly to be identified. The export credit manager must keep up to date on political, economic and financial events in the markets in which his company trades. An excellent source of market risk information is *International Risk & Payment Review* published by Dun & Bradstreet, either on-line or in book form, and updated monthly. All major banks provide intelligence reports on markets, as does the Overseas Trade Services operation of the Dept. of Trade and Industry.

Varying amounts of protection against market risks may be obtained from two sources — the use of secure payment terms and the operation of a credit insurance policy. Both these subjects are covered in separate chapters. It is necessary to point out however that these forms of protection may not be available in cases of extreme risk and they should not be regarded as alternatives. If a confirmed Letter of Credit cannot be obtained, it will be very difficult to obtain credit insurance cover. There are a number of markets where NCM cover is only available for business on letter of credit terms.

Buyer risk

As in the home market, proper analysis of buyer risk depends on good information. The quality of information varies immensely, according to the

140

market in view. Not surprisingly, in the developed, industrial nations good information is easier to find than in the Third World countries. But there are also big differences within the industrial nations, most strongly evidenced between the USA and Europe. The reason for this is the comparative weakness and low standing of the credit profession outside the USA, where to be seen as being credit-worthy is a highly-prized asset, both for companies and for individuals.

Nonetheless some progress is being made. In 1986 FECMA was formed (Federation of European Credit Management Associations), its purpose being to promote and develop co-operation on all aspects of credit management and to uplift the status of the profession. By 1997, credit management organisations existed in eleven European countries plus Israel. Membership directories are published regularly by the Institute of Credit Management.

Information sources on the commercial risk are as follows:

1 Company accounts.
2 Credit reporting agencies.
3 Banks.
4 Official sources.
5 Agents.
6 Credit contacts.

Each of these will be examined in detail.

Company accounts

North America

Balance sheet information in the USA is normally readily available. If a company refuses financial information it is reasonable to assume that there is something to hide — unlike in Europe where firms are not used to being asked to disclose. Accounts can often be obtained directly from a buyer, but they are frequently included in credit agency reports. It is common practice for many corporations to send copies of their quarterly financial statements direct to the reporting bureau. The position is similar, although not so well developed, in Canada.

Europe

Some knowledge of the forms of business organisation found in Europe is helpful, as well as facts about the legal requirements, availability and interpretation of accounts. While the principle of the limited liability company is accepted everywhere, each European nation has developed its own business structure.

Within the EU steady but slow progress has been made towards the harmonisation of company law, to facilitate the establishment of a single internal market.

There follows a brief survey of EU countries, identifying the different types of business organisation. It is worth noting that as a general principle companies are not accustomed to being approached by potential or existing suppliers and asked for financial inforamtion. During the 1990s there were over 200,000 business failures in Europe every year, so the understanding of how business operates in these countries is of great importance to the credit manager.

France   The treat majority of French businesses are small, family-controlled enterprises with a strong tradition of secrecy.

There are two forms of limited liability company, the SA (Société Anonyme) and the SARL (Société à responsibilité limitée). SAs and SARLs are classified according to their size as small, medium-sized or large companies. Large companies are those with a balance sheet value exceeding FF10 million, turnover exceeding FF20 million and more than 50 employees. Detailed balance sheets and profit and loss accounts must be filed. Small and medium-sized companies (turnover below FF3 million and between FF3 million and 20 million respectively) are permitted some modification in the filing of accounts. The AGM must be held within six months of year-end, and two copies of the accounts have to be filed with the local court within one month of the AGM. A copy of the accounts has to be filed at the Registry of the local commercial court (where it is available for public inspection). Copies are also filed and available for inspection at:

Institut National de la Propriété Industrielle,
32 Rue de la Trois Fontanets,
92016 Nanterre.

Despite these legal requirements, it difficult to obtain up-to-date balance sheets in France. Around one-third of all French companies are registered in the Paris area, causing great administrative congestion which is aggravated by the fact that most companies close their accounts on 31 December.

A personal visit may be made to the local Registry or photocopies of accounts can be requested through the post. Accounts are usually available between six and 12 months from the balance sheet date.

A translation of French accounting terms appears in the Appendix to this chapter.

Partnerships are a more common form of business than in the UK. The two principle forms are:

a   *SNC (Société en nom collectif)*   This has a separate legal existence, but partners are both jointly and severally liable for its debts.

b   *SCS (Société en commandité simple)*   This includes sleeping partners whose liability is limited to the amount of contributed capital.

There are no legal requirements for the publication or filing of accounts by partnerships.

One other form of business worthy of mention is the GIE (Groupement d'interest economique). This is a kind of joint venture, having a separate legal existence. Members are jointly and severally liable for the debts of a GIE.

Germany   German industry has a number of distinguishing features. The most important of these is the power exercised by the banks. They have very considerable shareholdings, and management decisions can be vetoed if the bank holds over 25 per cent of the equity.

There are two types of limited company: The AG (Aktiengesellschaft) and the GmbH (Gesellschaft mit beschränkter Haftung). Limited companies are classified according to size as large, medium-sized or small. Large companies must fulfil at least two of the following criteria: sales exceeding DM32 million, balance sheet value exceeding DM15.5 million, more than 250 employees. Detailed accounts must be filed at the local Commercial Register and, for large companies, in the Federal Gazette. Small companies (sales below DM8 million, balance sheet up to DM3.9 million and below 50 employees), do not have to have their accounts audited but must file balance sheets at the Commerical Register. Medium-sized companies must have their accounts audited and must file summarized balance sheets and profit and loss accounts at the Commercial Register.

A translation of German accounting terms is given in the Appendix to this chapter. German accounting practice is particularly conservative in its treatment of assets and reserves.

Another major feature of German industry is the frequent use of partnerships as a form of organisation. There are several different types of partnership, including:

a   *OHG (Offene Handelsgesellschaft)*   Partners are jointly and severally liable.

b KG (Kommanditgesellschaft) A limited partnership. Only fully liable partners can participate in management.

c GmbH & Co. KG A partnership in which the wholly liable partner is a GmbH.

No accounts have to be filed by partnerships unless two of the following three criteria are met — sales exceed DM250 million, balance-sheet exceeds DM125 million, over 5,000 employees.

Because of the strong influence of the banks, German companies do not expect to be asked to disclose their finances to creditors.

Netherlands Dutch companies are either NV (Naamloze Vennootschap) or BV (Besloten Vennootschap). The former is roughly equivalent to a public limited company and the latter to a private limited company.

NVs are classified according to size as large, medium-sized or small companies. Large companies must fulfil at least two of the following criteria — sales exceeding DFL35 million, assets exceeding DFL17 million, over 250 employees. Small companies are those with sales below DFL8 million, assets below DFL4 million and fewer than 50 employees. Small companies are permitted to file an abbreviated balance sheet at the local Chamber of Commerce, all others must file full balance sheets and profit and loss accounts.

Balance sheets may be obtained by writing to the Chamber of Commerce appropriate to the region where the company is situated. Some information is also available on-line from a central database operated by Vereniging van Kamers van Koophandel en Industrie in Nederland, Watermolenlaan 1, 3447 Gt. Woerden.

A translation of Dutch accounting terms is given in the Appendix. Dutch accounting practice is fairly close to that of the UK, and interpretation of balance sheets presents no special problems.

Belgium A feature of Belgian industry is the power of a small number of holding companies. Consolidated accounts are not required, and it is often difficult to assess a company's worth. Limited companies are either SA/NV [and also SCA — a form of limited partnership — and SC (Société Cooperative)].

Limited companies are required to file annual accounts with the local commercial court. Accounts are available for inspection locally and at the central bank (BNB — Centrale des Bilans, Boulevard du Berlaimont 5, 1000 Bruxelles). Small companies (i.e. those meeting two of the following criteria — balance sheet total below BF70 million, turnover below BF145 million, fewer than 50 employees) are permitted to file abridged accounts. Accounts are written in either French or Dutch. There are a number of accounting terms particular to Belgium (in both languages). These are given in the Appendix.

144

Luxembourg Business organisations are very similar to those in Belgium, companies being SA or SPRL. Accounts for all limited companies must be filed at one of the two Tribunaux d'Arrondissement within one month of the AGM and are available for inspection.

Companies are classified according to size, as follows (two criteria being required):

	SMALL	MEDIUM	LARGE
Balance sheet total	Below FLUX77m	FLUX77–310m	Over FLUX310m
Turnover	Below FLUX160m	FLUX160–640m	Over FLUX640m
Employees	Below 50	50–250	Over 250

Both small and medium-sized companies are permitted to file abridged annual accounts.

Italy Two types of limited company are found — the SpA (Società per Azioni) and the SRL (Società a responsabilità limitada). The former requires a minimum share capital of L200 million and the latter L20 million. Accounts are prepared with the sole object of reducing the incidence of taxation, with the result that assets are frequently undervalued. Italian balance sheets do not always balance and accounts have to be considered unreliable. There is no clear legal distinction between current and fixed assets and the profit and loss account is often given in a condensed form due to the lack of proper accounting principles. A translation of Italian accounting terms is in the Appendix.

Both SPAs and SRLs have to file annual financial statements at the local civil court, where they are available for inspection. Due to the unreliability of the postal service, accounts are best obtained through a bank or reporting agency. There is no distinction between small, medium and large companies.

Other forms of business include SNC (general partnership), SAS (limited partnership), SCRL (a co-operative with limited liability) and SCRIL (a co-operative with unlimited liability). None of these organisations have to file accounts.

It is an old joke that if you ask an Italian for his company's balance sheet he will reply, 'which one do you want?' The truth is that in Italy two or even three sets of accounts are maintained — the official one for the tax authority, the real one for the shareholders and perhaps one for the bank. The same practice occurs in Spain and South America.

Denmark The organisation of Danish industry is relatively similar to that of the UK. Limited companies are either A/S or ApS requiring a minimum capital of DKR300,000 and DKR80,000 respectively (all subscribed on formation).

Annual accounts must be filed within one month of shareholders' approval with the registrar of companies in Copenhagen and are available for public inspection.

Companies are classified according to size by the following criteria:

	SMALL	MEDIUM	LARGE
Balance sheet total	Below DKR2m	DKR2–30m	Over DKR30m
Turnover	Below DKR4m	DKR4–60m	Over DKR60m
Employees	Below 50	50–250	Over 250

Both small and medium-sized companies are permitted to file abridged annual accounts.

Forms of partnership in Denmark include I/S (Interessentskab — limited partnerships) and KA/S (partnership limited to the extent of contributed shares). No accounts have to be filed.

A translation of Danish accounting terms is in the Appendix.

Spain Two types of limited company exist in Spain — the SA (minium share capital of 10 million pesetas) and the SRI. (private limited company, minimum capital 500,000 pesetas). Both are required to file accounts at the local mercantile registry where they can be inspected.

Around 40 per cent of Spanish industry is owned by the banks which means that companies in trouble are often supported to a far greater degree than would otherwise be expected.

Greece Both limited companies (AE or SA) and limited partnerships (EPE) are required to file annual accounts in the local offices of the Ministry of Commerce or the local First Instance Court of Justice respectively

Portugal The majority of businesses are either public companies (SA) or private companies (SPA). SAs must have a minimum share capital of ESC.5 million, and SPAs a minimum of ESC.400,000.

Annual accounts must be filed with the local Conservatória do Registo Comercial and with the Ministry of Finance (SAs only), and with the Dineccao-General das Contribuicoss e Impostos (tax authority). SAs also have to file their accounts with the Diario da Republica (official gazette).

Ireland Limited companies follow the UK pattern and are either Plc or Ltd. All such companies must file their accounts at the Companies Registration office in Dublin.

Companies are classified according to size by the following criteria:

	SMALL	MEDIUM	LARGE
Balance sheet total	Below IR£1,250,000	IR£1,250,000 to 5m	Over IR£5m
Turnover	Below IR£2.5m	IR£2.5m to 10m	Over IR£10m
Employees	Below 50	50–250	Over 250

Both small and medium-sized companies are permitted to file abridged annual accounts.

Sweden, Finland and Norway

Limited company accounts (companies with the suffix AB, OY or AS respectively) are available for public inspection and reliable credit information can be obtained. Of these three, Norway is not an EU member.

Austria and Switzerland

In Austria only public limited companies (AG) are required to file accounts. In Switzerland only limited companies quoted on the stock exchange (AG/SA or GmbH/SARL) are required to do so. Switzerland is not an EU member.

Eastern Europe

The break-up of the communist bloc in 1989 and the gradual move towards capitalist economies in the 1990s present more problems and opportunities to UK exporters.

The difficulty for the credit manager is immense. The amount of financial information available is still fairly meagre. In the countries making the most progress in privatizing industry — the Czech Republic, Poland and Hungary — limited company accounts are sometimes available, less frequently in the last-named. Banks can often be helpful in obtaining information, notably in Poland. In the other countries of Eastern Europe, reliable information is much more difficult to obtain. Throughout the area, firms are often willing to supply the names of established Western companies as trade references.

Other markets

This embraces Australia, New Zealand, South Africa, Japan, where company accounts are available reasonably easily, and all the 'developing' nations of

South America, Africa and Asia, where balance sheets are generally hard to find. Even when they do come to hand, the credit analyst must not place too much reliance on them for two reasons. Firstly, as in many European countries, accounts are prepared because the law demands them and this becomes a tax-avoidance exercise. Secondly, the standards of accountancy and auditing fall far below those of Western nations.

Reporting agencies

Many UK credit reporting agencies offer a service on overseas markets. A few are good and many are poor. Successful overseas reporting is a very expensive business, since an agency must take pains to ensure that its contacts and agents all over the world are working actively to obtain up-to-date information. Only experience will tell a credit manager which agencies give good value. What must be borne in mind is the availability of financial information, which varies from market to market.

It is good practice to use two or three different agencies, rather than to rely on one. Most West European countries have their own credit reporting businesses, and it can be worthwhile to obtain reports direct on the local markets. Some of these have been acquired in recent years by the major multinational agencies, the best of which (such as Dun & Bradstreet) have on-line reports available for most European markets in either English or the local language.

Most UK and European agencies offer two types of report: the 'normal' and the 'special'. The normal report at best runs to two or three pages, including particulars of directors, partners, company operations, etc., and (if available) the latest financial information. Where the subject of a report does not have to publish accounts (especially common in Germany), the financial information is extremely limited. Another common form of normal report is a pre-printed matrix of categories and values, on which the appropriate answers are ticked. 'Special' reports are much longer (and quite expensive), but of questionable value if no financial data is available. Direct approaches by reporting agencies to a company, asking for financial information, are rarely successful outside the USA or the UK, because there is no tradition of exchanging or supplying information.

By contrast, credit reports in the USA are full of information, often including complete balance sheets for the last three years, lengthy biographical notes on executives and up-to-date payment reports from existing suppliers. Reports on companies in Japan, Singapore, Hong Kong, Australia and New Zealand can be obtained (on-line from Dun & Bradstreet) and are usually of good quality.

Credit reporting outside the countries so far mentioned is very difficult. Problems in obtaining balance sheets have already been referred to. Direct approaches to companies in these markets for financial information are not often successful, partly because of fears that any information given will somehow find its way to the tax authorities. Often all that can be achieved is a report on the local reputation and scale of business of the subject.

Banks

American banks, inside and outside the USA, are good sources of credit information, because the need to establish a sound credit reputation is recognised in the USA, and banks are allowed more discretion in divulging information.

By contrast, European banks are far more reticent about their customers' finances, but even so they are more helpful than UK banks. In most countries there is a recognised code of practice which prevents a banker from releasing balance sheet information or details of a precise nature about clients' accounts, unless the client authorises it. This leaves the bank freedom to provide background information about a client's business and reputation.

When seeking help from a bank, the credit manager should take pains to phrase his question as specifically as possible, e.g. 'Do you consider XYZ GmbH a good risk for up to DM50,000 credit on net 60-day terms?'

Official sources

Official sources include the commercial offices of UK embassies and consulates abroad and the Export Intelligence Service operated by the Department of Trade and Industry. The information provided is not financial but commercial, covering the local reputation and scope of a company's business, coupled with background data on local trading conditions and regulations. This service is of more value in the developing markets. Even if business is to be conducted on secure terms it is necessary to find out whether a buyer has a genuine, established business.

Agents

A firm's own agent, whether he covers one territory or many different markets, should be a prime source of information. He will often be the only person with direct contact with the customer, so his opinion and assessment of the buyer's ability to pay on due date are important. The opportunities for credit people to visit overseas customers are rare, so the credit manager must make sure, firstly, that it is a recognised part of an agent's job to obtain whatever financial information is available and, secondly, that he has an opportunity to brief the agent on what to look for and what questions to ask.

Credit contacts

As in the home market, a network of trusted credit contacts is invaluable. These are more difficult to establish because of language and distance, but there are two organisations through which export credit information can be exchanged.

1 *Institute of Credit Management* (The Water Mill, Station Road, South Luffenham, Oakham, Leics. LE15 8NB.) Through its many branch meetings throughout the UK and through the medium of its monthly journal, the ICM keeps its members well-informed on all important export credit topics.

2 *Federation of European Credit Management Associations* (FECMA, contact via the ICM above). Its membership directory, published by the ICM, contains an invaluable list of potential contacts.

3 *Finance, Credit and International Business* (known as FCIB: the European branch of the National Association of Credit Management; 475 Park Avenue South, New York 10016)   Membership of FCIB is by company (as opposed to the ICM of whom membership is individual). Three meetings a year are held in different European cities. FCIB started these conferences in 1967, and they provide a meeting place for credit and financial managers from all over the Western world.

While the emphasis in FCIB meetings is on market risk and the published transcripts rarely refer to companies by name, of equal if not greater value are the informal talks between credit people on all aspects of credit management.

Public buyers

The credit manager dealing with the 'Public Sector' buyers in the UK rarely has a problem — providing his documentation is perfect — but this is not the case in many overseas markets. While government buyers in the industrial nations (and in Comecon countries) can generally be regarded as safe, outside these areas the position is quite different.

The fact that the buyer is a government ministry or department by no means eliminates the possibility of payment problems. Quite apart from political or transfer risks, there is the danger that the individuals negotiating a contract may not have authority to commit their government to

150

expenditure. Another department's approval may be needed before finance is allocated. Further aspects of public buyer risk are examined in Chapter 17.

Conclusion

Some of the most valuable information files are only available to companies who have decided to pay for risk protection, either through export credit insurance or through factoring. Where neither of these is available, the credit manager has to reach a decision from the facts derived from the sources described in this chapter. Time is always against him. It is rare for reliable up-to-date information to be obtained in under two weeks, unless the prospect is a major concern in an industrial market. Credit decisions often cannot wait that long. In the next two chapters terms of sale will be examined, and it will be seen that some of these give the partial or complete security which must be sought when large amounts are to be risked with unknown faraway buyers. Chapter 14 examines export credit decisions in the light of risk assessment and payment terms.

Appendix: accounting terminology used in overseas balance sheets

These lists are not exhaustive, but include all the most commonly found terms in company accounts. Where terms are entirely or virtually the same in English as in the local language they are omitted, e.g. 'Réserve légale' in French.

FRENCH–ENGLISH

French	English
BILAN	**BALANCE SHEET**
Montant brut	Gross amount
Amortissements ou provisions pour dépréciation	Depreciation
Montant net	Net total
ACTIF	ASSETS
Frais d'établissement	Formation expenses
Immobilisations	Fixed assets
Terrains	Land
Constructions	Buildings
Matériel et outillage	Machinery and tools
Mobilier et matériel de bureau	Furniture and fittings
Matérial de transport	Vehicles
Immobilisations incorporelles	Intangibles (i.e. goodwill, etc.)
Autres valeurs immobilisées	Other 'non-current' assets
Prêts (or créances) à plus d'un an	Long-term receivables
Titres de participation	Investments
Dépôts et cautionnements	Guarantee deposits
Valeurs d'exploitation	Stocks
Matières premières et fournitures	Raw materials and supplies
Produits semi-ouvrés	Work-in-progress
Produits finis	Finished goods
Valeurs réalisables à court terme ou disponibles	Current assets
Fournisseurs — avances	Advance payments to suppliers
Clients	Debtors
Impôts et taxes	Taxes
Comptes d'associés	Associate company debtors
Sociétés mères et filiales	Parent and subsidiary company debtors
Comptes de régularisation — actif	Pre-paid expenses
Effets à recevoir	Bills receivable
Titres de placement et bons	Marketable securities and bonds
Banques et chèques postaux	Cash at bank
Caisses	Cash in hand
Perte de l'exercice	Loss for the year

152

PASSIF	LIABILITIES
Capitaux propre et réservés	Capital and reserves
Capital social ou personnel	Capital
Primes d'émission d'actions	Share premium
Report à nouveau	Brought forward
Situation nette (avant résultats de l'exercice)	Total capital and reserves (before this year's results)
Subventions d'équipement	Plant subsidies
Provisions pour pertes et charges	Provisions for losses and expenses
Dettes à court terme	Current liabilities
Fournisseurs	Creditors
Clients — avances	Advance payments from customers
Personnel	Debts due to staff
Impôts et taxes	Taxes and duties
Autres créanciers	Other debtors
Obligations et emprunts à moins d'un an	Obligations and loans due within one year
Effets à payer	Bills payable
Banques	Owing to the bank
Bénéfice de l'exercice	Profit for the year

COMPTE DE PERTES ET PROFITS	PROFIT AND LOSS ACCOUNT
Perte (bénéfice) d'exploitation	Operating loss (profit)
Pertes (bénéfices) exceptionnelles	Exceptional loss (profits)
Impôts sur les bénéfices	Tax on profits
Perte (bénéfice) nette (net) comptable	Net loss (profit)
Compte d'exploitation générale	Trading account
Stock au début de l'exercice	Opening stock
Achats	Purchases
Frais de personnel	Wages and salaries
Travaux fournitures et services extérieurs	Supplies and services
Frais divers de gestion	Administrative expenses
Frais financiers	Interest charges
Dotation	Depreciation
Stocks à la fin de l'exercice	Closing stock
Chiffre d'affaires	Turnover
Ventes	Sales
Ventes de déchets	Sale of scrap
Ristournes, rabais et remises obtenus	Discounts and allowances

Notes

1 French companies use a pre-printed set of documents — the *Bilan*.
2 Stocks are not included under the heading 'Current Assets', but are shown separately.
3 Because of the common practice of paying by bill of exchange, the total creditors have to be obtained by adding *Fournisseurs* to *Effets à payer*. Similarly trade debtors will include *Clients* and *Effets à recevoir*.
4 While the various sub-headings under 'Stocks' have been shown, these are actually found on page 5 on the *Bilan*, on the Trading Account.
5 The *Bilan* only shows one year's accounts. To make comparisons, each year's accounts must be obtained separately.

GERMAN-ENGLISH

German	English
German	**English**
AKTIVA	ASSETS
Anlagevermögen	Fixed assets, long-term loans and investments
Sachanlagen und immaterielle Anlagewerte	Fixed and intangible assets
Grundstücke und grundstückgleiche Rechte mit Geschäfts-, Fabrik- und anderen Bauten	Land and property rights with office, factory and other buildings erected
Grundstücke und grundstückgleiche Rechte ohne Bauten	Land, etc. without buildings
Maschinen und maschinelle Anlagen	Machinery and installations
Betriebs- und Geschäftsausstattung	Factory and office equipment
Werkzeuge	Tools
Anlagen in Bau und Anzahlungen auf Anlagen	Construction in progress and advance payments for same
Konzessionen, gewerbliche Schutzrechte und ähnliche Rechte	Intangible assets
Finanzenlagen	Financial assets
Beteiligungen	Investments
Wertpapiere des Anlagevermögens	Securities
Ausleihungen mit einer Laufzeit von mindestens vier Jahren — davon durch Grundpfandrechte gesichert	Loans granted for at least four years — amount of such loans secured by mortgages
Umlaufvermögen	Current assets
Vorräte	Stocks
Roh-, Hilfs- und Betriebsstoffe	Raw material and supplies
Unfertige Erzeugnisse	Work-in-progress
Erzeugnisse und Waren	Finished goods
Andere Gegenstände des Umlaufver-mögens	Other current assets
Geleistete Anzahlungen	Prepayments to suppliers

Forderungen aus Lieferungen und Leistungen — davon mit einer Restlaufzeit von mehr als einem Jahr . . .	Trade debtors, of which due in more than one year . . .
Wechsel	Bills receivable
Schecks	Cheques
Kassenbestand, Bundesbank- und Postscheckguthaben	Cash in hand and bank deposits
Andere Bankguthaben *or* Guthaben bei Kreditinstituten	Other short-term deposits
Sonstige Forderungen	Sundry debtors
Forderungen an verbundene Unternehmen	Amounts due from associate companies
Sonstige Vermögensgegenstände	Other current assets
Rechnungsabgrenzungsposten	Pre-paid expenses
Geschäftswert	Goodwill
Abschreibungen	Depreciation

PASSIVA

LIABILITIES

Grundkapital	Share capital
Offene Rücklagen	Capital reserves
Gesetzliche Rücklagen	Legal reserves
Freie Rücklagen	Other reserves
Wertberichtigungen	Allowances or provisions
Rückstellungen	Accrued liabilities
Verbindlichkeiten mit einer Laufzeit von mindestens vier Jahren	Long-term debts (at least four years)
Anleihen	Loans
Verbindlichkeiten gegenüber Kreditinstituten — davon durch Grundpfandrechte gesichert	Bank loans — secured by mortgage
Lastenausgleichsvermögensabgabe	Tax equalisation reserve
Sonstige Verbindlichkeiten	Other liabilities
Kurzfristige Verbindlichkeiten	Current liabilities
Verbindlichkeiten aus Lieferungen und Leistungen	Trade creditors
Wechselverbindlichkeiten	Bills payable
Verbindlichkeiten gegenüber Kreditinstituten	Bank loans and overdrafts
Verbindlichkeiten gegenüber verbundenen Unternehmen	Accounts due from associate companies
Steuern	Taxes

Bilanzgewinn	Retained earnings
Umsatzerlöse	Turnover
Aufwendung für Roh- Hilfs- und Betriebsstoffe	Cost of goods sold
Gesamtleistung	Total revenue
Rohertrag (Rohaufwand)	Gross profit (loss)
Löhne und Gehälte	Wages and salaries
Zinsen und ähnliche Aufwendungen	Interest and financial charges
Jahresüberschuß (Jahresfehlbetrag)	Profit for year (loss)
Sonstige Erträge	Other income
Sonstige Aufwendungen	Other expenses

DUTCH–ENGLISH

Dutch

ACTIVA

Duurzame produktiemiddelen *or* vaste activa

Terreinen

Gebouwen

Machines en installaties

Werktuigen

Kantoorinventaris *or* Kantoorinrichtingen

Woonrechten

Afschrijvingen

Immateriële activa

Deelnemingen met direct realiseerbare waarden

Vlottende activa *or* vlottende middelen

Voorraden

Grondstoffen

Goederen in bewerking

Gereed produkt

Handelsdebiteuren

Vorderingen op geleverde ondernemingen

Wissels

Vooruitbetalingen

Overige vorderingen *or* diverse debiteuren

Liquide middelen

Kase, banken *or* belegde middelen

PASSIVA

Kortlopende schulden *or* schulden op korte termijn

Crediteuren *or* handelsverplichtingen

Bankverplichtingen

Belasting op de winst

English

ASSETS

Fixed assets

Land

Buildings

Machinery and equipment

Tools

Furniture and fittings

Leasehold properties

Depreciation

Intangibles

Investments — other non-current assets

Current assets

Stocks

Raw material

Work-in-progress

Finished goods

Trade debtors

Intercompany receivables

Bills receivable

Payments in advance

Sundry debtors

Cash and marketable securities

Cash in hand and at banks

LIABILITIES

Current liabilities

Trade creditors

Bank overdrafts

Tax

Verplichtingen tegenover gelieerde ondernemingen	Debts due to subsidiaries
Verplichtingen moedermaatschappij	Debts due to parent company
Te betalen kosten	Accrued expenses
Winstuitkering	Dividends payable
Schulden op lange termijn	Long-term debts
Aandelenkapitaal	Share capital
Ingehouden winsten	Retained earnings
Eigen vermogen	Shareholders' funds
Voorzieningen	Provisions
Obligatieleningen	Debentures

VERLIES — EN WINSTREKENING	**PROFIT AND LOSS ACCOUNT**
Omzet	Turnover
Bedrijfswinst *or* bedrijfsresultaat	Operating profit
Betaalde interest	Interest paid
Winst voor aftrek van belasting	Profit before tax
Winst na aftrek van belasting	Profit after tax
Nettowinst	Net profit

FLEMISH–ENGLISH

Flemish	English
ACTIVA	**ASSETS**
Vastliggend *or* vaste activa	Fixed assets
Onstoffelijk *or* immateriele vaste activa	Intangibles
Effectenbezit	Investments
Beschikbaar en omzetbaar	Current assets
Klanten	Trade debtors
Ontangen wissels	Bills receivable
Inventaries	Stocks
Handelsgoederen	Merchandise
Werk aan de gang	Work-in-progress
Fabrikaten	Finished goods
Beschikbaar	Cash
Verwezenlijkbaar	Liquid assets
Niet eisbaar	Shareholders' funds
Hypothecaire lening	Mortgage loan
Leveranciers	Trade creditors
Betalen dividenden	Dividends payable
Fiskale provisie	Tax provision
Verscheidene schuldeisers	Sundry creditors
Resultaat	Retained earnings
VERLIES — EN WINSTREKENING	**PROFIT AND LOSS ACCOUNT**
Overgedragen saldo	Balance brought forward
Overdracht op nieuw	Carried forward
Kapitaal is volstort	Capital is fully paid
Tantièmes	Directors' fees
Bedrijfsonkosten	General and administrative expenses
Brutowinst	Gross profit

160

BELGIAN/FRENCH–ENGLISH

Belgian/French

English

ACTIF

ASSETS

Belgian/French	English
Immobilisé brut	Fixed assets
Amortissements	Depreciation
Actifs circulants	Current assets
Réalisable	Stocks, debtors and investments
Inventaire *or* magasins	Stocks
Travaux en cours	Work-in-progress
Disponible	Cash
Non exigible *or* fonds propres	Shareholders' funds
Exigible à court terme	Current liabilities
Emprunt hypothécaire	Mortgage loan
Prévision fiscale	Tax provision
Divers créditeurs	Sundry creditors
Bénéfice brut	Gross profit
Résultat	Retained earnings
Le capital est entièrement libéré	Capital is fully paid
Comptes d'ordres	Contingent liability
Participations	Permanent investments in other companies

ITALIAN–ENGLISH

Italian	English
ATTIVO *or* ATTIVITÀ	ASSETS
Immobilizzi	Fixed assets
Terreno	Land
Macchinario	Machinery
Impianti	Plant
Fabbricati	Buildings
Automezzi	Vehicles
Attrezzi	Equipment
Arr. uff & attr *or* mobili d'ufficio	Fixtures and fittings
Ammortamenti	Depreciation
Titoli a reddito fisso	Fixed interest securities
Partecipazioni portafoglio titoli	Investments and marketable securities
Attivi currenti	Current assets
Magazzino *or* scorte	Stocks
Materie prime & merci	Raw material and supplies
Prodotti in corso di fabbricazione	Work-in-progress
Prodotti finiti	Finished goods
Clienti	Debtors
Anticipi a fornitori	Payments in advance
Cambiali attive *or* effetti attivi	Bills receivable
Cassa	Cash
Depositi bancari	Bank deposits
Crediti versi consociate	Owed by subsidiaries
Attivi immateriali	Intangibles
Avviamento	Goodwill
PASSIVO	LIABILITIES
Debiti correnti *or* debiti a breve termine	Current liabilities
Fornitori	Creditors
Effetti passivi	Bills payable
Anticipi di clienti	Prepayments
Debiti verso società collegate	Due to associate companies
Debiti verso banche *or* scoperti bancari	Bank overdrafts
Debiti verso il fisco	Current taxation
Debiti a lungo e medio termine	Medium and long-term debt

Accantonamenti	Provisions
Capitale sociale	Share capital
Riserve	Reserves
Obbligazioni	Debentures

PROFITTI E PERDITE — COSTI	**PROFIT AND LOSS ACCOUNT — COSTS**
Acquisti *or* costo dei materiali	Purchases
Spese generali	General expenses
Vendite	Turnover
Imposte *or* oneri tributari	Taxation
Proventi finanziari	Interest received
Oneri finanziari	Interest charges
Utile dell'esercizio *or* utile netto	Net profit
Avanzo a nuovo	Balance carried forward

DANISH–ENGLISH

Danish	English
AKTIVER	**ASSETS**
Anlægsaktiver	Fixed assets
Fast ejendom	Land
Maskiner og inventar	Machinery and equipment
Aktier	Shares
Værdipapirer	Securities
Afskrivninger	Depreciation
Omsætningsaktiver	Current assets
Kassebeholdning	Cash
Varedebitorer	Debtors
Veksler	Bills receivable
Forudbetaling til leverandører	Advance payments to suppliers
Varelager *or* varebeholdninger	Stocks
Igangværende arbejder	Work-in-progress
Andre fordringer	Other debtors
PASSIVER *or* **GÆLD**	**LIABILITIES**
Kortfristet gæld	Current liabilities
Kreditorer	Creditors
Vekselgæld	Bills payable
Forudbetaling fra kunder	Advance payments from customers
Bankgæld	Bank overdraft
Skyldigt udbytte	Dividends due
Skyldige skatter	Taxes due
Langfristet gæld	Long-term liabilities
Prioritetsgæld	Mortgages
Udskudt skat	Deferred tax
Udbyttegivende gældsbreve	Debentures
Udbytte til aktionærerne	Dividends due to shareholders
Investeringsfonds	Investment funds
Egenkapital	Net capital
Bunden egenkapital	Fixed capital
Aktiekapital	Share capital
Lovpligtig reservefond	Legal reserves
Fri egenkapital	Free capital
Overførsel til næste år	Retained earnings
Garantiforpligtelser	Contingent liabilities
Varesalg	Sales

Vareforbrug	Purchases
Bruttofortjeneste *or* bruttooverskud	Gross profit
Finansieringsomkostninger	Financing costs
Udbytte	Dividend
Renteomkostninger	Interest paid
Ordinært driftsresultat	Operating profit
Årets driftsresultat	Profit for year
Selskabsskat	Company tax
Årets nettoresultat *or* regnskabsmæssigt overskud	Net profit
Sidste år	Preceding year

SWEDISH–ENGLISH

Swedish	English
Swedish	**English**
ACTIVA *or* TILLGÅNGAR	ASSETS
Omsättningstillgångar	Current assets
Växelfordringar *or* främmande växlar	Bills receivable
(Konto) fordringar	Debtors
Fordringar hos koncernbolag	Associate company debtors
Förskott till leverantörer	Advance payments to suppliers
Varulager *or* varor	Stocks
Färdiga varor	Finished goods
Halvfabrikat	Work-in-progress
Råvaror	Raw material
Materialier	Supplies
Kassa	Cash
Bankfordringar *or* banktillgodo *or* bankkonto	Bank balances
Anläggningstillgångar	Fixed assets
Jordområden *or* jordfastigheter	Land
Byggnader	Buildings
Industrifastigheter	Plant
Maskineri	Machinery
Inventarier	Fixtures and fittings
Avskrivning	Depreciation
Investeringstillgångar	Investments
Värdepapper	Securities
PASSIVA *or* SKULDER OCH EGET KAPITAL	LIABILITIES
Kortfristiga skulder	Current liabilities
Växelskulder	Bills payable
Bankskulder	Bank debts
Leverantörsskulder *or* kontoskulder	Creditors
Skulder till koncernbolag	Associate company creditors
Skatt	Taxation
Erhållna försäljningsförskott	Advance payments from customers
Langfristiga skulder	Long-term debts
Pensionfund *or* pensionskassa	Pension fund

Inteckningslån	Mortgage loan
Obligationslån	Bond loan
Utvecklingsfond	Development funds
Dividender	Dividends
Reserving för kreditrisker *or* kreditförlustreserv	Bad debt reserve
Skattereservfond	Tax reserves
Aktiekapital	Share capital
Reservfond	Capital reserves
Från föregående år vinst	Brought forward balance on profit and loss
Vinstsaldo	Profit balance
Årets vinst	This year's profit
Ansvarsförbindelser	Contingent liabilities
Fakturerad försäljning	Turnover
Tillverknings-, försäljnings och administrationskostnader	Cost of sales, sales and administrative expenses
Bruttoresultat	Gross profit
Rörelsresultat	Operating profit
Redovisad nettovinst	Net profit

SPANISH–ENGLISH

Spanish	English
ACTIVO	**ASSETS**
Inmovilizado	Fixed assets
Terreno	Land
Inmuebles	Property
Maquinaria	Machinery
Útiles y herramientas	Tools
Inversiones	Investments
Activo circulante	Current assets
Cuentas corrientes	Current accounts
Deudores	Debtors
Efectos a cobrar	Bills receivable
Almacenes *or* existencias	Stocks
Obra en curso *or* trabajos en curso	Work-in-progress
Fabricación existencias	Finished goods
Materia prima	Raw material
Caja y bancos	Cash and bank balances
Cartera de valores	Securities
Anticipos en compras	Advance payments to suppliers
Realizable a largo plazo	'Long-term' current assets
Realizable a corto plazo	'Short-term' current assets
PASIVO	**LIABILITIES**
Exigible a corto plazo	Current liabilities
Saldos acreedores	Creditors
Proveedores	Suppliers
Créditos bancarios	Bank credit
Efectos a pagar	Bills payable
Imptos. y s.s.ptes de pago	Taxes and social security payable
Dividendo	Dividend
Exigible a medio y largo plazo	Medium and long-term liabilities
Fondos propios	Shareholders' funds
Capital social	Share capital
Reserva	Reserve
Amortizaciones	Depreciation

CUENTA PÉRDIDAS Y GANANCIAS

Beneficio
Remanente ejercicio anterior
Impuestos
Provisiones
Ingresos de explotación
Resultado bruto de explotación
Gastos financieros

PROFIT AND LOSS ACCOUNT

Profit
Balance from previous fiscal year
Tax
Provisions
Gross revenue
Gross profit
Financial expenses

NORWEGIAN–ENGLISH

Norwegian	English
EIENDELER *or* AKTIVA	ASSETS
Anleggsmidler *or* anleggsaktiva	Fixed assets
Bygninger	Buildings
Maskiner og inventar	Machinery and equipment
Obligasjoner og andre verdipapirer	Bonds and other securities
Investeringer	Investments
Omløpsmidler *or* omløpsaktiva	Current assets
Lager	Stocks
Lager av råvarer	Raw materials
Halvfabrikata under tilvirkning *or* materiale under bearbeiding	Work-in-progress
Varer beregnet til videresalg	Finished goods
Debitorer	Debtors
Vekselfgordringer	Bills receivable
Kontanter, bankinnskudd og innestående på postgiro	Cash in hand, bank and post giro account
Forskudd til leverandører	Prepayments
GJELD OG EGENKAPITAL	LIABILITIES AND EQUITY CAPITAL
Kortsiktige forpliktelser *or* kortsiktig gjeld	Current liabilities
Kreditorer	Creditors
Vekselgjeld	Bills payable
Kassakreditt	Bank overdraft
Utliknet skatt	Taxation
Forskudd fra kunder	Advances from customers
Langsiktig gjeld	Long-term debt
Egenkapital *or* aksjekapital	Share capital
Reservefond	Reserves
Årsoverskudd *or* årsunderskudd	Year's profit or loss
Pantstillelser	Mortgages
TAPS- OG VINNINGSKONTO	PROFIT AND LOSS ACCOUNT
Salgsintekter *or* omsetning	Sales
Innkjøp	Purchases

Avskrivninger	Depreciation
Brutto salgsinntekt	Trading profit
Renteutgifter	Interest paid
Netto inntekt etter skatter	Net profit after tax

PORTUGUESE–ENGLISH

Portuguese	English
ACTIVO	ASSETS
Imobilizado	Fixed assets
Imóveis	Property
Móveis e utensílios	Furniture and fixtures
Incorpóreo	Intangible assets
Disponível	Liquid assets
Caixa	Cash
Bancos	Bank balances
Realizável	Current assets
Clientes	Debtors
Prov. p/cob. duvid	Bad debt provision
Letras a receber	Bills receivable
Fornecedores	Paid in advance to suppliers
Remanescentes *or* armazena	Stocks
Armz. mat. primas	Raw material
Armz. prod. p/recup	Work-in-progress
Prov. p/depr. exist	Provision for stock depreciation
Reintegrações	Depreciation
Custos antecipados \	Pre-paid expenses
Devedores diversos	Sundry debtors
PASSIVO	LIABILITIES
Exigível	Current liabilities
Fornecedores	Creditors
Clientes	Customers
Letras a pagar	Bills payable
Empréstimos terceiros	Loans to third parties
Imposto	Tax
Imp. transacções	Added value tax
Rendas	Income
Contas de ordem	Contingent liabilities
Letras descontadas	Discounted bills
Ganhos e perdas *or* lucros e perdas	Profit and loss
Vendas	Sales
Custo da mercadoria vendida	Cost of sales
Despesas c/o pessoal	Labour costs
Encargos financeiros	Financial charges

Despesas gerais de fabrico	Production costs
Despesas gerais administrativas	Administration expenses
Despesas de viaturas e distribuição	Transport and distribution costs

FINNISH–ENGLISH

Finnish	English
OMAISUUS	ASSETS
Käyttöomaisuus	Fixed assets
Investoinnit	Investments
Varat	Current assets
Varasto	Stocks
Keskeneräiset työt	Work-in-progress
Tilisaatavat *or* velalliset	Debtors
Käteinen *or* käteistä	Cash
VELAT	LIABILITIES
Tilivelat *or* velkojat	Creditors
Pankkivelat	Bank overdraft
Lyhytaikaiset velat yhteensä	Total current liabilities
Verot	Tax
Osakepääoma	Issued capital
Varaukset	Reserves
Omapääoma	Shareholders' funds
Lainat	Loans
Vieras pääoma	Loan capital
Voitto	Profit
Myynti	Sales
Ostot	Purchases
Liikevoitto	Trading profit
Maksetut korot	Interest paid
Voitto ennen veroja	Profit before tax
Voitto verot vähennettyinä	Profit after tax
Päättynyt tilikausi	Year ended
Yhteensä	Total

Chapter 12

Contract terms, documentation, payment terms and letters of credit

Compared to the domestic market, the export trade offers a bewildering choice of terms. The credit manager must not only understand how they work, but also how to make the most appropriate choice.

Export terminology

Before examining these terms, it is essential to understand the basic terminology and documents of the export trade. Full coverage of these leads into the study of contract, mercantile and international laws, which is beyond the scope of this book. The recognised authority on these and other related subjects is *The Export Trade* by Clive Schmithoff (Stevens and Sons Ltd).

Shipping terms and their meaning are known as *Incoterms* — defined by the International Chamber of Commerce and accepted throughout the world. All quotations and invoices should state that Incoterms apply. The principal terms which the credit manager should be familiar with are as follows:

Ex-works

The price will include packing for export. The buyer must arrange for collection from the seller's premises and all carriage and insurance costs to his own premises. Property and risk pass from the seller when the buyer is notified that the goods are at his disposal. From a credit viewpoint, these are the best contract terms. So long as the buyer or his agent signs for the goods, there can be no problem about proof of delivery. No delivery period is involved so the credit period is clearcut.

FOB (free on board)

The principal obligations of the seller are:
a To place on board ship the specified goods.
b To pay all handling and transport charges.
c To cover all expenses incurred to that point.
d To notify the buyer to enable him to arrange marine insurance.
e To bear any costs and charges in passing Customs.
   The principal obligations of the buyer are:
a To advise the seller in good time which ship is to be used — in time to meet delivery requirements.
b To ensure space is available in the vessel.
c To bear any costs and charges in passing out of port.
d To provide substitute vessels if necessary and to bear any costs arising therefrom.
   Other points to note are:
a Buyer must arrange and pay for freight and marine insurance.
b Property in goods passes when goods cross the ship's rail — unless otherwise stipulated.
c Unless otherwise stated, it is seller's responsibility to obtain an export licence.

CIF

A CIF contract does not really relate to the sale of goods but a sale of the documents relating to the goods. *Delivery of shipping documents is equivalent to delivery of the goods*. The principal obligations of the seller are:
a To ship to the port of shipment the specified goods.
b To procure a contract of affreightment under which goods will be delivered to the specified destination.
c To arrange appropriate insurance.
d To make out a proper invoice.
e To render these documents to the buyer so he may obtain delivery or claim for loss or damage.
   The principal obligations of the buyer are:
a To bear all risks after goods have passed the ship's rail — provided seller has tendered proper documents.

b Take up the documents — if in order — and pay according to the contract terms.

c Pay even *before* arrival, receipt or examination of goods.

d Take delivery at port of destination and bear costs of unloading and any freight not included in the seller's invoice.

e Bear all cost incurred during voyage (except freight included in seller's invoice), including any demurrage.

f Obtain any import licence or other necessary document.

g Bear all costs of customs duties, taxes, etc.

CFR (formerly C & F)

As for CIF, except that the arrangement of insurance, paragraph *c* under CIF, is an obligation of the buyer rather than the seller.

DDP (formerly Franco)

Delivered duty paid followed by the delivery address of the buyer, this gives the seller the responsibility of all costs 'door to door'.

Documentation (See also Appendix 2 — SITPRO)

Export documentation is many an exporter's nightmare. Payment delays are frequently the result of documentation errors, and while the credit manager will probably not be responsible for preparing documents, it is good practice for all export paperwork to be checked and despatched by the credit department. This should certainly apply to all documents going to a bank. The principal documents to consider are:

1 Commercial invoices.
2 Consular invoices.
3 Insurance certificates.
4 Bills of lading.
5 Airways bills.
6 Forwarding agent's receipt.
7 Certificates of origin.
8 Trust receipt.

Commercial invoices

Apart from the standard information which appears on all invoices, the following must also be included:

a Type of contract, e.g. C & F Antwerp, after the invoice value.

b   Shipping marks and number.

c   Name of vessel.

d   Currency of invoice.

e   Declaration of origin of goods (commonly required by importing authorities).

f   Customer VAT no. for shipments to the EU.

Some countries require commercial invoices to be legalised by their embassy in the exporter's country or be certified by an authorised UK Chamber of Commerce.

Consular invoices

These are a common requirement in South America. A special form has to be obtained from the appropriate embassy in the UK and completed by the exporter. It then has to be stamped by the embassy, who will make a charge. There are specialist agencies providing a service in this field which can sometimes reduce or avoid bureaucratic delays through their use of regular contacts.

Insurance certificates

An insurance company's certificate is needed as evidence of insurance in any contract beyond C & F in terms of the exporter's responsibility. It is not sufficient to have a cover note or broker's certificate; these are not accepted by banks handling documents as evidence of insurance.

Bills of Lading

The most important documents in overseas trade, since they are both a receipt for goods by the shipping company and also documents of title. Whoever possesses an original Bill of Lading is considered the owner of the goods. Bills are raised in sets, usually three or more originals plus copies. The presentation of one original is sufficient to obtain the goods. If goods are sold on open account terms, the Bill of Lading accompanies the goods with another original mailed direct to the buyer so that he can take possession on arrival in his country. If documentary terms are operating, the exporter must ensure that Bills of Lading are only given to the importer against payment or acceptance. In the 'Consignee' box, the word 'order' should be entered, and the exporter must endorse the reverse of the document. Alternatively, the words 'to order of the bank' (or another third party, if required under the terms of a Letter of Credit) may be entered — in which case ownership of the goods will not pass until the bank adds its endorsement. If the goods are to be sent direct to the buyer on open account terms, the name of the buyer is entered in the consignee box and the Bill of Lading is not a negotiable document.

A Bill of Lading is said to be 'clean' if it is signed by the shipping company without qualification. If goods or packing are received damaged or, in some respect, inconsistent with the Bill of Lading, the Bill will be 'claused' appropriately and it ceases to be a clean Bill. This is of great importance where payment is to be made under a Letter of Credit, as a clean Bill of Lading is normally a prerequisite. Clausing will also occur if dangerous goods are involved or goods are stowed on deck. To avoid this problem in trades such as chemicals, the buyer must try to have a Credit worded so as to allow shipment on deck.

Similarly a Letter of Credit may demand a 'shipped' Bill of Lading, which means that the word 'shipped' must be included. It can happen that instead of 'shipped' the Bill says 'received for shipment', which may mean that the goods are still at the docks awaiting loading. Any such endorsements must be dated by the shipping company and any alterations properly authenticated.

A problem frequently encountered is the difficulty in getting Bills of Lading to the bank within the time specified under a Letter of Credit. If no time limit is stipulated, banks will accept documents within 21 days of document date. This should be sufficient time but credits do sometimes demand presentation within a shorter period. Forwarding agents (who deal with the shipping company for the exporter) are not always able to meet such deadlines, unless prior arrangements are made. If sufficient attention is paid to this, the credit manager should be able to obtain Bills of Lading within three to four days.

Another common problem which can result in payment being withheld by the bank is the omission of the words 'freight prepaid' on the Bill of Lading on CIF and C & F contracts. Unless a credit account has been established, the seller is obliged to pay the shipping company or forwarding agent *before* Bills of Lading are handed over. Not being aware of this until too late is a frequent reason for late presentation of documents. Even where credit terms exist, payment is usually required within a very short period and special arrangements have to be made. The credit manager would do well to check on all the terms operating with the company's shipping lines or forwarding agents.

There are a number of special types of Bills of Lading, depending on the method of shipment and the route involved. Unless specifically prohibited in the terms of a Letter of Credit, the following types of Bill are accepted by the banks as being documents of title:
1   Short Form Bill of Lading.
2   Through Bill of Lading (also known as Combined Transport Document).
3   Multi-modal Bill of Lading.

179

Types of Bill *not* acceptable to a bank unless specifically authorised by a Credit are:
1 Bill of Lading issued by forwarding agents.
2 Charter-party Bills of Lading.
3 Bill of Lading covering shipment by sailing vessel.

The following types of bill of lading do not give title to the goods — Sea Waybill, House Bill of Lading.

Airway Bills, road or rail consignment notes

None of these documents give title. In order to retain control over goods until payment is received, the exporter must consign the goods to a third party (e.g. a bank or an agent) who has agreed to accept responsibility for them.

Forwarding agent's receipt

As the name indicates, this does not give evidence of shipment but only of receipt for shipment.

Certificate of origin

A declaration of the origin of the goods is frequently required from the exporter by the importing country. Sometimes a signed statement on the commercial invoice is sufficient. Some markets required a combined certificate of value and origin, others demand a separate document usually issued and stamped by a Chamber of Commerce.

Trust receipt

Where a bank is asked by the buyer to release title documents or goods before payment is made, on a 'documents against payment' transaction, it may choose to do so against a trust receipt. This binds the buyer to take the goods into safe keeping and to make the outstanding payment within an agreed period. Banks only accept trust receipts from customers of undoubted standing, since failure to pay leaves the bank fully responsible to the exporter.

Choosing payment terms

There are two principles to observe. The first is to set the shortest possible terms compatible with winning or retaining business. The second is to use documentary terms (i.e. letter of credit or bills of exchange) unless selling to a credit-worthy buyer in a market free from political or foreign exchange risks.

The following payment terms will be considered in this chapter.

1   Cash with order.
2   Cash on delivery.
3   Letter of Credit.

Bill of Exchange and open account terms will be examined in Chapter 13.

Cash with order

This is obviously the safest method of trading, but its use is generally confined to 'one-off' orders from unknown buyers. Exchange control regulations in a number of markets do not permit advance payment, e.g. France (except by the approval of the Bank of France).

Cash on delivery

The success of COD terms depends largely on the efficiency of the postal service in the buyer's country, since there is no alternative to the Post Office if goods are to be sent on this basis. Other transporters and carriers will usually not handle goods if payment has to be obtained from the buyer at the time of delivery. It may be possible to have the parcel delivered to a bank in the buyer's locality, with instructions for it to be released only against payment. This method depends entirely upon a prior arrangement with the bank, and the exporter must not assume that an overseas bank will accept such an arrangement.

Putting the above two terms (CWO and COD) aside, conditions of payment are either documentary or open account. Documentary terms have been developed over many years as a means of enabling traders unknown to each other to buy and sell with varying degrees of security. This has been made possible by the international banking system acting as an intermediary. Banks operate under rules laid down by the International Chamber of Commerce, in particular the *Uniform Customs and Practice for Documentary Credits* (UCP 500) and the *Uniform Rules for Collection*. These booklets are essential references for the export credit manager. They may be obtained from the International Chamber of Commerce, 14–15 Belgrave Square, London SW1X 8PS, or any UK clearing bank.

Letters of Credit

A documentary credit is an undertaking by the buyer's bank to pay an agreed sum of money to the seller under certain precisely defined conditions. This has clear benefits to both parties. The seller is now certain of payment from a bank — providing he complies with the Credit in every respect — as opposed to hoping for payment from an unknown buyer in an unknown market. The buyer knows that payment will only be made on his behalf against the evidence he is demanding.

For a buyer to agree to Letter of Credit terms he must first arrange that his bank will issue a credit. This will only be possible if the buyer has adequate facilities with his bank. Refusal by a buyer to open a credit (in a market where it is normal practice) may therefore be interpreted by the exporter as an indication of strained resources, and requests for less secure terms should be examined cautiously. In some markets the issue of Letters of Credit is controlled by the central bank, and in time of economic stress, regulations may be imposed aimed at restricting the outflow of currency. Thus in the Nigerian Budget of April 1978 no credit could be opened without the importer first depositing 100 per cent of the value with the central bank. In 1976 the Government of Brazil made a similar ruling, linking it with the issue of foreign exchange.

It should not be forgotten that the buyer also benefits from Letter of Credit terms. The precise documentation requirements which the buyer dictates will ensure that payment need only be made if the price, despatch dates, ports of loading and unloading, condition and description of the goods is exactly as ordered.

The confirming or advising bank acts strictly as an agent of the issuing bank, and it has no responsibility beyond checking the documents. It has been known for payment to be made under a credit, yet on arrival and inspection the goods are found to be totally incorrect, e.g. bananas instead of radios. The bank can only be held liable if it fails to detect a discrepancy or lack of conformity in the documents. The basic principle is that banks deal in documents, not in goods.

There are four types of Credit:

1 *Revocable Credits*   Very rarely used, since they offer no protection to the seller. Once established they can be amended or cancelled either by the buyer or by the issuing bank.

2 *Irrevocable Credits*   Once opened, an irrevocable credit cannot be modified or cancelled without the consent of both buyer and seller.

3 *Unconfirmed Irrevocable Credits*   Payment remains the responsibility of the issuing or opening bank. The issuing bank in the buyer's country will

normally contact the seller via an 'advising bank' in the seller's country. The advising bank has no obligation to pay the beneficiary, but it will generally do so providing first, that the conditions of the credit are complied with and, secondly, that it has no serious doubts about being reimbursed by the issuing bank without delay. When advising unconfirmed credits, a bank usually adds the words 'this credit does not bear our confirmation' (or similar).

4 Confirmed Irrevocable Credits   For the exporter these are the only safe type of credit. The advising bank is requested by the opening bank to 'add its confirmation'. By doing so it becomes the 'confirming bank' and assumes all the obligations of the issuing bank. Providing the beneficiary presents documents in complete conformity with the credit, the confirming bank has to pay — regardless of any doubts that may have arisen about reimbursement.

There are two advantages to the exporter in having a confirmed credit. Firstly, it eliminates any doubts about the standing of the opening bank. Commercial standards and regulations in some parts of the world fall far below those of the UK and not all establishments calling themselves banks are worthy of the name. Some markets are notorious for producing banks whose existence goes no further than the name on their notepaper. A useful reference book is the *Bankers' Almanac*, an annual publication listing the principal banks of the world. A summary of the latest balance sheet is given, details of branches and the names of London and New York correspondents. Extreme caution should be exercised in dealing with any bank not listed in the *Bankers' Almanac*.

The second advantage is that the transfer risk is removed. The exporter, having contracted to receive payment in sterling or another currency of his choice and having obtained a Letter of Credit, must overcome the final problem of how to bring payment into his own bank. Confirmation by a UK bank solves their problem since payment is assured against correct presentation of documents. When this protection is most needed, however, it is often not available. There comes a point when shortage of foreign exchange in a market becomes so acute that UK banks will refuse to confirm credits because they can see a high risk of not being repaid by the issuing bank. This situation arose with credits opened by Turkish banks in 1977–9. Unless the opening bank actually had sterling funds in London which a UK bank could draw on, confirmation was not possible. It is not normally considered necessary to seek confirmation of credits raised by first-class banks, particularly when the advising bank is a branch or even the head office of the opening bank. This rule does not apply, however, if there is a severe foreign exchange problem in the buyer's country. Confirmation should always be sought in that situation.

It follows from the above that an exporter, on receiving an unconfirmed credit, is entitled to find a bank willing to confirm. The correct procedure is for the seller to try and arrange that the UK bank's confirmation is requested by the opening bank (on instructions from the buyer).

In this situation the seller should be prepared to pay confirmation costs. These will vary but will generally be as much again as the original opening cost. 'Silent confirmations' can sometimes be arranged by a specialist broker.

Payment under Letter of Credit

Payment may be 'at sight', i.e. on presentation of specified documents or at a fixed future date up to 180 days from sight. The exporter must be wary of a credit requiring presentation of documents at the issuing bank. This can add considerable delay to receipt of payment and, more importantly, the documents move outside the direct control of the UK bank. In either case the credit may call for bills (sight or term) to be drawn, usually on the advising bank but sometimes on the buyer or on the issuing bank. The exporter enjoys the same security with a term bill as with a sight payment, since the documents are only passed to the customer after the bill is accepted. An accepted bill, drawn on the advising bank under a Letter of Credit, may be discounted by the exporter — at a fine rate because it bears the bank's name. A term bill drawn on the buyer may be negotiated by the exporter in the UK before it has been accepted but at a higher rate of interest, since it does not carry the bank's name although the issuing bank is ultimately responsible. Term bills drawn on and accepted by the issuing bank can be discounted, and the beneficiary is paid at sight by the advising bank. These different ways of obtaining payment before maturity are summarised as shown in Exhibit 12.1

Exhibit 12.1

Term bill drawn on	Acceptance necessary?	Beneficiary obtains payment by
(a) Advising bank	Yes	Discounting bill with advising bank (or his own bank) at a fine rate
(b) Issuing bank	Yes	Sight payment from advising bank
(c) Buyer	No	Negotiating bill with advising bank at ordinary market rate

When a Letter of Credit calls for term bills, it is sometimes referred to as a Documentary Acceptance Credit. This should not be confused with an Acceptance Credit (see Chapter 16).

Opening the credit

It is normal for a buyer to request a pro-forma invoice containing details to be included in the Letter of Credit. At this stage the exporter should do his utmost to ensure a favourable credit. Points to note are as follows:

a   Allow as big a safety margin as possible in the shipment date. If the credit expires too soon after the promised date, the exporter may have to seek an extension which can take a long while to arrive. If the validity of the credit is linked to the expiry of an import licence or the availability of foreign exchange, extension or renewal may be refused.

b   Specify that shipment may be made from any UK port. A dock strike could prevent shipment from the original chosen port. 'UK' is better than 'English' in this context.

c   If there is any possibility that part-shipment of trans-shipment may be necessary, request permission to be given in the credit.

d   Ask that the buyer instructs his bank to advise the credit through the exporter's bank, with a request that the latter be asked to add their confirmation. If the exporter's bank is not a correspondent of the opening bank this will not work, but it is worth trying.

e   The seller must check his pro-forma carefully for any spelling errors, incorrect part numbers, descriptions, etc. If there are any, they will be repeated on the credit which can easily lead to problems.

Checking the credit

The Letter of Credit is generally received by the sales office. Copies should immediately be given to the credit department and the shipping department. All these offices should have a checklist, and the credit must be examined line-by-line to ensure that its conditions can be fulfilled and payment obtained. A specimen checklist is given in Appendix I to this chapter.

If discrepancies or errors are found, the buyer must be asked to arrange an amendment, if time permits. Some errors, such as incorrect spelling, may be easier to accept than have amended, providing the same errors are repeated in the documents. Any amendment request must be made direct to the buyer, since he alone can instruct the opening bank.

Serious problems arise when a necessary amendment has not arrived before the expiry date for shipping. If the buyer has cabled that the amendment is 'on its way', the exporter must decide whether to ship or whether to await the amendment. When sailings to the buyer's country are infrequent or it is difficult to book shipping space at short notice it is tempting to take a chance, especially if failure to deliver on time could mean missing an opportunity. In this situation, however, the exporter would be well advised *not* to take a chance unless his relationship with and knowledge of the buyer gives sufficient confidence in the buyer's good faith. Even when this confidence exists, however, the exporter must check that any import licence or exchange control regulations are not being infringed.

Presenting the documents

Bankers never grow tired of telling exporters about the high percentage of documents containing errors. If thorough checks are made in providing information to the buyer to open the credit and against the credit when it arrives, the chances of error on presentation are greatly reduced.

While the task of obtaining, preparing and collating documents will usually fall to the shipping office or possibly the invoice department, the credit manager should have the final responsibility of getting the documents to the bank. This is because part of the credit manager's job is to ensure that payment of all sales arrives on time. In export business this demands close relationships with all banks who are involved in the payment process. Nonetheless, situations will occur where documents do not comply with the credit terms, such as where the Bill of Lading is claused or where documents are presented outside the validity of the credit. Some errors can be corrected by the exporter, providing there is sufficient time. These include for example the omission of the words 'freight prepaid' on a Bill of Lading (necessary on C & F and CIF contracts), or omitting to endorse the Bill of Lading. When discrepancies occur which cannot be put right, the exporter has a choice of one of three actions:

1 Ask the advising/confirming bank to cable the issuing bank for approval to pay or accept despite the errors.
2 Ask the advising/confirming bank to send the documents to the issuing bank on a collection basis.
3 Ask the advising/confirming bank to pay against an indemnity, either from the exporter or from his bank. (That is, the bank has recourse to the beneficiary or his bank if the opening bank refuses to accept the documents.)

The first of these is generally preferable to the others, although in some markets inefficient banks can take weeks to reply to a cable. Sending documents out on a collection basis means surrendering the protection of the credit. The issuing of indemnities, while sometimes unavoidable, is a bad practice because if it is done often, it inevitably encourages careless handling of documentation.

A bank has a duty to examine all documents stipulated in the credit, but will disregard any other documents submitted.

Documentary credits always have a time limit, beyond which documents will not be accepted. Sometimes two expiry dates are given, one for the latest shipment date and one for presentation of documents. If no deadline is indicated for presentation of documents, under the *Uniform Customs and Practices for Documentary Credits*, the exporter must submit documents within 21 days of the date of shipment. This 21-day period is nonetheless subordinate to the final expiry date of the credit.

The exporter can request his buyer to renew or extend the validity of a credit. It should be noted that the renewal of confirmation of a credit is not given automatically when the credit itself is renewed. An example of this occurred in 1977 with credits which had been opened by Turkish banks with UK confirmation before the foreign exchange crisis. Exporters who subsequently applied for renewal of these credits found that confirmation by the UK banks was no longer available, except in those cases where the opening bank still had funds in the UK which had approval from the Central Bank of Turkey to be used against the credits in question.

Credits opened in foreign currency operate in precisely the same way as those in sterling. Since the exporter receives payment in foreign currency, he will probably want to eliminate his exchange risk through a forward contract. This is explained in Chapter 18.

There are a number of special kinds of credit, details as follows:

Revolving credits These enable a series of payments to be made, usually within a fixed period, up to a maximum figure for each presentation. A payment of £10,000 against a revolving credit of £100,000 results in an automatic topping-up or renewal to the full £100,000. This is a useful facility where a series of regular shipments are to be made within a known period, whose total value is unknown. Another form of revolving credit is where regular payments of fixed amounts (of say £10,000) have to be made over a fixed period of time. The credit will be opened for £10,000, available on each presentation according to the agreed timetable.

Transferable credits The beneficiary of a transferable credit is entitled to instruct the advising bank to transfer all or part of the value of the credit to a second beneficiary. The second beneficiary obtains payment by presenting documents to the bank, in accordance with the terms of the credit. By this is meant that an export agent in the UK can ensure that his UK suppliers obtain payment out of the credit, leaving a balance (representing the agent's profit) to be drawn directly by the agent.

Appendix 1: Checklist for Letters of Credit

A *Preparing information on which customer opens Letter of Credit*

1 Allow sufficient time for possible production delays, e.g. request Letter of Credit to be valid one month beyond scheduled delivery date.
2 Ensure all particulars are complete and accurate.
3 State whether part-shipment and trans-shipment must be permitted.
4 For FOB contracts ask that the payment be made against presentation of freight forwarder's receipt.
5 If your goods are specially made to customer specification, ask for the Letter of Credit to be opened and in your possession *before* you start manufacturing.

B *On receipt*

1 Is the Letter of Credit *irrevocable*? It must be.
2 Is the Letter of Credit *confirmed by a UK or US bank*? It is infinitely preferable but not mandatory. Please contact credit department if it is not.
3 Is our name and address correct — spelling particularly?
4 Is the name of our customer correct and spelled correctly?
5 Do validity, expiration and shipping dates give sufficient time to get documents together in time to assure payments, special attention to the juxtaposition of these dates and shipping and airline schedules?
6 Is the Letter of Credit amount enough to cover our quotation? Check:
   a Cost of goods plus profit.
   b Inland transport to dock or airport, including wharfage and handling charges.
   c Ocean/airline transportation charges.
   d Forwarding fees.
   e Consular charges.
   f Insurance costs.
   g Miscellaneous charges.
7 Is description of goods correct? If you decide not to ask for amendment then the customer's description of the goods must appear on all documents as well as your description.
8 Is quantity of goods correct?
9 If required, is partial shipment permitted?
10 Is shipment required at a given rate or amount? If so, can you conform?
11 Is shipment permitted from any place in the UK or only from one named place?
12 Does named destination (port of discharge) you quoted, or you and buyer agreed on, agree with Letter of Credit?

13 Do you require export licences?
14 Is the import licence shown? (It is usually required to be shown on the invoice.)
15 Is the Letter of Credit in a foreign currency? If so, please contact credit department.
16 Are guarantees of any sort required by buyer?
17 Can properly executed documents be obtained to conform with Letter of Credit in the language of the buyer if required?

    Bill of Lading
    Air waybill
    Parcel post receipt
    Invoices — commercial, preferential, consular, legalised
    Packing list
    Certificate of origin
    Insurance policy certificate
    Certificate of inspection
    Certificate of Quality

    Is any specified agency required to issue or authenticate any of these documents?
18 Can you comply with cover of insurance risks required by the Letter of Credit? Does credit require policy or certificate?
19 Compare the conditions of the contract of sale with the Letter of Credit.
20 Where is payment to be made? If not in UK, does the expiry date allow sufficient time for documents to be presented at the overseas bank?

If, after having made examination of the Letter of Credit against this checklist and having compared the sales contract with the Credit, you find need for amendment or clarification of the Credit, cable your customer requesting necessary clarification or amendment, bearing in mind shipping and validity dates and the chance of amendments being received in time to honour shipping and validity dates.

Appendix 2: SITPRO

A considerable amount of work on export documentation has been done by SITPRO (Simplification of Trade Procedures), 151 Buckingham Palace Road, London, SW1 9SS. It has published *Systematic Export Documentation*, which shows how exporters can both improve efficiency and save money by streamlining their documentation systems. In recent years SITPRO has devoted considerable effort to developing the use of EDI (electronic data interchange) in international trade. The ultimate objective is to replace all forms of export documentation by a paperless system that will enable both exporter and importer to conduct business from quotation through to receipt of payment via a computer link.

Appendix 3: Case Study on Letters of Credit

A UK company, based in Bromsgrove in Worcestershire, received an order for computer software value £14,000 from South Korea. The buyer was a subsidiary of a US multi-national company. Payment was to be by unconfirmed letter of credit. This was their first order from this market.

The supplier's sales office was at a different Bromsgrove address from the credit control department, which was also the Head Office. This was to cause two problems:

a   The buyer only knew the sales office address and gave this to his bank. This resulted in 2–3 days' delay before credit control had sight of the Letter of Credit details (relayed by fax by the supplier's bank).
b   The invoice address was different from that on the packing-list and other documents.

When the Letter of Credit was examined by credit control, two problems were found.

a   Shipment was specified as being 'FOB Bromsgrove airport'.
b   The last date for shipment was only four working days away.

The buyer was immediately cabled and asked to instruct the bank to amend shipment to 'FOB Birmingham airport' and to expand the despatch date by seven days. Both amendments were actioned promptly by the buyer, but there was a delay with the Korean bank. In the meantime the sales office continued to prepare to ship.

The Letter of Credit amendments arrived just in time for the freight forwarder to collect the goods and meet the shipment deadline. Documents were delivered to the bank on the last permissible day and the following problems appeared:

a   Goods were actually shipped from Heathrow, since there was no flight from Birmingham to Korea.
b   The packing list was inadequate, in that the description of goods did not match that on the invoice nor on the Letter of Credit.
c   The invoice address differed from that on the packing-list and air waybill.
d   The airway bill had two dates:
   i)   the date of collection by the freight forwarder, which was inside the Letter of Credit deadline
   ii) the actual flight date which was not.

Because of these discrepancies the UK bank were not able to pay. Nine days later the UK bank advised that approval to pay had been received. A total of £242 was deducted in bank charges.

Chapter 13

Payment terms (continued) — Bills of Exchange and open account

Bills of Exchange

The legal definition (*The Bills of Exchange Act, 1882*) cannot be improved: 'An unconditional order in writing, addressed by one person to another, signed by the person giving it, requiring the person to whom it is addressed to pay on demand or at a fixed or determinable future time a sum certain in money to, or to the order of a specified person, or to a bearer'.

The exporter raises a Bill as the 'Drawer' and the buyer is the 'Drawee'. The 'Payee' is usually the exporter but can be a third party. If payment is to be made 'on demand' the bill is known as a *sight draft*. Payment at a future date makes it a *tenor, time* or *usance bill.*

Sight drafts

Payment by documentary sight draft gives the exporter a good measure of security, without the full protection afforded by a Letter of Credit. The only real disadvantage is that there is no safeguard against the possibility of the buyer refusing to take up the goods on arrival.

The procedure to be adopted in a sight draft transaction is as follows: When the goods have been despatched, the exporter must gather together all the required documents and raise a sight draft on the customer. Drafts are

191

usually raised in sets of three, each one being identified as 'this first of exchange (second and third of same date being unpaid)', etc. All documents are then sent to the exporter's bank (the remitting bank) under cover of an instruction schedule (or bank lodgement form). The exporter's bank is thereby instructed to release documents to the buyer against payment. To perform this duty the remitting bank sends the documents to a bank in the buyer's country (the collecting bank). The name of the collecting bank may already have been provided by the exporter — normally when the buyer has requested the use of a particular bank. If no instructions have been given, the remitting bank will select a correspondent bank. However the collecting bank is chosen, it acts as the agent of the remitting bank and is fully responsible for handling and disposing of documents in accordance with the instruction schedule.

An alternative method, offered especially by American banks in the UK, is known as *direct collections*. The exporter's bank gives the exporter a supply of lodgement forms which the exporter completes and sends with all the documents direct to the collecting bank. A copy of the lodgement form goes to the remitting bank, who then assumes the usual responsibilities for following up. Time is clearly saved by this method, but the exporter loses the benefit of his own bank checking documents prior to sending them overseas. This checking procedure is *not* part of the remitting bank's responsibilities, but it is often undertaken as part of the bank's service to its customers.

Careful completion of the instruction schedule by the exporter is important. The following points should be noted:

a   Is the bill to be presented on receipt or should presentation await the arrival of the vessel? In some markets it is normal practice for payment (or acceptance) of bills to be deferred until the goods arrive.

b   Is payment or non-payment to be advised by cable or by airmail? To minimise costs, it may be considered sufficient for non-payment only to be advised by cable.

c   How is payment to be remitted? By airmail or by cable? The interest-saving on a cable transfer will outweigh the cost on payments over a certain level (see Chapter 14 for further consideration of this point).

d   Who should the collecting bank contact in 'case of need', i.e. if payment is refused or some other problem occurs? This will normally be the exporter's local agent. What powers does he have in determining the action to be taken?

e   Is the bill to be protested? This is examined later in this chapter.

f   What action is the bank to take with regard to the care and disposal of the goods if payment is not made?

g   Are the charges of both collecting and remitting banks to be paid by the buyer or by the exporter, or are they to be shared? The intention of the exporter can also be expressed through the use of a clause on the bill (see 'clauses' below).

192

The term 'cash against documents (CAD)', is sometimes used as an alternative to payment by sight draft. The difference is that CAD terms do not involve the raising of a Bill of Exchange. The exporter sends all the documents to his bank for release against payment. There may be a cost saving for the buyer in respect of local stamp duties on bills, but the exporter gains nothing. The absence of a properly numbered and dated Bill of Exchange from the exporter's records can also be inconvenient.

The term 'cash against goods' is occasionally encountered. The exporter is required to send documents with the goods, having first arranged that the buyer will either pay or accept a Bill of Exchange on receipt of documents. The bill is thus a clean bill, and the whole transaction is really a form of open account, since the exporter has no control over goods and relies entirely on the good faith of the customer. It occurs generally in situations which would normally call for documentary terms. Because goods arrive ahead of documents, the customer cannot clear them through customs. To avoid this problem, 'cash against goods' may be suggested. Unless the buyer is entirely trustworthy, the procedure is not recommended. A variation on this idea is to address the Bill of Lading to the collecting bank, sending it as before 'in the ship's bag'. For this method to be successful, it is essential to make prior arrangements with the bank, which will need to be located in the port of disembarkation (or near to the frontier in the case of an overland shipment).

Term bills

Term, tenor or usance bills are drawn by the exporter to be paid, either at a fixed future date or at a calculable future date, e.g. '90 days from Bill of Lading' or '60 days after sight'. There is clear advantage in commencing the credit period from Bill of Lading date, and in the absence of any specific arrangements to the contrary the exporter should always do this. Expressing a bill as payable '90 days after sight' means that the period of shipment and dock clearance is effectively added on to the credit period. Also the exporter does not know the due date until advised by the collecting bank.

Under a term bill arrangement the buyer is permitted to receive documents (and therefore goods) only after 'accepting' the bill for payment on the due date. Regardless of the credit period, accepted bills are usually held by the collecting bank until maturity unless the exporter is arranging to discount them. If a collecting bank releases documents to a customer before the bill is paid or accepted and the bill is not honoured on presentation, the collecting bank is held responsible.

Term bills sometimes require documents to be released against payment. For example, on a 90-day D/P bill, after the bill is accepted the goods are placed in a bonded warehouse and the buyer has 90 days in which to pay. During this period he has an opportunity of finding customers ready to take delivery and pay him as soon as he pays the bank and takes possession of the goods.

Payment before maturity of a term bill may be obtained by the seller by negotiation through his bank. The exporter sells his bill to his bank — normally before acceptance has been obtained from the customer. If payment is not made on due date, the bank has recourse to the drawer. A sight bill may also be negotiated if the exporter prefers not to suffer the one or two months' delay normal with sight payments. If less than 100 per cent of the face value of a bill is paid by the bank, this becomes an advance rather than a negotiation.

The act of 'discounting' a bill is different. A bill must be accepted first and be payable in the locality of the discounting bank. Discounting is usually restricted to bills drawn on banks under Letters of Credit.

Bill clauses

The addition of a clause to a bill enables the drawer to give precise instructions about payment. Clauses in common use include:

'Payable with interest at . . . per cent per annum from the date hereof until arrival of funds in London.' This was known as the Eastern Clause, because it was frequently used in trade with the Far East which involved long delays in the transmission of funds.

'Payable at the current rate of exchange for sight drafts in London.' This ensures that the buyer must provide sufficient local currency to meet the sterling value of the bill on due date.

'Payable with all bank collection charges.' This assumes that the buyer has agreed to meet these costs.

'Payment may be made in local currency pending exchange control approval for the transfer of sterling.' In practice, collecting banks, unless instructed to the contrary, release documents against local currency payments without such a clause.

While the exporter can include any of the above instruction clauses on the bank lodgement form, there is clearly an advantage in entering them on the bill itself. They remain in full view to any person handling the bill, whereas a lodgement form can become separated from the bill.

Bills of Exchange problems

Demurrage

A frequent problem is demurrage, by which is meant costs imposed by port authorities when goods arrive ahead of documents and cannot be cleared from the docks. When the shipment period is only a few days, i.e. for all European and Near Eastern destinations, the exporter must either ensure that documents are obtained from the forwarding agent within 24 hours or make an arrangement with the collecting bank. By no means are all banks equipped or prepared to take delivery of goods and store them.

Article 6 of the *Uniform Rules for Collections* states: 'In the event of goods being despatched direct to the address of a bank or consigned to a bank for delivery to a drawee against payment or acceptance or upon other terms without prior agreement on the part of that bank, the bank has no obligation to take delivery of the goods, which remain at the risk and responsibility of the party despatching the goods.'

Shipments by air, road or rail

Complete security in documentary transactions is only possible where documents of title are passed to the collecting bank. (The phrase 'complete security' is not strictly accurate, since it takes no account of the possibility of fraud.)

Where shipment is by rail or road there is no document of title unless a Combined Transport Bill of Lading is used or, in the case of container deliveries, a Multi-modal Bill of Lading. When shipment is by air, the Airway Bill is not a document of title.

The usual answer to the question of security in these situations is that the goods should be consigned to a bank. Very often this is either not possible or not acceptable to the buyer. As far as air-freight is concerned, the prime object is speed — to deliver goods as fast as possible to the buyer. If a bank has to take possession (assuming a prior arrangement has been made), this adds considerably to the time. Some countries permit airlines to operate on a 'cash-on-delivery' basis, but many do not. Not all airlines are willing to undertake this responsibility.

Release against local currency

It is normal practice for the collecting bank to release documents (on a 'D/P' collection) against payment in local currency, although Article 12 of the *Uniform Rules* only permits this if the amount paid can be remitted immediately. Since the buyer has parted with his money, from his point of view it is entirely reasonable that he be allowed to take possession of the merchandise. For the exporter, however, the picture is quite different. In markets that are short of foreign exchange, there can be long delays before payment is permitted. To guard against the possibility of the exporter losing as a result of a devaluation of the local currency between the lodging of local currency and its transfer to the seller, the collecting bank should be asked to release documents only against a 'shortfall undertaking', i.e. the buyer guarantees to provide enough additional local currency as is needed to produce the right value for the exporter.

For example, a UK exporter supplies goods to a Ghana importer on documentary sight draft, value £1,000. The importer pays enough cedis (Ghanaian currency) to buy £1,000 and obtains the documents also giving a shortfall undertaking to the collecting bank. No sterling is available for six months, and during that time the cedi is devalued by 20 per cent. In accordance with the shortfall undertaking, the buyer must give the bank additional cedis so that the total held will still buy £1,000.

Often, however, these undertakings are not effective. Local controls may prevent extra payments being made or long delays can occur, depending on the degree of priority given by the central bank to the merchandise.

The solutions to this problem are either to sell under a Letter of Credit, confirmed by a UK bank, or to continue on a bill basis under the protection of an export credit insurance policy. Neither of these solutions is satisfactory, since in extreme cases — those that cause the most problems — UK confirmation is not available, and it may not be possible to obtain credit insurance on occasional business at short notice.

Dishonour of bills

When sending a bill to the bank, the exporter must at that time decide whether to have it protested in the event of non-payment. Protesting is done by having a notary public complete a deed of protest to the effect that payment has been refused on due date. This evidence of non-payment can be produced in court, and in many countries it is a necessary first step towards court action for the recovery of payment.

The regulations for protesting bills vary from country to country, some requiring protest to be made within 24 hours of presentation and others allowing several years before the right to protest disappears. Information on protest regulations in different markets may be obtained from the Exports Bank.

The effect of protest also differs according to the market. In some countries the protesting of a bill is tantamount to an act of bankruptcy on the part of the buyer, and in others his reputation will be severely damaged.

It is, therefore, important that the exporter should check both on the protest regulations and on the effect of protesting in all markets where bill terms are used and to mark his records accordingly. If a credit insurance policy is held, the exporter is normally expected to protest bills, since failure to do so may mean that the legal right to sue for an unpaid account is lost.

Using an Aval

More security is given to an accepted term bill if the customer agrees to arrange for his bank to add its acceptance to the bill. This is called an aval. An avalised bill can be discounted, the cost depending on the quality of the accepting bank and the perceived market risk.

Open account

When the buyer is an established company with a good reputation in a market free from serious political or transfer risks, goods may be supplied on open account. The carrier is instructed to deliver direct to the buyers, documents of title (where existing) accompanying the goods. The payment terms may be on arrival of goods, or at an agreed number of days after invoice date or after arrival.

The decision on the period of credit to be offered will be influenced by the local practice and by competition. Terms of 60 or 90 days are common in France, sometimes being stretched even further by the use of complicated arrangements, such as 'payment on the 10th or the 20th of the third month following the month of invoice'. Such requests should be resisted by the credit manager because credit costs money, which reduces profit margins, and because control over unpaid accounts becomes more difficult the older they are. If a market is to be entered where it is known that long terms will be expected, prices must be adjusted to cover this. Italy is such a market and terms of 90 or 120 days are frequently encountered. Broadly speaking, the further south one goes in Europe the longer the terms tend to be. A further problem is caused by the period of shipment, since many buyers will start counting the credit period from the date of receipt of goods. Shipments by sea to the USA, for instance, will take up to 14 days to arrive, and then there is a further delay before the goods arrive at the customer's premises. There are two alternative ways of tackling this situation. Terms can be set at 30 days from receipt of goods. This may suit the customer, but the exporter can never precisely fix the due date, unless a special arrangement is made with the carrier. It may be better to agree on, say, 60 days from invoice date providing that the total delivery period is within four weeks.

It is the practice in some European countries to agree discount terms, often with an alternative. Thus in Germany one often finds buyers offering to pay '2 per cent 10 days, 30 days net'. In other words the buyer has the option of a 2 per cent discount for paying in 10 days from invoice date or paying net after 30 days. Generally these arrangements are not recommended because with a short period such as ten days, most or all of that time will elapse before the customer receives the invoice. Any benefit to cash flow will therefore be lost.

The credit decision, as to payment terms and credit limit, is examined in Chapter 14 together with the question of export cash-flow.

Credit decisions and export cash-flow

The previous three chapters have been devoted to risk evaluation and payment terms. When the credit manager has satisfied himself on these issues, the moment of credit decision has arrived.

There are a number of guidelines which can help in deciding on the right payment terms and controls, and these should be followed in a logical sequence. Assuming that a new enquiry is received, the following questions should be asked:

Is there a serious political or transfer risk in the importing country?

If yes, terms should be Confirmed Irrevocable Letter of Credit. If a credit period is demanded, this can be given by term bills under the Letter of Credit. If the market risk appears acceptable:

Is the buyer of high standing and good reputation?

If yes, then credit can be given, either on open account terms or by the use of term bills. Open account is generally reserved for well established buyers in Europe or the USA, where reliable commercial information is obtainable.

If the answer to the second question is no, the choice is generally between documentary sight draft or Letter of Credit (lack of confirmation may be acceptable assuming the absence of serious market risk). Where the product is made-to-measure against customer specification, a Letter of Credit is preferable. Providing work is not started until the credit arrives, the pre-shipment risk can be avoided. If the contract is ex-works or FOB, however, there is still the danger that the buyer will decide not to arrange for collection or for shipment. Where non-standard goods are involved and the buyer is unknown, it is always advisable to quote CIF or delivered terms, payment to be made by Letter of Credit.

Some markets, especially amongst the developing countries, present difficulties even though there are no serious political or transfer risks. Incompetent banking systems or a corrupt and inefficient bureaucracy (or both) frequently result in payment delays which can drag on for months. To recognise these problems and be prepared for them is part of the credit manager's job. Through regular liaison with other exporters (already discussed in Chapter 11) and expert advice from his bank, the credit manager must be able to meet these difficulties and to find answers.

Complete freedom of choice of terms is often not possible. Regulations may be imposed on importers by their governments, attempting to limit the outflow of foreign exchange. The exporter will then be expected to offer more liberal terms in order to do business. The terms offered by competitors can also have an effect. In a market where similar products are sold on 90-day terms or 30 days less 3 per cent discount (often found in Germany), the exporter who insists on 30 days net will find it hard to win orders.

While a detailed consideration of credit insurance services is reserved for Chapter 15, it is important to note that the holding of a credit insurance policy can play an important role in the choice of terms. Markets which would otherwise demand Letter of Credit terms may sometimes be sold to on documentary bills under the protection of credit insurance. To insist on a Letter of Credit will certainly mean extra costs for the buyer. Also the conditions specified in the Letter of Credit may be so strict that compliance by the exporter is almost impossible. The alternative of term bills with credit insurance cover may be very attractive.

Credit decisions often have to be made quickly with no time available for comprehensive information gathering and detailed risk evaluation. At such times, just as in the home market, the credit manager has to live on the telephone, and his ability to make good decisions will depend very much on the contacts and information sources he has developed. The following example illustrates this.

In the late afternoon of Day 1, a UK manufacturer of automotive parts (G) received a telephone order from a company in West Germany asking for despatch on Day 3 of goods to the value of £11,000. The buyer was totally unknown. Within 24 hours credit clearance had been given, and the goods were despatched on Day 3. This was the result of several telexes and telephone calls to credit agencies and insurance companies. While G did not hold a credit insurance policy, discreet enquiries established that credit insurance had no file on the buyer. A UK credit agency had no information. Direct approaches to two German reporting agencies produced a few basic facts which together indicated that the company was small (3–4 persons), long established (30 years) and of good reputation. No details of net worth, turnover of profitability were available, since it was registered as a sole trader.

Telephone calls direct to the buyer (who spoke no English) revealed he was willing to pay on a 45-days documentary sight draft basis, but there was no time to contact his bank to make the necessary arrangements. Without insurance cover, this was clearly a very marginal case, and the credit manager would have preferred that documentary terms were used.

The decision was made to ship, payment to be by 45-day clean draft. Payment was received on due date.

Credit limits

When credit terms are given, either open account or on term bills, credit limits should be set. The same principles should be observed as in the home market, questions being asked in the following sequence:

On the payment terms agreed or requested, what credit limit is needed to cater for the expected volume of business?

A problem not generally encountered in the domestic market is the period of shipment, which can vary from a few days to several weeks. This may be built into the terms, as when documentary bills are dated from Bill of Lading date, or when 60 days from invoice are agreed in place of 30 days from date of arrival.

A further complication can be the slow movement of funds back to the UK, which will distort the credit period. If a delay of four weeks is commonly experienced in receiving the proceeds of a 60-day term bill from a particular market, should the credit limit be increased to allow for this? While a 60-day bill may run from Bill of Lading date, the goods may have left the factory three weeks earlier and been at the docks waiting for a vessel.

Fortunately, as far as documentary terms are concerned, where the credit manager would aim to build in an extra month for slow payment with a domestic buyer, that extra month can be used to cover delays in shipping, since he will have a bill accepted for payment on the due date. Thus, for a buyer on 60 days sight averaging £5,000 monthly, a credit limit of £15,000 should be sufficient. While the payment itself may not arrive until several weeks after due date of the bill, the collecting bank will send a telex advice if payment is not made, and an immediate hold can be placed on further deliveries.

Should a bill not be accepted within a reasonable period, this in itself will alert the credit manager to a potential problem.

Open account customers present a slightly different set of problems. On the one hand, being on open terms should mean that the delivery period is relatively short. The risk of shipping delays is normally less with container traffic across Europe than with ocean transport. Against this, the absence of a bank advice about payment plus transfer delays can prolong the period of uncertainty before payment actually arrives.

Experience with different markets will give the credit manager a guide as to where payment delays can be expected. Market conditions change, and the prudent credit manager will look as much at the financial strength of his customers as at the liquidity problems of their territories.

As a general rule, a credit limit for a buyer on open account needs to be high enough to cover the credit period plus an extra month.

Can this credit limit be justified on the information available?

As we saw in Chapter 11, hard financial information is difficult to obtain. Judgements often have to be made on business reputation rather than balance sheet figures. Selling into Germany, for example, very frequently means dealing with firms who have no legal obligation to publish accounts. To insist on documentary terms may result in lost business since they expect to be granted open terms. Unless he is protected by an export credit insurance policy, the credit manager has a very difficult task in these situations. There is no formula for the right answer. All he can do is to develop to the maximum the sources of information that are available and hope that his past experience does not lead him to false judgements. In many cases he will open an account on a small limit and aim to increase it gradually as the customer proves his ability and intention to pay.

Is the credit limit to be a restriction or a guideline? What risk category is the customer to be allocated?

As in the domestic market, these decisions determine the nature of order-referral controls.

Category A is reserved for government buyers (Western industrial markets only!) and national/international companies of the highest standing. The principles followed in the UK are not always applicable, even to the Western industrial markets. Italian hospitals, for example, should on no account be given 'blue-chip' status.

Category C will include any buyers whose credit limit is restrictive. Because of information problems, this category will probably include a bigger proportion of overseas customers than the domestic sales ledger.

Category B will include all those not coming under 'A' or 'C', and order referral limits will be set to ensure that credit limits are not breached.

Market risk limits

In selling to markets with a transfer risk, on sight draft or unconfirmed Letter of Credit, it is prudent to set a credit limit which is, firstly, related to the buyer and, secondly, to the market.

An example from real life concerns a UK supplier (W) of a standard product to a Portuguese buyer (F) in 1977–8. The credit standing of F was rather low. When this was put against the background of Portugal's financial problems, terms of documentary sight draft were clearly well justified. In late 1977 the Portuguese government increased its already strict controls over foreign exchange, import licences and Letters of Credit. F applied for credit terms because of the internal liquidity squeeze. A term Letter of Credit was considered, but UK confirmation was doubtful, and, more importantly, Portuguese restrictions on the use of credits would have made it almost impossible for W to arrange the required delivery programme. Eventually the following steps were taken:

1   F provided a bank guarantee, initially from a West German bank but later from a Portuguese bank, which could be called in the event of W not receiving sterling funds in the UK. [This was far better than merely guaranteeing payment by F, since local currency might have been paid, thus releasing the bank from its obligation. It can be regarded as similar in effect to a confirmed Letter of Credit, but without the restrictions and conditions of a Letter of Credit.]
2   Payment terms were set at 90-day documentary bills.
3   A credit limit of £100,000 was set. Not only did this match the value of the bank guarantee, but it also represented the maximum value W was prepared to ship and risk having returned to the UK should bills not be accepted.

Operating the controls

It is clear that even more flexibility is needed than with home customers, because of the additional problems of shipping, documentation and payment delays.

The credit manager needs to have some knowledge of shipment methods and also of documentation. This is often complicated and can easily lead to delays which will make nonsense of a credit limit system. With regard to delays in the transfer of funds, this is a subject on its own covered later in this chapter.

Special care is needed where non-standard problems are involved, since the amount at risk must be calculated to include work-in-progress and finalised stock.

The following examples (from practical experience) illustrate this:

1   An American company (B) wished to order specially-made engineering products from S, a UK firm. S was eager to have this business which could well develop into a substantial volume within a few years. On the other hand, the status information on B was not good, showing losses over recent years and a very poor liquid position. Normal terms for the product were 30 days from arrival of goods. A Letter of Credit was suggested but turned down by B (because of lack of bank support). Shipments would be required monthly, at an average value of £17,500.

One big advantage was that B, being a US company, was fully aware of the need to prove its credit standing. Accounts up to the last half-year were produced, plus evidence of US government contracts which needed the UK product. The other advantage was that S had credit insurance with Trade Indemnity, which included work-in-progress cover.

It was eventually agreed that the account would be opened on a limit of £35,000 on terms of 45 days from date of invoice. This was both the minimum amount that would permit the required sales to be made and also the maximum figure that could be insured. Careful controls were set up to ensure the amount at risk did not exceed £35,000, which had to cover both unpaid deliveries, any finished goods, plus work-in-progress.

2   A French buyer (L), purchasing non-standard products on 60 days' open account from a UK supplier (B), ran into financial difficulties. The existing debt was frozen under a form of moratorium, but L wished to continue buying. The proprietor of L had given B his personal guarantee on part of the outstanding debt. He offered to buy on cash terms for a price artificially increased by 20 per cent, this extra amount being set against the frozen debt. B agreed, since not only would the debt be reduced, but more product would be sold at no risk.

Over a period of 12 months the debt was reduced by nearly 50 per cent, but the system was not trouble free. Imports into France cannot be paid for on 'pro-forma' terms without Bank of France approval. To avoid this, on receipt of a cable advice of the next shipment value, L would give his bank an irrevocable instruction to remit the required amount to B, when his bank received the necessary customs entry document. Because the product was 'made-to-measure', B would not start manufacture until L's bank advised that they had the money available against receipt of documents. B then had to arrange for the transporter to deliver the customs document to the bank immediately after customs clearance, so that payment could be sent to the UK. A lengthy and cumbersome procedure but it did work. The alternative for B (apart from accepting the terms of the moratorium and not supplying any further goods) was to take L's proprietor to court for his personal guarantee. Doubts about the costs involved and whether he had sufficient personal assets persuaded B to choose the method described.

This is also an interesting reflection on the value of personal guarantees. They should never be taken if it seems likely they will be called, unless a very careful check has been made of the legal procedures and costs involved in the country concerned. In the example above, it was fortunate for B that the existence of a guarantee (and the threat of calling it) was sufficient in itself.

Distributor credit

A common feature of export marketing is the appointment of a distributor to be responsible for selling in a particular market.

The credit manager should be contributing to this decision by the provision of information. A major problem is often the amount of credit to be given and on what terms, since distributors usually expect better terms than direct buyers to enable them to build up stocks and give a good service to the market. The nature of the end-market will have a big effect on the amount of distributor credit granted. If a distributor has to give 2–3 months' credit to his customers, he will expect at least the same from his UK supplier; otherwise he will be forced to borrow locally to maintain his cash-flow. Borrowing costs, which may be high, reduce his profit margin. By the nature of their business, distributors usually have little in the way of fixed assets, so the exporter is often confronted with the choice of limiting credit to what the balance sheet will stand, thereby restricting sales and preventing expansion in the export market and giving more credit with some form of security. It may sometimes be possible to take a first charge on the distributor's receivables.

If a credit insurance policy is held, this can be particularly valuable in financing distributors. Providing a full disclosure is made and the insurer can be persuaded that the customer is fundamentally sound and healthy, a credit limit can often be obtained which would be completely unjustifiable to a supplier without insurance cover.

Payment methods

Regrettably, many companies believe that fixing the payment terms is all that needs to be done. As a result of this, control of export cash-flow is very neglected and misunderstood.

We have already seen how the international banking system enables exporters and importers to trade with varying degrees of security. It is vital that the credit manager understands how to use this system so that the transfer of funds from the customer to the seller's bank is achieved with the

Exhibit 14.1

Payment methods	Documentary terms	Open account
Customer's cheque	No	Yes
Bank cheque	Yes	Yes
Bank transfer	Yes	Yes
SWIFT	Yes	Yes
Clean bill	No	Yes

minimum delay. Payment methods can be matched to different payment terms as shown in Exhibit 14. 1.

Sterling payments

1 *Customer's cheque*   Cheques drawn by overseas buyers on their local bank are expressed in the currency of that country, with one exception. This exception is when the buyer's bank is operating a sterling hold account, having obtained permission from the appropriate monetary authorities on the grounds that there is sufficient volume of sterling transactions (both imports and exports). Such a sterling account is classed as an external account.

If possible, buyers should be dissuaded from making this type of payment because 'cleared funds' cannot be provided by the exporter's bank until the cheque has been returned to the bank it is drawn on, presented and cleared. While the exporter's bank may often be prepared to give immediate face value, this will be with recourse and is equivalent to the negotiation of a bill of exchange drawn and payable abroad. A delay of at least one week is unavoidable between receipt of the cheque in the UK bank and receipt of cleared funds, and this period can easily stretch to two or even three weeks depending on the location of the buyer's bank and the efficiency of the local clearing system. If, at the end of this period, the exporter is told that the cheque has bounced, he has lost all that intervening time and may even have shipped further goods. His bank will also charge interest on the money advanced pending clearance, plus commission and postage.

2 *Bank cheque*   The only type of cheque payment which is satisfactory is a cheque drawn on a UK bank, usually a branch of the customer's own local bank. Cleared funds can be obtained within two to three days, since the UK bank is merely honouring a cheque raised by its overseas branch or by a correspondent. This method of payment is commonly known as a banker's draft. Problems can still arise with this system, since the UK paying bank

may refuse to give value without a covering advice from the issuing bank abroad.

3 Bank transfer This is achieved by the buyer instructing his bank to transfer funds to the bank of the seller. This method is generally used for the payment of documentary bills as well as for open account transactions. While apparently simple, bank transfers give rise to a high volume of frustration and bitterness amongst UK exporters, who invariably blame the banking system when payments take longer than expected. Many complaints can be avoided if some trouble is taken at the outset to determine the timing and routing of transfers. Some points to note are as follows:

a   *Type of transfer* A high proportion of bank transfers are sent by mail (abbreviated as MT), because without other instructions this is the normal method. The time taken for an MT to be credited to the exporter's bank will vary greatly, depending on the number of banks involved in the transfer and on the efficiency of those banks. A minimum period of one week should be expected. While most MTs should arrive within two to three weeks, longer delays are not unknown.

    The alternative is to request a SWIFT payment or telegraphic transfer (TT). SWIFT is a system of inter-bank communication and payment to which most major banks throughout the world belong. However, this does not mean that all branches of member banks are on the system. The transfer period for either SWIFT or TT is a minimum of two working days, depending on how many banks are involved in the chain. Apart from its speed, the advantage of SWIFT or TT payment is greater security. Costs are higher than for a mail transfer and are normally paid by the sender unless otherwise arranged. If large customers are unwilling to pay by this method, the credit manager could offer to pay the bank charges.

    It is worth remembering that the customer's bank account is debited at precisely the same time regardless of whether MT or TT is used.

b   *Precise instructions* The customer should be asked to give his bank full particulars of where and how the payment is to go. An example of inadequate instructions is:

'Please pay £5491.65 to General Manufacturers Ltd, 99 Oxford Street, London, England.'

This should be worded:

'Please pay by SWIFT or TT £5491.65 to National Westminster Bank Plc, 100 Oxford St, London, England, sort-code xxxxxx, for the credit of A/C No. 1234567 General Manufacturers Ltd.'

This identifies the account number and the name and the branch of the supplier's bank. If the exporter also wants to receive a separate advice of payment, the following should be added:

'Under advice to General Manufacturers Ltd, 99 Oxford St, London, England.'

c   *The banking chain*   The more banks a payment has to pass through, the longer it will take and the more chances there are of error and mishandling. The first step in establishing payment arrangements with a new buyer is to check whether his bank (or one of his banks) has a direct relationship with, i.e. is a correspondent of, the exporter's bank. A common problem arises when the customer is using an out-of-town branch and payment has to come to the local branch of the exporter's bank. The sequence of events can be as follows:

i   Buyer instructs local branch to pay.

ii   Local branch passes instruction to main office.

iii Main office transfers to UK correspondent.

iv   UK correspondent transfers to main office of supplier's bank.

v   Main office transfers to supplier's local branch.

Even when the original instruction is to pay by TT, delays will occur in this type of situation because a transfer instruction only covers the movement of funds between two international centres, e.g. Paris to London. A payment which starts in Société Général in Evreux and has to move via Paris and London to Banbury is only on cable between Paris and London. Where the use of a local branch at both the start and the finish of a bank transfer is unavoidable, several extra days will be added to the two days' cable transfer period.

If there is a choice of banks for the importer to use, it will help the supplier to request that payment be remitted from a bank which is a correspondent of his bank. Failing this, it can sometimes be quicker to request the buyer to arrange payment by a bank draft drawn on a London bank

208

with instructions for the funds to be telephoned to the exporter's bank on arrival in the UK.

The same principles apply with the transfer of funds from the payment of bills. Delays tend to be longer because documentary transactions are more common in distant markets where communications are poor and standards of banking competence are low compared to the industrial nations.

A final point to remember is that customers have to buy sterling in order to pay it. Very few markets can offer the facilities taken for granted in the City of London for the purchase of currency.

4 *Clean bill* In a number of European markets it is normal practice for domestic payments to be made by clean bill. By this is meant a Bill of Exchange drawn by the seller on the buyer, dated to mature at an agreed future date, which is accepted by the buyer and 'domiciled', i.e. the buyer enters the name and address of the bank where payment will be made. No documents are attached to the bill, which is merely a means of payment as opposed to a method of controlling the delivery of goods. Its use is common in France, Belgium, Portugal and Norway and less frequent in Spain, Italy and Germany.

Payment by clean bill for goods exported on open account terms offers a number of advantages over payment by cheque or bank transfer:

a   Acceptance of a bill gives a limited amount of security. The customer knows it will be presented to his bank on the due date, and he will probably ensure that funds are available. To have a bill dishonoured is regarded as an extremely serious offence in all overseas markets.

b   The exporter does not have to remind the buyer to send a cheque or transfer. It is easier to omit to send a bank transfer on due date than to ignore the fact that a bill is falling due.

c   An accepted bill fixes the amount which has to be paid.

d   It can be used as a form of security where documentary terms are not practicable. For example, an order is received from a customer in Norway who has a history of slow payment on open account. The supplier accepts the order *subject* to acceptance of a clean bill dated to mature 30 days (the normal credit period) from the agreed despatch date. Only when the bill is returned accepted will shipment be made. This avoids the usual problem with clean bills of releasing the goods and then having no leverage on the customer to accept the bill.

209

An accepted bill should be presented for payment through the exporter's bank, with clear instructions about the disposal of funds, advice of non-payment, etc., and whether the bill is to be protested. Since the customer will be choosing the paying bank, there is no way of minimising transfer delays, which can easily be lengthy when the exporter's bank has no account with the buyer's bank.

A country with its own payment peculiarities is France. While payment by clean bill is normal practice, French buyers have a habit of amending, i.e. retarding, the due date on a bill so that 60-day terms turn into 90. This is especially likely to happen on a bill dated to mature in August. The whole of French industry and commerce appears to close for the month and bills are pushed into September. It is also quite common for a French customer, who has agreed open account terms, to raise his own *billet à order* or *traite*. This is a promisory note, which is payable by the customer's bank on the date indicated. It cannot be discounted but may be negotiated with recourse by a bank.

German buyers occasionally request their suppliers to draw a Bill of Exchange on them for the same value as the payment which has just been made for goods supplied. If payment terms are 90 days, the draft would be payable at that maturity and the cheque or bank transfer payment would have a discount deduction. The buyer then has a bill which can be sold to his bank at 2–3 per cent below the rate of interest for overdraft borrowing. It is a method of financing which has developed because of the difference in interest charges. The drawer of the bill has, of course, been paid for his goods, but he has a contingent liability until the bill is paid on maturity.

In Italy there is a payment method known as 'Ricevuta Bancaria'. This is used like a bill of exchange or promissory note and can be raised either by the supplier or by the customer. Once accepted for payment by the customer of a fixed amount on a fixed date, it is sent for payment through the banking system. However, it has no legal validity and is not protestable, and is therefore only suitable for use with buyers of undoubted credit standing. Its advantage — and indeed the reason for its existence — is that it requires stamp duty of only L.3500, compared to a charge of 1.2 per cent on bills and promissory notes.

5 *Promissory notes* A promissory note is an unconditional promise to pay a fixed amount, on a fixed date to, or to the order of, the beneficiary. It is raised by the customer and, like a bill of exchange, it can be avalised by a bank or protested for non-payment. It is preferred to a bill of exchange in some markets because it does not attract stamp duty.

Foreign currency payments

Many exporters invoice in the currency of the buyer or in a third currency. The reasons for doing so and the problems and benefits arising are examined in Chapter 18. In this chapter we are concerned with the handling of currency payments. Two basic principles must be observed.

The first is to remember that every currency payment into the UK has to be cleared through its country of origin. Thus all US dollar payments have to be routed through and cleared by a bank in the USA (generally in New York), regardless of where the buyer is located. Similarly payments in German marks or French francs have to come from a bank in Germany or France.

The second principle is that there must be a market for the foreign currency when it arrives in the UK. A buyer in Ghana will be delighted to pay in cedis, but the UK exporter will not be able to convert them into the required amount of sterling.

1 Customer's cheque   This is to be avoided for the same reasons that applied to receipt of a sterling cheque from an external account. All cheques must be cleared in the country in which they are domiciled.

If sales are being made to a number of buyers in a particular market, it may be advantageous to open an account in the appropriate currency. Thus an exporter with many customers in France could arrange to open a franc account in Paris. Customers would be asked to send their cheques (or arrange bank transfers) in francs to that account. At agreed intervals — daily, weekly or monthly — the balance can be transferred back to the UK. There is a saving on bank charges because of the reduction in transfers. If required, the exporter can arrange to have a daily telex listing payments received so that control over credit limits and overdue accounts is maintained. This arrangement also overcomes a problem which can arise in markets operating strict exchange control regulations. For example, payments from France are not valid unless the paying bank has checked the evidence of import before authorising the despatch of funds. An exporter who goes to Paris and brings back a cheque direct from his customer may find the cheque is dishonoured because it lacks the bank's approval.

2 Other methods   Payments by bank draft, bank transfer and clean bill have the same characteristics whether they are made in sterling or in the currency of the buyer.

Additional problems occur when payment is made in a third currency. A big proportion of world trade is conducted in US dollars. All dollar payments have to be cleared through a bank in the United States. The result is that the clearing system in New York has an enormous volume of business to handle which often results in delays.

The most common cause of delays in bank transfers, however, is that the customer's bank at the end of the chain is not in direct correspondence with the same US bank which is finally crediting funds to the exporter's bank. For example, a UK supplier sells to a customer in Greece on documentary sight draft terms in US dollars. In order to take up the documents, the customer instructs his bank to pay $1 million to the UK supplier. The Greek bank has a dollar account with a New York bank and an instruction is given to transfer $1 million from that account to the Midland Bank, London, for the account of the exporter.

Providing there are sufficient funds in the Greek bank's New York account, the New York bank makes the transfer. But if the New York bank's account with the Midland, London, is temporarily overdrawn, the transfer will be routed via another New York bank which makes the final transfer to London. This chain of events can easily be lengthened if the Greek buyer has to deal through his local branch and if the UK supplier banks with an out-of-town branch of the Midland.

Payment methods — conclusions

1 Payment by SWIFT or TT is usually the fastest method — providing there are not going to be too many banks in the chain.
2 Payment in local currency into a currency hold account may be worthwhile if there is sufficient volume.
3 Delays are frequently the result of too many banks handling a transfer.

Exporters often find that it pays to use several different banks. The City of London has the biggest and most diverse banking community in the world. Many banks have developed from specialising in particular markets or areas — West Africa, South America, the Middle East, the Far East, etc. As a result, their knowledge of these markets is first-class and they often have a strong branch network. An exporter with a concentration of business in a particular area should find out which bank has the expertise and then take advantage of it. It is generally not necessary to open an account in order to have collection work done. A number of banks, including the UK clearers, some UK merchant banks and some US banks in London, offer a cash management service which may include advice and help on a wide range of topics, such as documentation, currency invoicing and market risk in addition to the basic function of accelerating cash flow. A publication 'Cash by Express' produced by SITPRO in 1987, based on a survey by Barclays Bank plc, is highly recommended.

Overdue accounts

Everything said so far about payment methods assumes that customers are paying in accordance with the agreed terms. It is now necessary to look at how the exporter should tackle overdue accounts. This will be covered under the following headings, relating primarily to open account customers:

1 Invoices.
2 Statements.
3 Interest.
4 Letters.
5 Telephone.
6 Fax.
7 Visiting.
8 Agents.
9 Collection agents.
10 Legal action.
11 Political and transfer problems.

Invoices

Should export invoices be designed or presented differently from home trade? The UK supplier traditionally expects his overseas buyers to understand English, but it is worth considering whether a little trouble taken to present an invoice in the buyer's language might not have a beneficial effect on the timing of payment. This is particularly true where sales are made to small buyers. The problem of language occurs throughout the collection cycle. While English may be readily understood by multinational companies, this knowledge begins to fade the lower down the scale the contact exists. Some countries are renowned for their understanding of English, e.g. Holland, Denmark and Germany, but even so, it is wrong for the UK exporter to presume that he can correspond with and talk to these customers as if they were in Birmingham or Leeds.

It is not difficult to produce invoices with headings and pre-printed information in the main European languages — French, German, Dutch, Spanish and Italian. The invoice should carry a clear instruction about the method of payment, including full details of the bank account where funds are to be sent.

Statements

The UK practice of monthly statements is not followed on the Continent, with the exceptions of Belgium and Norway. In Austria and Germany, however, it is normal for customers to be sent a statement on or shortly after the due date.

This non-usage of statements derives from the fact that payment terms are invariably X days from the invoice date, in contrast to the UK custom of monthly accounts. If statements are to be sent, to be of any value they must include the due date of every invoice.

Interest

Statutory interest charges are likely to be introduced into the the UK by the year 2000 (see Chapter 3 for more details).

In Europe interest charges are accepted as normal commercial practice in Scandinavia, Austria and Switzerland.

Suppliers suffering from bank transfer delays should not hesitate to charge interest to the banks responsible, providing that definite proof can be given that the bank was at fault.

Letters

Collection letters are not an effective way to chase overdue accounts, whether the customer is in Manchester, Munich or Milwaukee. But sometimes they have to be used, perhaps because there is no practicable alternative or because of the volume of accounts. The first rule must be to write in the buyer's language — unless that language is not one of the major European languages, in which case English must be used. Many buyers do understand English, but the chances of receiving a reply are much higher if they are addressed in their own language.

Telephone

Unless the credit manager is fluent in the appropriate language, there is no point in chasing by telephone without first knowing (a) the name of the person who can help and (b) that he can speak English. As mentioned previously, there is a good chance of finding English speakers in Holland, Germany, Denmark, Sweden, Norway and in any multinational company, but this is of little use unless the language is spoken by the individuals controlling payment. Where there is no language problem, as with the USA, one five-minute call establishing a personal contact is worth more than a dozen letters. In some parts of the world, cultural differences can make telephone communication difficult. For example, in areas such as Greece, Turkey, Cyprus and the Middle East it is not considered fitting to discuss business with a woman.

Fax

The preferred method of follow-up by many exporters is by fax, but here again it pays dividends to use the buyer's language and to address it for the attention of the particular person known to be in a position to help.

Visits

Not many credit managers have the opportunity to visit overseas buyers, but the economics of an occasional trip should be examined. A one- or two-day visit will be expensive but if the result is the clearance of many thousands of pounds several months earlier than expected, such a trip is easily justified. An alternative is to ask the export sales manager to include the problem on the agenda for his next visit. My experience with this option is that payment problems are put on the bottom of the agenda and that time does not permit their discussion.

The agent

Just as an agent should regard the gathering of information as part of his job, so should he be ready to assist in the follow-up of overdue invoices.

An agent covering a market or group of markets should be sent details of all overdue accounts in those areas every month. Those he cannot visit, he can telephone, with the advantage of speaking their language. Where an agent's commission on sales is not payable until the sales have been paid, this provides an excellent incentive!

Collection agencies

Many collection agencies in the UK (and others overseas) offer to collect export debts. The credit manager should be very wary of these offers. While the debt will probably be handled on a 'no collection — no charge' basis, a great deal can be lost if, after six months, the agency passes the debt back, having failed to collect.

The credit manager must find out exactly what arrangements the collector has in the market in question. Preferably he should obtain the names of 'satisfied clients' and check on the experience. Collection rates are inevitably higher for overseas debts — between 10 and 25 per cent are not uncommon.

Legal action

The last resort is to take the customer to court. This will be very expensive and will probably drag on for many months. Choosing a solicitor is the first problem. It is clearly preferable to use an English-speaking lawyer and the best way is by recommendation. A number of points need to be agreed with the lawyer at the outset, including how frequently he will report on progress, what costs are likely to be, what documentation will be needed, whether it is better to seek judgement in a UK court or in the debtor's country and how long the entire procedure is likely to take.

Assistance in obtaining legal aid is also often provided by the commercial section of British Consulates and Embassies. Full details of the help available should be requested from the Department of Trade and Industry.

Political or transfer problems

Non-payment due to political reasons or lack of foreign exchange is a hazard of exporting which few companies succeed in avoiding at one time or another. The reasons for these problems were examined in Chapter 11.

There is very little the credit manager can do when told by his bank that his customer in Zaire has paid in local currency but no sterling will be available for an indefinite period. Nonetheless he should take the following steps:

a   Ensure that sales and marketing department are fully aware of the problem, and that no further business is sought or accepted unless on a Confirmed Irrevocable Letter of Credit. If a credit insurance policy is held, any restrictions imposed on policy holders must, of course, be adhered to.

b   Keep checking (through the bank and the press) on the status of blocked debts. A recommendation may well be required at year-end on the amount of bad debt provision to be made.

c   Keep his ear to the ground for news of possible ways of getting round the problem.

Chapter 15

Export credit insurance

Protection against the various forms of export credit risk is available to UK exporters from a number of insurers in the private market.

The purpose of this chapter is to survey the facilities offered for short-term business (up to 180 days' credit) and to consider how the decision to seek protection should be reached. Over 80 per cent of UK exports fall under the heading of short-term.

The benefits of export credit insurance

The primary and most obvious benefit of export credit insurance is to protect the exporter's cash flow and profits from non-payment arising either from insolvency or from political causes.

There are, however, other possible advantages, summarised as follows:

a The exporter can be assisted in the identification of high-risk buyers and markets.

b Policy holders can obtain credit information on their buyers quickly; this information is likely to be more comprehensive than anything obtainable from a reporting agency.

c Guidance on the most suitable payment terms is available.

d Insurance is often a pre-requisite for obtaining export finance.

(This last topic is dealt with in Chapter 16, *Export Finance*).

The value of these additional services to exporters is being increasingly emphasised by insurers. The concept of a policy which only comes to life when a claim is made or at the renewal date is being replaced by the idea of a continuous service in the form of credit information, advice and opinions and debt collection.

The insurance market

The development of the European Union in the early 1990s led to the concept of all EU countries being one domestic market, but the reality is that UK firms still treat sales into the EU as exports. This is a thoroughly realistic attitude, in view of the multitude of different business practices, legal entities and procedures and trading currencies. Underlying all of these there are also many cultural and linguistic differences which can entrap the unwary exporter. Company failures within the EU rose by over 50 per cent between 1990 and 1994.

Nonetheless, one result of this concept of one market has been to prompt the major credit insurance companies to offer cover on European buyers – and on buyers in other OECD countries – under a single policy, without drawing any distinction between 'home' and 'export'.

The major provider of insurance to UK exporters is NCM, a Dutch-owned company which took over the business of the Insurance Services Group from the Export Credits Guarantee Department (ECGD) in 1991. In 1994 over £15 billion of UK exports were covered by NCM. Euler Trade Indemnity Plc is the second largest provider, with over £6 billion exports covered in 1994. Other insurers, such as Coface LBF (French-owned), Gerling Namur (German), Hermes (German) and FCIA (American) also offer short-term export protection. The role of ECGD is now limited to the provision of cover for medium to long-term exports; this is examined under *Export Finance* in Chapter 16.

The other part of the credit insurance market concerns the brokers. Most insurers and policy-holders prefer to operate through a broker on the basis that a skilled professional intermediary brings added value to a relationship. His knowledge of the market enables him to present a client with all the relevant policy options, both at inception and at renewal. Conversely insurers are saved a lot of time and expense by the work of a broker in only putting forward suitable clients.

Protection offered

Protection comes under two headings:
a   Buyer risk (normal cover is up to 90 per cent of invoice value)
  • Insolvency
  • Protracted default (i.e. failure to pay within six months after due date)

- Failure or refusal of the buyer to accept goods despatched in accordance with contract terms (in these cases, the exporter must bear a first loss of 20 per cent, before the 90 per cent indemnity applies).

b Political risk (normal cover is up to 95 per cent of invoice value)
- Action by the government of the buyer's country which prevents contract performance, in whole or in part
- Political events, economic difficulties, legislative or administrative measures which prevent or delay the transfer of payment
- War, civil war or revolution outside the UK which prevents contract performance
- Cancellation or non-renewal of an export licence by the UK government or the imposition of new restrictions on exports after the date of contract
- The failure or refusal of a public buyer to fulfil any of the terms of the contract.

In addition to the above, cover can usually be arranged for pre-credit risks, i.e. where special goods are being made and the buyer becomes insolvent before the goods have been shipped. NCM can also arrange protection for other export services and activities as follows:
- Technical or professional assistance
- Refits, conversions and repairs (applicable to ships, aircraft and other major items)
- Royalties due under licensing or franchise agreements
- Sale of goods via overseas subsidiaries
- Sale of goods from overseas stock or exhibitions.

Cover is also available for losses incurred in meeting foreign exchange commitments. Exporters are generally allowed some latitude to exclude parts of their turnover, to particular markets and/or buyers, providing the insured turnover offers the insurer a reasonable spread of risk.

How policies work

Insurers generally operate either a credit limit service or an aggregate first loss system. The latter is more suitable for large exporters with established credit control procedures. Claims are not paid until an agreed aggregate loss is reached. Premium rates are lower on this type of policy, since insurers are less exposed to claims and have lower administration costs.

With a credit limit system, all export buyers are vetted by the insurer, unless there is an agreed threshold below which the exporter is allowed to set his own limits, on the basis of satisfactory information or trading experience.

As in all forms of insurance, the exporter must ensure that the buyer is correctly identified, that terms and conditions have been agreed and that goods have been despatched and invoiced in accordance with contract terms.

Claims are only paid after thorough investigation of all circumstances of the loss, including whether the exporter exercised good credit control and whether all policy terms were strictly complied with.

The essence of this is that a credit insurance policy is not a substitute for credit management, but rather a safety net.

Credit insurance for smaller exporters

Companies with exports exceeding £1 million p.a. have a wide choice of policies, but those below this level are not so well catered for, particularly where exports are less than £250,000.

The introduction by NCM in late 1995 of a new Compact Policy was a major step towards meeting this need. The principal features of this policy are as follows:

- companies with export turnover of any value up to £1 million are eligible, regardless of the number of buyers
- buyer risk cover is 90 per cent and political risk 95 per cent
- minimum premium is £1500 with no extra charge for credit limits
- credit limits may be obtained on-line from a terminal in the exporter's own office or through a broker.
- The policy document is written in plain English and minimum paperwork is required.

The alternatives to the above are mainly a small number of 'managed policies' available to companies offering at least £250,000 export turnover. Both Barclays Bank and Intrum Insurance Services provide this type of facility, under a master policy with NCM. Client companies are relieved of the burden of administration in return for an annual fee (typically £500), in addition to premium on turnover. Firms whose exports are below this threshold may be eligible if there are good growth prospects. Another option is Trade Indemnity's Multi-Market policy, which does not require a minimum export turnover but a minimum total turnover of 350,000 in the UK and OECD combined.

How to decide about credit insurance

As with domestic credit insurance, the first step towards a decision should be a careful analysis of risk, firstly by market and then by buyer within each market.

If a high percentage (say 75 per cent) of business is in Western Europe, market risk will not be significant and the chief criteria will be the financial strength of the buyers and the spread of risk between them. The case for credit insurance will be considerably stronger for a firm whose exports are concentrated amongst a small number of large buyers than for one whose business is well spread.

Conversely, an exporter supplying mainly to third-world markets (e.g. South America, Africa and the Middle East) will have a high level of political risk, whether or not the actual buyers are financially sound. In such circumstances there is a *prima facie* case for insurance which can only be ignored if business is normally conducted on secure terms of payment (i.e. confirmed letters of credit). It should be noted, however, that some markets are 'uninsurable' and cover on others is dependent on the use of relatively secure terms (e.g. unconfirmed letters of credit).

The costs of export credit insurance

Premiums are charged either as a percentage on insured turnover (normal with a 'credit limit' type of policy) or as a percentage on outstanding balances (more often found with aggregate first loss policies). Premium rates vary considerably, depending on a number of factors:

- the spread of risk
- the industry the exporter is supplying
- the exporter's bad debt experience
- the volume of turnover
- the payment terms
- the perceived quality of credit management.

Special premium rates may also be charged on selected markets, often combined with a requirement for special payment terms. Some insurers also charge for each credit limit.

Nearly half of UK exporters do not credit insure. Some of these believe it to be too expensive and 'not available' when most needed. The majority, however, have not seriously considered it, do not fully understand the risks and regard the failure of a major buyer as 'something that happens to someone else'. This attitude usually accompanies the lack of any professional credit management.

Chapter 16

Export finance

In most export sales the gap between shipment and payment is greater than in domestic business. This may be caused either by a longer credit period agreed with the buyer and/or by a series of seemingly unavoidable delays in the export cycle. These delays may be the consequence of long journey times, poor communications between exporter, freight forwarder, customer and banks, inefficient banking procedures controlling the movement of money, foreign exchange problems and slow payment by the buyer.

Ways of closing, narrowing or tolerating this gap in the cash-flow are all forms of export finance.

Short-term finance

Overdraft

Many exporters rely upon existing overdraft facilities, particularly if their business is on short open account terms (i.e. up to 90 days). This option clearly has limitations, particularly if exports are growing and there is not much head-room in the overdraft limit. Banks will normally restrict advances from a sales-ledger linked overdraft facility to between 30 and 50 per cent of total debtors.

Overdraft rates vary between one and four per cent above base lending rate, with three per cent being typical. To this must be added annual arrangement or renewal fees, usually between 0.75 per cent and 1.5 per cent of the total facility value. So for an exporter with high borrowing costs, funding through bank overdraft is expensive, and of course all overdrafts are repayable on demand.

Bank finance

Several UK clearing banks provide finance to exporters trading on terms up to 180 days, providing sales are credit insured and subject to certain minimum volumes.

Credit insurance may be either through an exporter's own policy (generally NCM or Trade Indemnity), through the bank's own policy or through a 'managed' policy held by Intrum Justitia.

The minimum export turnover required is normally £2 million, but all the banks will consider situations down to at least £250,000.

Up to 100 per cent of invoice value is available on proof of shipment, of which 90 per cent is without recourse – providing the debt is fully insured. Exporters can select which transactions they wish to be financed.

Bill of exchange finance

1 Advances The exporter's bank may be willing to advance a percentage (normally between 80 and 90 per cent) of the face value of documentary bills submitted for collection. Normal overdraft rates will apply and the bank has recourse to the exporter in the event of non-payment.

2 Negotiation All the clearing banks will purchase documentary sight or term bills for 100 per cent of face value at the time they are lodged for collection or acceptance. CAD transactions (i.e. sight drafts without bills) and clean bills (i.e. bills without documents) may also be negotiated. The negotiating rate is normally the exporter's overdraft rate, calculated on the time between the bank paying the exporter and the actual date of customer payment. Negotiation is done with recourse to the exporter should the bill be dishonoured.

3 Discounting This is similar to negotiation, except that bills must have been accepted by the drawee. The bank buys at a discount (say 95 per cent of face value) and the exporter gives up the remaining 5 per cent as the price for having immediate payment. This facility is often encountered where the bill is drawn under a Letter of Credit, in which case discounting will normally be without recourse. Similarly any bill that carries a bank acceptance may be discounted without recourse. Bills that bear the *aval* (guarantee) of a first class bank (usually arranged by the buyer) may be discounted at advantageous rates.

Acceptance credits

An alternative to the negotiation or discounting of individual bills is an arrangement whereby the exporter obtains finance by drawing a series of clean bills on his bank which are immediately discounted at very fine rates in the London discount market. The underlying security for these bills is provided by actual export transactions which are covered by documentary bills lodged with the bank for collection.

The main benefits of acceptance credits are flexibility and low cost, since the exporter can use them as and when funds are needed, and his bank's acceptance ensures that interest costs are minimal. Banks prefer to see that the risk is covered by credit insurance.

Risk distribution

Another possible source of short-term finance is risk distribution, available to exporters using documentary credits, and offered by the Midland Bank and some European banks. In situations where a single bank is unable to add its confirmation to a Letter of Credit, due to the market risk and/or the size of the transaction, confirmation may be obtained through a syndicate of banks sharing the risk. The exporter only deals with one bank (normally his own) and is unaware that confirmation, and thus removal of all risk, has been made possible by syndication.

Confirming houses

A confirming house acts on behalf of an overseas buyer, placing the order with a UK exporter. The exporter is relieved of all credit risks and can usually obtain payment within 30 days or less. Confirming houses can often handle all shipping and documentation.

Invoice discounting and factoring

Confidential invoice discounting was referred to briefly in Chapter 10. Most factoring companies offer this service, which may be regarded as a suitable alternative or addition to overdraft finance, since cash advances are available for up to 80 per cent of export invoices, compared to a normal maximum of 50 per cent on overdraft. A minimum export turnover of £500,000 is generally required and there is an administration charge of up to 0.75 per cent on turnover. If bad debt protection is required this can be provided (at extra cost) or the exporter may operate his own credit insurance policy.

Full factoring services for exporters are described in Chapter 10. A minimum export turnover of £250,000 is normally required.

Both invoice discounting and factoring are more attractive to exporters selling on open account terms than to those using letters of credit and bills of exchange, because of the easy availability of bank finance for the latter categories.

Medium and long-term finance

ECGD supplier credit scheme (SCF)

This is a UK government-backed facility available for specific contracts for capital or semi-capital goods with a value between £25,000 and £20 million, requiring finance of between 2 and 5 years. Contracts above £20 million will almost certainly be catered for by ECGD Buyer Credits (see below).

Several UK banks, including Barclays and Midland, operate this service. The main features are as follows:

a The bank provides up to 85 per cent of contract value, subject to contract approval by ECGD.
b The remaining 15 per cent normally has to be paid by the customer on contract signature. The bank may also be able to finance this.
c The exporter can obtain pre-shipment protection from ECGD if required.
d The exporter receives payment on shipment or on an agreed stage payment basis.
e The customer pays the UK bank through a series of bills of exchange or promissory notes, which are often guaranteed by the customer's bank.

The advantages to the exporter are as follows:

a The customer is provided with the finance he wants.
b All premiums, costs and interest rates are fixed in advance and can be built into the contract price.
c The exporter enjoys good cash-flow on a non-recourse basis.

ECGD Buyer Credit

ECGD Buyer Credit facilities are intended for contracts of £5 million and over, relating to major projects or the supply of high value capital goods.

Loan finance is provided by the exporter's bank directly to the overseas buyer or his bank. Credit periods can extend for up to 10 years, and repayment is in six-monthly instalments on bills of exchange or promissory notes.

As with a supplier credit scheme, 15 per cent of contract value is

226

normally payable up-front. The remaining 85 per cent is paid to the exporter at the agreed contractual stages out of the loan proceeds administered by the UK bank. All charges and interest rates are fixed at the outset for the duration of the contract. ECGD protection is arranged by the UK bank.

Buyer credits are complex arrangements, involving often lengthy negotiations between the exporter, the banks, the customer and ECGD. Because of this it is essential for exporters to start discussions at the earliest possible date.

ECGD lines of credit

Under the heading of buyer credit there are two further types of ECGD facility to assist overseas buyers.

1 Project line of credit This covers purchases by one overseas buyer from a number of UK exporters in connection with a specific project. One or more UK banks (called a syndicate) take responsibility for providing loan finance to the buyer, and arranging for the exporters to be paid on shipment or performance.

2 General purpose line of credit This operates in a similar way, except that finance is provided to a number of overseas buyers. The UK bank (or syndicate) provides a loan to an overseas bank which coordinates and satisfies the requirements of the individual buyers.

Under line of credit arrangements, individual contracts of relatively small value (sometimes as low as £20,000) can be financed. By its nature the successful establishment of line of credit finance relies considerably upon government support. The Department of Trade and Industry regularly publishes details of lines of credit, either new or with unused capacity, indicating the type of products and services which would be eligible.

Leasing

An exporter wishing to provide his customer with equipment on lease can sell the goods either to a UK or a foreign leasing company which will then set up a leasing agreement with the overseas buyer. Leasing can be an attractive alternative to outright purchase because the payments will be spread over a longer period. Also equipment which quickly becomes obsolete (e.g. computer hardware) can be replaced or up-graded with the original lease being rolled-over or amended. In some countries there are also tax advantages.

Export Finance Companies

Export finance companies provide two- to five-year finance to overseas buyers for the purchase of capital and semi-capital goods, in situations where the exporter does not wish to or is unable to arrange this. This service can be especially useful where several exporters are supplying the same buyer. The export finance company will handle all administration and provide the exporters with cash on shipment.

Forfaiting

Forfaiting is the purchase by a bank of trade debt without resource to the exporter. The debt is evidence by bills of exchange or promissory notes which are guaranteed by the overseas customer's bank. The guarantee usually takes the form of a simple wording known as an *aval*.

Credit periods between 30 days and 7 years may be accommodated. The exporter is paid as soon as the bills are available, less a discount at an agreed rate. Rates will reflect both the standing of the avalising bank and the underlying market risk. No minimum contract values apply, but banks prefer to deal in high values, usually for capital goods.

Unlike credit insurance, forfaiting provides 100 per cent protection of contract value. Both buyer risk, political risk, interest rate risk and foreign exchange risk are covered. Alternatively, an exporter using ECGD supplier credit finance for 85 per cent of a contract may be able to offer his customer finance for the remaining 15 per cent through forfaiting.

Countertrade

Restrictions in the availability of conventional export finance and shortages of foreign exchange in many under-developed markets have encouraged the development of countertrade; this is basically the exchange of goods with little or no exchange of money directly between buyer and seller. It is a generic term, encompassing barter, counter-purchase, compensation, bi-lateral trading and switch trading.

For example, a very sophisticated form of countertrade operated in Zimbabwe in the 1980s. Normal trading with the UK and other Western nations was prohibited for political reasons, but Zimbabwe wanted to import vehicles, chemicals and other goods and to export tobacco. The solution was to supply tobacco to intermediaries in Eastern Europe who in turn purchased Western European goods for onward supply to Zimbabwe. No international regulations apply to countertrade. As a result there is no standard format and each new situation produces a different solution.

Another form of countertrade takes place when a UK exporter contracts to build a plant or to install equipment, say in the former Soviet Union, and agrees to be paid in the product of the completed project.

For UK exporters seeking to break into new markets which cannot obtain enough sterling or other hard currency, and where credit insurance cover is limited or non-existent, countertrade may be the only way forward, providing the overseas market has a surplus of some kind for which a demand exists.

High risks and high costs are unavoidable in all countertrade transactions, since a third party is normally involved, and neither importer nor exporter can expect to receive the same price as would be available under normal trading conditions. In return for this, however, the importer may find an outlet for surplus goods which will fund the purchase of essential imports. The exporter can develop new markets and increase his turnover.

Chapter 17

Contract risks and bonds

A number of market risks facing the exporter were examined in Chapter 11, principally the dangers of disruption of trade, the lack of foreign exchange and restrictive government regulations. Difficult as these problems can be, they only represent a part of the story as far as exporters of capital goods and contractors working overseas are concerned.

In this chapter an attempt will be made to summarise these additional hazards and to indicate how far protection can be obtained from ECGD and what facilities are available in the private market.

The private market concerned with political risk insurance consists of Lloyd's Underwriters and a number of American and European insurers.

Pre-contract signing problems

Nature of the market

The first task facing the UK exporter is the need to understand something of the market. Business methods and business ethics are not the same the world over, and the exporter who neglects to study his market and gain some understanding of its customs and traditions will suffer the inevitable fate of someone who has not done his homework. Traditionally the Near and Middle East are the areas most likely to give concern to exporters, but business with any non-Western industrial market demands close attention to local practice and law. Sources of information include the Department of Trade and Industry.

Identity and status of the buyer

Unlike in the UK or Europe, the standing of the buyer is frequently not clear. The distinctions between sole traders, companies, consortiums and even local or central authorities are not always clear-cut, especially in the Middle East. It is most important to establish whether the other party is a 'public buyer', since ECGD bond support or cover does not extend to private buyers who require 'on-demand' bonds. This will be covered in more detail later in the chapter.

Reliable financial information on private buyers in the developing countries is very hard to obtain, but the exporter may be no better off dealing with a public buyer. It is not unknown for a government official — supposedly representing a ministry or department — to be dismissed and negotiations carried out in his name to be ignored or dishonoured.

The agent

It is often necessary for a UK firm to use a local agent. The extent of his authority should be clearly defined in writing. Commission will doubtless have to be paid, both as an agreed percentage of contract value to the agent and as part of his expenses. In many instances this will be pure and simple bribery, and the exporter must recognise that in many countries commerce could not exist without it. The only safeguard is to have enough in the price to cover it. With regard to commission which is directly related to contract value, the seller must be careful to avoid any commitment to pay it all at the front-end of the contract. An arrangement whereby commission is paid pro-rata to the receipt of stage payments is preferable; otherwise cash-flow can be seriously affected.

Taxation and profits

In a construction project — or any project that requires employees to be resident in the overseas country — liability to local taxation must be examined. Some countries impose withholding taxes on money remitted from them, and others have tight regulations about the remitting of locally earned profits back to the supplier country.

These matters may not appear to be relevant to the job of the credit manager, but all too often it falls to him to provide the answers because no one else in the company has thought of the questions.

Bid or tender bonds

The purpose of a bid bond is to give the buyer confidence that the seller is financially able to carry out the contract if it is awarded to him. Frivolous tenders are thus avoided. The bond is normally for 5 per cent or less of the bid and it has to accompany the bid. As for other types of bond, bid bonds may be issued either by banks or by surety companies. The main differences are:

1 Banks are less concerned with the underlying questions — can the bidding company be considered competent to do the work? They issue bid bonds against the counter-indemnity of the exporter, having first satisfied themselves that his balance sheet is strong enough.

2 Surety companies only issue bid bonds if they are satisfied that the bidder is technically and financially competent to undertake the contract.

A bid bond is normally returned for cancellation if the contract is not awarded or replaced by a performance bond (see below) if the tender is successful. Bid bonds are generally acknowledged to be justified and do not cause serious problems. Support from ECGD in the issue of a bond is examined below under the heading 'ECGD bond support'.

Contract problems

The content of a major contract with an overseas buyer gives rise to many problems, some of which are beyond the scope of this book. Those which the credit manager should be aware of are dealt with below. The exporter will very often be asked to submit a draft contract. It is most important that clauses with wording most favourable to the seller can be prepared quickly.

Payment terms

Contracts for capital goods are either on 'cash' terms, i.e. under Letter of Credit or short-term bills, or credit (supplier or buyer credit).

A typical cash contract might have the following payment terms, the *wording* of which is important:

> 15 per cent of contract value, paid in sterling within 30 days of contract signature by cable transfer to Exporter's Bank Ltd, High Street, Anytown, for the credit of UK Exporter Ltd A/C No. . . . 85 per cent of contract value to be covered by an Irrevocable Letter of Credit confirmed by a UK bank, to be opened and lodged with the confirming bank within 30 days of contract signature. Payment to be made on presentation of the following documents (all in quadruplicate):

Commercial invoice
Certificate of origin
Insurance certificate (on CIF or Franco terms)
Full set clean Bills of Lading
   or
Forwarding agent's or warehouse receipt (for ex-works and FOB contracts)
Packing note
Seller's Inspection Certificate

The Letter of Credit will permit part-shipment to be made from any UK port and will permit documents to be presented up to 21 days from date of Bill of Lading.

In a credit contract, payment terms will be more complicated. Assuming that ECGD support is being provided, the wording for a supplier credit might be:

15 per cent of contract value paid within 30 days of contract signature by cable transfer to Exporter's Bank Ltd, High Street, Anytown, for the credit of UK Exporter Ltd A/C No. . . . 10 per cent of contract value to be paid on shipment out of an Irrevocable Letter of Credit confirmed by a UK bank, to be opened and lodged with the confirming bank within 30 days of contract signature. Payment to be made on presentation of the following documents (all in quadruplicate):

Commercial invoice for 10 per cent of each shipment value
Certificate of origin
Insurance Certificate (on CIF or Franco terms)
Full set clean Bills of Lading
   or
Forwarding agent's or warehouse receipt (for ex-works and FOB contracts)
Packing note
Seller's Inspection Certificate

The Letter of Credit will permit part-shipment to be made from any UK port and will permit documents to be presented up to 21 days from date of Bill of Lading.

The remaining 75 per cent of the total contract price will be paid by ten Bills of Exchange against each shipment, each of equal value, maturing at intervals of 6, 12, 18, 24, 30, 36, 42, 48, 54 and 60 months from the shipment date.

The cost of opening and confirmation of the Letter of Credit shall be for the account of the buyer.

Advance payments bonds and performance bonds

It is becoming normal practice for overseas buyers to require an advance payment bond to be provided as a condition of agreeing to any pre-shipment payment. The purpose is to ensure that, should the exporter fail to complete the contract, any such payment will be recovered. Performance bonds also insure the buyer against losses should the exporter fail to perform. While advance payment bonds are issued for the amount of down-payment, varying from 5 to 30 per cent, the value of a performance bond is expressed as a percentage of contract value, usually 5 or 10 per cent.

Bonds are either 'on-demand' or conditional. A conditional bond requires the buyer to prove that the exporter is in default, and generally provides for payment up to the extent of the actual loss suffered. This type of bond may be issued either by a bank or a surety company. It does not present a problem because payment will not be made unless the buyer can prove default. Regrettably, overseas buyers are prone to insist on 'on-demand' bonds, under which the issuer is required to pay the amount claimed on the buyer's first written demand — without having to show that default has occurred. This type of bond is rarely issued by a surety company. It is left to the banks who are generally much happier with 'on-demand' bonds than with conditional ones, since they wish to avoid having to exercise any form of judgement on contract performance. An example of a typical 'on-demand' bank bond is given in Exhibit 17.1. A bond issued by an American bank takes the form of a Standby Letter of Credit, which is illustrated in Exhibit 17.2. This latter example attempts to make the bond conditional, but in fact is 'on-demand' since the bank promises to pay 'against your written statement'. Exhibit 17.3 shows a conditional bond, drafted by Credit and Guarantee Insurance Co. Ltd, who introduced this service to exporters in 1977.

It is common practice to require bonds to be issued by a local bank in favour of the buyer. The exporter's bank consequently issues a counter-indemnity in favour of the local bank. This places the vital issue of calling and paying of bonds at arm's length from both buyer and seller. The validity of a demand turns entirely on the wording of the bond and the need for banks to be seen to be honouring their bonds one to another in accordance with international banking practice.

In considering the issue of a bond, a surety company has regard to the following:
1 How competent is the exporter/contractor to perform the contract satisfactorily?
2 Has he sufficient plant and equipment available to do the work?
3 Are the contract conditions reasonable?
4 Is the contractor financially strong enough to pay the bond?

Exhibit 17.1 'On demand' bank bond

We understand that our customer ... has been awarded
a Contract for the supply of....

We are informed that in this connection a Bank
Guarantee for..., being...% of the Contract value, is
required.

We, ... Bank Ltd, hereby guarantee to pay you an
amount not exceeding ... upon receipt of your first
written demand, certifying that in your absolute
judgement... have failed to fulfil their obligations
under the above-mentioned Contract.

This Guarantee expires on completion of the Contract
or on..., whichever is the earlier. Any claim under
this Guarantee must be submitted to us before the
expiry date.

Any dispute over the interpretation of this Guarantee
shall be subject to the laws of... (Buyer's country).

---

5 If sub-contractors are involved, what protection does the contractor have
against a possible failure?

Banks regard bonds issued as part of their customer's credit facilities. They
are less concerned with the ability of their customer to perform his contract.
Refusal to issue a bond will only result from the customer's reaching his
overdraft limit or for some other reason directly related to the customer's
financial position.

ECGD bond support

An exporter who cannot obtain a bond from his bank or from a surety
company may be able to claim assistance from ECGD in the form of an
indemnity to a bank or surety company to encourage the issue of a bond.
Before ECGD will consider such support, the contract must be worth at least
£250,000, basic ECGD insurance cover must be available and taken up, and
the terms of payment must be cash or near-cash (thus ruling out any business
under supplier or buyer credit). Support for on-demand bonds is only
available for public sector buyers. If these criteria are satisfied, ECGD will

thoroughly examine the exporter's finances and the proposed contract and the ability of both the exporter and any sub-contractors to perform it.

ECGD's premium rate is 1 per cent p.a. for bid bonds and 1¼ per cent p.a. for all others (with a minimum of one year's premium). If an ECGD-backed bond is called and paid, ECGD repay the surety within 30 days plus interest since the date of payment.

ECGD has the right of recourse to the exporter in the same way as a bank or surety company after paying an unsupported bond, although it is not usually exercised immediately.

This scheme was introduced in 1975 primarily to assist companies with large Middle East contracts who were having difficulty in raising bonds. Originally there was a minimum contract value of £20 million, reduced over

Exhibit 17.2　Standby Letter of Credit (Performance Bond)

Upon request of... (hereinafter referred to as the Seller), we hereby issue this irrevocable Standby Letter of Credit in your favour, for their account, up to.... This Performance Bond will be payable against your written statement that the Sellers have failed to perform subject to the Sellers having become liable to supply...to... (hereinafter referred to as the Buyer). Also subject to ..., being 15% of the total net contract price, having been paid to the Seller in accordance with the terms of an agreement made with the Buyer.

We hereby agree to repay to you in Sterling any amount for which the Seller shall be so liable under the above-mentioned agreement up to a total of .... The amount payable shall be calculated on a reducing basis pro-rata to the value of the goods supplied up to date if and when this Bond is called. This Bond may be called if the Seller fails to meet his obligations under the agreement, except those obligations which are excluded or qualified under 'Force Majeure' of the agreement. This Bond will expire when the final delivery has been made, and in any event not later than....

We confirm this Letter of Credit and thereby undertake that all claims will be duly honoured by us, if presented to the negotiating bank not later than....

Exhibit 17.3

Credit & Guarantee Insurance Company Limited

Colonial House, Mincing Lane, London, EC3R 7PN
England

GUARANTEE

THIS GUARANTEE is issued by **Credit & Guarantee Insurance Company Limited** (the Guarantor) to the Indemnified Party stated in the Schedule.

WHEREAS the Supplier stated in the Schedule has paid to the Guarantor a premium as consideration for this Guarantee and whereas the Indemnified Party and the Supplier have entered into the Contract specifically described in the Schedule.

THE GUARANTOR hereby undertakes subject to the provisos stated overleaf and the terms conditions and endorsements contained herein to indemnify the Indemnified Party against loss not exceeding the amount stated in the Schedule in the event of the Supplier defaulting in the performance of the Contract.

THE GUARANTOR undertakes to settle liability under the terms of this Guarantee within thirty days of receipt of evidence that the Indemnified Party has exercised all legal rights and remedies against the Supplier and that the loss suffered is not recoverable from the Supplier.

THE LIABILITY of the Guarantor shall be paid in the currency stated in the Schedule through a Bank in the United Kingdom as nominated by the Indemnified Party whose receipt of such payment shall discharge the Guarantor from further liability.

Date

....
Authorised Signatory

....
Underwriter for the Guarantor

Provisos *

1 This Guarantee shall only be valid provided it is delivered by the Guarantor to the Indemnified Party through a Bank in the United Kingdom as nominated by the Indemnified Party.

2 The Indemnified Party is not aware of the Supplier being in any financial difficulties at the date of acceptance of this Guarantee and has no reason to doubt that the Supplier will be able to perform the Contract.

3 The Indemnified Party shall not amend the Contract nor exercise any right to amend the Contract nor grant any indulgence thereunder without the prior written approval of the Guarantor.

4 The loss relating to this Guarantee shall have been directly and naturally suffered by the Indemnified Party as a result of a default by the Supplier during the validity period stated in the Schedule.

5 The Indemnified Party shall upon request of the Guarantor irrevocably assign to the Guarantor all rights in regard to any loss claimed under this Guarantee but such assignment shall only become effective on the date the Guarantor settles liability.

* The Provisos incorporated in this Guarantee are conditions precedent to any liability of the Guarantor.

Conditions

1 In the event of the Supplier defaulting in the performance of the Contract or any part thereof or the Indemnified Party having knowledge that the Supplier is unlikely to perform the Contract the Indemnified Party shall immediately take such action as is possible and prudent in the circumstances to require the Supplier to perform the Contract and immediately notify the Guarantor by telex or telegram and confirm such notification in writing. Thereafter the Indemnified Party shall in consultation with the Guarantor take all reasonable and prudent steps to mitigate any loss which may be suffered. The Indemnified Party shall if so required by the Guarantor allow the Guarantor to perform the Contract and shall credit and transfer to the Guarantor all monies and benefits due or to become due to the Supplier notwithstanding any terms of the Contract which entitles the Indemnified Party to retain such monies and benefits.

2 Evidence of loss suffered by the Indemnified Party shall include:—

    (a) an award of an Arbitrator in accordance with an arbitration provision incorporated in the Contract or

    (b) an unsatisfied Judgement Debt against the Supplier awarded in favour of the Indemnified Party by a Court in the United Kingdom or

    (c) written evidence from a Liquidator of the Supplier that the loss suffered by the Indemnified Party is a debt which will be admitted to rank against the insolvent estate of the Supplier or

    (d) written evidence in accordance with a procedure as detailed by the Guarantor in a special endorsement typed on this Guarantee.

3 The Indemnified Party shall at all times make available to the Guarantor and allow the Guarantor to examine or take copies of any letter accounts or other documents in the possession or control of the Indemnified Party relating to or connected with this Guarantee or any transactions between the Indemnified Party and the Supplier and the Indemnified Party shall at the request of the Guarantor supply the Guarantor with any information in the possession of the Indemnified Party or take any reasonable steps to obtain for the Guarantor any information or the sight of any documents in the possession of any third party relating to or connected with this Guarantee or any transaction between the Indemnified Party and the Supplier.

4 If the Indemnified Party makes any claim knowing it to be false or fraudulent as regards amount or otherwise this Guarantee shall become void and all claims under it shall be forfeited and any sums previously paid by the Guarantor under this Guarantee shall forthwith become repayable by the Indemnified Party.

5 The liability of the Guarantor shall cease at the expiry of the validity period stated in the Schedule except for any loss which directly relates to a default previously notified to the Guarantor under the terms of Condition 1 of this Guarantee.

6 This Guarantee shall be governed by the Laws of the United Kingdom whose Courts shall have exclusive jurisdiction in any dispute doubt or question arising hereunder.

Exclusions

1 The Guarantor shall not have any liability under this Guarantee in respect of loss directly or indirectly occasioned by happening through or in consequence of war invasion acts of foreign enemies hostilities (whether war be declared or not) civil war rebellion revolution insurrection military or usurped power or confiscation or nationalisation or requisition or destruction of or damage to property by or under the order of any government or public or local authority.

2 The Guarantor shall not have any liability under this Guarantee in the event of the Indemnified Party or any associated concern or subsidiary of the Indemnified Party obtaining any form of control or financial control of the Supplier or the Indemnified Party having failed to comply with the terms of any contract with the Supplier or any associated concern or subsidiary of the Supplier.

Exhibit 17.3 (cont)

The Schedule

Guarantee Number:	
	(Please quote this number in all communications to the Guarantor)
The Indemnified Party:	
The Supplier:	
The Contract:	Contract Value:
	Terms of Payment:
Maximum Liability of the Guarantor:	
Currency for payment of liability:	
Validity Period of this Guarantee:	

Date:

Checked:

SPECIMEN

_____
Authorised Signatory

_____
Underwriter for the Guarantor

the years to the present £250,000. The amount of information required by ECGD is generally not so great as that called for by banks or surety companies.

Unfair calling of bonds

The great risk of an on-demand bond is that it can be called without notice and without good cause. Underwriters will never forget the events of 1969 in Libya when the new Ghadaffi regime arbitrarily called guarantees given on behalf of contractors (notably Italian but also UK). This was a 'political' act and, therefore, not predictable according to ordinary commercial expectations.

Another instance of unfair calling occurred in 1977, also in Libya. An English exporter, Edward Owen Engineering Ltd, contracted to supply goods to a Libyan buyer against a Confirmed Letter of Credit. The buyer required an on-demand bond, which was issued by Barclays Bank International Ltd *before the Letter of Credit was opened*. The Letter of Credit was *not* opened, the exporter refused to ship and the bond was called. The bank paid and its action was upheld in the Court of Appeal. Lord Denning, Master of the Rolls, ruled that a bank's obligation on a performance bond is absolute and commented 'these performance guarantees are virtually promissory notes payable on demand'.

Protection against unfair calling may be sought either from ECGD or from the private market. A major point to be aware of is that neither ECGD nor Lloyd's cover offers a clear-cut advantage over the other.

1 ECGD's premium rate is invariably lower than the private market, but it is charged over the whole contract, whereas Lloyd's premium is calculated pro-rata to the risk according to contract performance.
2 In some markets at times Lloyd's can offer better cover than ECGD. For example, in 1977 ECGD would only give protection for export to Libya against war risk. Lloyd's were able to give cover against contract repudiation (which was the chief worry of many exporters) and import/export embargo.

Another related problem with bonds is their validity period and the difficulties sometimes encountered in recovering the documents. Under Syrian law a bond remains valid until it is returned for cancellation by the buyer to the local bank of issue. Other markets where periods of validity extend to 10 or 15 years include Turkey, Thailand and Libya. UK banks are very reluctant to accept such terms, which give them an indefinite exposure. Counter-indemnities from the exporter are naturally required, which can often cause difficulties. Not many exporters can present such a solid appearance as to warrant a 15-year risk!

Retention bonds are sometimes required when a buyer releases the final instalment of the contract price or the retention element of monthly progress payments. The bond is required to cover the period between such a payment and the final expiry date of the contractor's obligations.

To conclude this examination of the bond problem, there follows a shortlist of checkpoints for the exporter:

1 Allow for the cost of bonding in the contract price.
2 Try to persuade the buyer to accept a surety company bond.
3 If an 'on-demand' bond is unavoidable:
    a Ensure there is an expiry date as close to contract completion as possible.
    b Try to make the bond value reduce pro-rata to contract performance.
4 Obtain quotations from both Lloyd's and ECGD (providing the contract itself is ECGD-covered) against unfair calling.

Force majeure clauses

A strong force majeure clause is essential in a contract. Exhibit 17.4 illustrates a long form of force majeure which has an exhaustive list of reasons preventing the supplier from incurring any obligations or penalties.

Many clauses provide for termination of the contract after a specified period of force majeure interruption. Losses resulting from such termination can be insured with the private market.

Contract ratification

A risk which cannot be covered by ECGD is the possibility of losses arising from work done or expenses incurred prior to the contract becoming operative, which are irrecoverable in the event of the contract collapsing. Under this heading also come losses arising from the enforced closing-out of a forward foreign exchange contract. (See Chapter 18 for further explanation.)

A Contract Ratification Indemnity policy may be obtained from Lloyd's.

Arbitration

One of the hazards of contracting abroad concerns the handling of disputes. It is normal to find overseas buyers insisting that a contract be subject to the laws of their own country. Even if a contract is made subject to the laws of England, enforcement of a favourable decision will often be impossible.

Exporters are strongly recommended to include the following arbitration clause (recommended by the International Chamber of Commerce):

'All disputes arising in connection with the present contract shall be finally settled under the Rules of Conciliation and Arbitration of the International

Exhibit 17.4   Long form of 'force majeure'

(a) If either party is delayed or hindered in or
prevented from performing any of its obligations
under the Agreement by reason of Act of God, fire,
flood, earthquake, epidemics, quarantine restrictions, accident, explosion, breakdown or failure of
plant or machinery, war, riot, civil disturbance,
strike, lockout, work slowdown, labour dispute, acts,
orders or regulations of Governments, failure
(whether partial or total) of or shortage in any of
the Company's or its suppliers' existing or contem-
plated sources of material (including parts and components) or fuel or labour or transport whether such
failure or shortage be existing or apprehended by the
Company, failure of any supplier or sub-contractor of
the Company to perform any contract with the Company
or by reason of any cause whether or not of the same
nature as the foregoing beyond its control, it shall
be under no obligation but the time for performing
the same shall be extended until the operation of the
causes preventing, hindering or delaying the performance thereof has ceased.

(b) Without prejudice to the generality of the foregoing, if manufacture or delivery by the Company is
delayed hindered or prevented, or if the quality of
the goods available for supply by the Company is
reduced by reason of any of the causes described in
paragraph (a) above the provisions of the said paragraph shall apply and the Company shall be entitled
to suspend deliveries in whole or in part and shall
not be obliged to purchase or otherwise acquire any
goods from any third party or to arrange for any
supply of goods by any third party.

Chamber of Commerce by one or more arbitrators appointed in accordance
with the said Rules.'

This standard clause may be supported by stipulations as to the place of
arbitration, the number of arbitrators and the national law applicable to the
contract.

Further information on this subject may be obtained from the International
Chamber of Commerce, 14–15 Belgrave Square, London SW1X 8PS.

Post-contract problems

Apart from the unfair calling of a bond, most of the 'post-contract' problems are those which prevent one side or the other from fulfilling their obligations. These are as follows:

1 Import or export embargo.

2 Contract repudiation.

3 Exchange transfer delays.

4 War, civil war, etc.

5 Expropriation of assets.

Losses arising from these causes may be covered either with ECGD or in the private market, depending on the view taken of the market in question. There are several important limitations however:

1 Control repudiation cover from ECGD is only available for public sector buyers.

2 Exchange transfer losses can only be claimed under a Lloyd's policy if transfer of the required currency to the UK is prevented by law or government regulation. Many transfer delays occur without any such official announcement.

The cost of protection

The costs of insurance cover, bank guarantees, etc., have all to be included in the contract price. The credit manager must be ready to provide these details to the commercial department as soon as they are available. Approximate costs should be obtained as far in advance of final negotiations as possible.

Exhibit 17.5 illustrates the costing of an actual contract quoted for Nigeria in late 1978. It is important to note that the rates quoted were only relevant to that particular contract at that time and are *not* intended as a guide to current rates.

The calculation of item 6, interest charges for the five-year loan, is based on the following formula:

$$\left(\frac{A}{B}\right) \div \left(\frac{CDE}{100}\right)$$

Exhibit 17.5

BASIC DATA

1 Contract value: £5 million.

2 Terms wanted: 15% down, 85% over 5 years under Supplier Credit.

3 Repayment by ten equal six-monthly instalments.

4 Interest rate: 7.5% p.a.

5 Shipment period: 3-15 months from date of contract.

6 Advance payment bond required.

COSTS £

1 ECGD premium (3% on £5 million)	150,000
2 ECGD premium for bank guarantee (9.32% on 85% of £5 million)	13,600
3 Bank fee (9.375% on 85% of £5 million)	15,937.50
4 Advance payment bond fee (1% on 15% of £5 million)	7,500
5 Premium for unfair calling cover (3% on 90% of 15% of £5 million)	20,250
TOTAL	£207,287.50
(4.1% of contract value)	
6 Interest charges	£876,562.50

where A is the amount of loan, B the total number of repayment instalments, C the number of instalments per year, D the rate of interest and E the sum of instalment number, e.g. $10 + 9 + 8 + \ldots + 55$. In the example given, the calculation is

$$\left(\frac{4.25\text{M}}{10}\right) \div \left(2 \times \frac{7.5}{100} \times 55\right)$$

$$= \text{£}876,562.50$$

Chapter 18

Currency and foreign exchange problems

There is an exchange risk in virtually every export transaction. If the UK exporter invoices in sterling, the customer has to buy pounds in order to pay. If prices are in a foreign currency, the seller has to convert his receipts back into sterling. In both situations one party is at risk because the prices at which currencies are bought and sold fluctuate in a generally unpredictable manner.

Sterling exchange rates against other major currencies fluctuated considerably during the 1990s. Exporters suffered serious problems in 1997 when the pound appreciated steadily against all European currencies. By the end of the century it seems likely that the UK will be committed to joining EMU (European Monetary Union) which will stabilize exchange rates. In the mean-time the risks still exist.

The role of the credit manager in currency transactions is twofold:

1   To give advice on which currencies to favour or avoid, on exchange rates and on how to use exchange rates in preparing quotations.
2   To ensure that incoming currency payments are handled properly. In some companies he may also be required to manage the exchange risk, although this is normally a function of the treasurer.

Exchange rates

Some basic knowledge of exchange control and the foreign exchange market is essential. What follows is not intended as a detailed explanation. The aim here is merely to sketch the framework, to give the credit manager some understanding of the market from the exporter's point of view. Further reading is suggested at the end of the book.

The exchange rate that the bank will use to change foreign currency into sterling is determined by the foreign exchange market. The London market consists of over 200 dealers (the clearing banks, merchant banks and foreign banks) who are in constant communication both with each other and with exchange brokers in the City and with banks in other financial centres. Currencies are bought and sold freely in the market and the price of one currency, say US dollars, in sterling is a reflection of the supply of and demand for those currencies. The majority of foreign exchange transactions are made 'spot', i.e. purchase and sale become effective in two working days. (This allows for time differences and local holidays in financial centres round the world.)

Spot rates

The exporter who receives $100,000 without having made any prior arrangements for its disposal and who wishes to convert it into sterling has to offer it to a bank. He will be quoted the spot rate. Small variations in the spot rate can be found from bank to bank, and within one day each bank will have a 'spread' of rates, the movement depending partly on changing demand by the bank for the currency through the day and partly on political/economic factors which affect the market's overall view of its strength or weakness. Not all currencies can be readily exchanged in the market, and it is very important for the exporter to be aware of this. As an example, an exporter to Ghana in 1978 would have been extremely foolish to agree to be paid in Ghanaian cedis, because there was no market for them. Officially, a sterling–cedi exchange rate is quoted, but this does not help the exporter if no one in the London foreign exchange market wants to buy cedis.

Virtually all international trade is conducted in a small number of currencies which are immediately convertible on the London market. The value of these currencies against the pound is quoted daily in the financial press. The list is as follows:

US dollars
Canadian dollars
Austrian schillings

Belgian francs
Danish kroner
Dutch guilders
French francs
German marks
Italian lire
Japanese yen
Norwegian kroner
Portuguese escudos
Spanish pesetas
Swedish kroner
Swiss francs
Irish punt
ECU

Forecasting of any kind is extremely difficult, and the exporter who arranges to be paid in currency and then does nothing to insure against the possibility of an exchange loss is a speculator. At times when sterling is losing value against, say, US dollars, it can seem entirely justifiable to anticipate that dollars arriving over the next 6–12 months will be worth more sterling than if they arrived today. Nonetheless, to rely on such a belief is speculation, and there are many exporters who have done this and have suffered severe losses, despite having followed the advice of 'experts'.

Forward rates

The alternative to speculating on the spot rate is to sell forward. In the foreign exchange market, banks quote forward rates as well as spot rates. The *Financial Times* each day gives a summary of the rates quoted on the previous business day, showing spot, one month forward and three months forward. In some currencies, notably US dollars, Deutschmarks, Swiss francs and Canadian dollars, forward rates can readily be obtained for the next 12 months or even further.

A forward rate of, say, three months is *not* the bank's forecast (or anyone else's) of what the spot rate will be in three months' time. It is the result of calculations done within the market using three known facts:
1 The spot rate.
2 The cost of the currency being sold in its country of origin.
3 The cost of the currency being purchased in its country of origin.
These last two factors are usually expressed as interest rates. The difference between interest rates in the two centres is the biggest factor in determining the difference between spot and forward rates. This difference is either a

premium or a discount. (If there is no difference between spot and forward, the currencies are said to be 'at par'.)

A three-month forward premium in US dollars against sterling means that a contract to deliver dollars to the bank in three months' time will produce more sterling than if those dollars were delivered today. The amount of forward premium is expressed in hundredths of a cent, as in the following example taken from the *Financial Times*, 24 April 1991:

APRIL 23	CLOSE	THREE MONTHS	% P.A.
US	1.7110–1.7120	2.29–2.26 c. pm	5.32

This tells us that at close of business on 23 April the banks were selling dollars spot at 1.7110 and buying them spot at 1.7120. If the banks were asked to buy dollars, i.e. to receive them from an exporter, on 23 July (three months' time), the cost would be 1.7120 less 2.26 cents = 1.6894. The letters 'pm' indicate a premium. When the bank is buying, the second or right-hand amount is deducted from the second or right-hand amount in the spot (or 'close') column. The final column indicates the annual percentage by which the dollar is appreciating against the pound. In this example, selling dollars three months forward is giving the exporter an exchange of profit of 5.32 per cent p.a. Applying these rates to a payment of $100,000 which the exporter is expecting on 23 July, gives the following result:

Selling $100,000 at spot (1.712)	= £58,411
Selling $100,000 3 months forward (1.6894)	= £59,193
Benefit	= £782.

The opposite of a premium is a discount and selling currency at a forward discount means receiving less sterling than would be available today. For example, on the same day this entry appeared:

APRIL 23	CLOSE	THREE MONTHS	% P.A.
SPAIN	183.45–183.75	63–78c dis	−1.54

The calculation involved in selling forward Spanish pesetas is as follows:

Selling Pts.100,000 at spot (183.75)	= £544
Selling Pts.100,000 3 months forward (183.75 *plus* 78 céntimos = 184.53)	= £542
Loss	= £2

The rules to remember in forward calculations are that premiums are deducted and discounts are added.

Currencies at a forward premium are often referred to as 'strong' currencies, those at a forward discount as 'weak' currencies. This classification often over-simplifies the relationships and is misleading. Exchange rates can of course be influenced by political events, but the underlying reason for one currency being weaker than another is always the interest rate differences. The cause of forward premiums and discounts is the difference between interest rates. On 23 April 1991, the UK minimum lending rate was 12 per cent compared to 6 per cent in the USA. This made the dollar at a premium against sterling.

It is a combination of forward rates and the movement of the spot rates which makes currencies strong or weak.

The exporter expecting to receive $100,000 in three months' time has, therefore, a choice. He can either wait until the payment arrives and then sell it 'spot', or he can take out a forward contract now, under which he is committed to deliver those dollars to the bank in three months' time *at a rate which is fixed today*. To wait and sell at spot is speculation, whereas to sell or cover forward is a form of insurance. A further alternative is to borrow the expected dollars and immediately sell them at 'spot' for sterling. When the payment arrives, it is used to repay the dollar loan.

Forward contracts

It is not usually possible to predict the exact date of a payment. To overcome this difficulty, the exporter can make an 'option contract' (as opposed to a fixed contract). Under this, the bank will accept the payment between any two fixed dates. The agreed forward rate will apply whenever payment is made within the option period. If there is a forward premium, the bank will fix the rate on the earlier date, and on the later date if a discount exists. For example, an exporter selling in dollars on 60-day terms might make an option contract to deliver to the bank any time between 60 and 90 days from date of invoice. If the payment arrives *after* the beginning of the option period, the bank obtains the benefit. It follows that the exporter should fix the start of an option period as far ahead as possible, to try and gain the maximum benefit from the forward premium. Thus if he knows that his buyer habitually pays one month late, he might decide to sell forward 90 option 120 days from invoice date. If, however, the payment arrives before the option period, the exporter will suffer a penalty for delivery early. An alternative to an option contract is to sell at a fixed date and then 'roll-over' or extend it as necessary. This will cost more in bank fees besides entailing more work.

If an exporter is unable to deliver the currency, perhaps because the buyer cancelled the order or returned the goods for credit, the forward contract has to be 'closed out'. This means buying the currency at spot in order to fulfil the contract. Depending on how the exchange rate has moved, there will be either a loss or a gain.

Currency options

Since the early 1980s a new form of protection against exchange risks has developed and become well-established. A currency option contract gives the exporter the right to buy or sell a specific amount of the nominated currency at a fixed price within a specific future period. The essential difference between this and a forward exchange contract is that an option carries no obligation to buy or sell.

An exporter may, for example, take an option contract to sell dollars in twelve months' time, when he expects to receive dollar payments from his customers. He can choose an option rate (called the strike price) to produce the required amount of sterling, but he will only exercise his right and sell the dollars under the option if the strike price is more favourable than the spot rate. If his dollar payments never arrive, the option merely expires without any penalty. Under the so-called American option, the right to sell can be exercised at any time up to the end of the agreed period. Under a European option the sale can only be made at the end of the period.

Options may be regarded therefore as a form of insurance, and a premium is charged whose cost is determined by the underwriter's view of the strike price relative to market conditions, the length of the option period and the volatility of the chosen currency. As an example, for a three-month option on US $500,000 with a forward premium of 2.05 cents, a premium of 2.7 per cent (American) or 2.67 per cent (European) was quoted (in July 1991).

Exporters must decide whether to cover their exchange risks by covering forward or by using an option. The latter is more expensive but far more flexible. The sections that follow on 'Currency quotations' and 'Operating forward contracts' are based on the assumption that forward contracts are used.

Currency quotations

Apart from the very large corporations, most companies do not employ more than a handful of people conversant with foreign exchange. It will frequently fall to the credit manager to assume the role of adviser on currency. If he is responsible for arranging forward sales and controlling the receipt of currency payments, this is a logical move.

Before examining in detail how exchange rates can be used in quotations, there are two basic principles which should be observed:

1   The decision to quote in currency should always be because it will help win business — never because of the prospect of exchange profits.
2   The choice of a conversion rate should be dictated with a view to long-term business rather than an immediate killing. Thus exporters who won business in the USA by quoting at around 1.60 found within a relatively short time that they had to choose between drastic profit erosion (as the rate moved into the 1.80–1.90 range) and the risk of losing business if they increased prices to keep pace.

When a currency quotation is prepared, there are a number of alternative methods:

a   Use an agreed fixed rate.
b   Use the spot rate.
c   Use a fixed rate with an exchange variation clause.
d   Use the forward rate.

An agreed fixed rate

The price is agreed with the buyer in both currency and sterling. The buyer then undertakes to pay sufficient currency to produce the required sterling figures. All the exchange risk is thus passed back to the buyer, who might just as well be paying in sterling. This is most unlikely to be accepted and needs no further consideration.

Spot rate

The exporter converts into currency at spot (at the time of quotation). If an order is obtained, any forward premium is extra profit. This may be good practice in a period of stable prices and low inflation, providing the currency price is not too high for the buyer. Problems are likely to occur, however, when price increases are required, unless the currency has weakened against sterling, thus making the original spot rate more beneficial to the exporter.

A fixed rate with an exchange variation clause

This involves sharing the exchange risk with the buyer. It is usually complicated to set up and administer, but it can offer a reasonable compromise in terms of unstable exchange rates.

Example A dollar price is agreed, based on a rate of 1.90 to the pound. Providing the spot rate at a date of shipment (or date of payment) remains within 5 per cent of 1.90, i.e. 1.805–1.995, no action is needed.

If the spot moves beyond that range, both parties may agree to share any profit or loss — measured either from the base point or from the edge of the range.

Forward rate

Using the forward rates is at once the most difficult and the most fruitful way of quoting. Difficulty arises because in the interval between quotation and receipt of order, both spot and forward rates may change significantly, and the exporter can do nothing about it because without a firm order he cannot sell forward. (For the moment, use of the ECGD Tender to Contract facility is ignored.)

The following example illustrates the use of forward rates:

Stage 1 British Widgets Ltd is seeking business in Germany. A potential buyer agrees to be quoted in Deutschmarks. Delivery will be wanted over a 12-month period on 60-day terms. Price competition is very fierce. The order at stake is 100,000 widgets.

Stage 2 The exporter must obtain a minimum unit price of £5 for the first six months, rising to £5.50 in the second half-year following labour and material price increases.

Stage 3 These facts are given to the credit manager. He telephones the bank and asks for 'indicated' rates for selling Deutschmarks at monthly intervals for 12 months beginning in three months' time. He should make it clear that the rates are only for indication.

Stage 4 The indicated rates are shown in Exhibit 18.1. Assuming an even spread of deliveries, the average rate is 3.4618.

Stage 5 The credit manager recommends that the Deutschmark price be based on 3.50. This is between spot and the average forward rate, thus building in a margin of safety in case the rates go against the exporter before an order arrives, i.e. in case the pound appreciates against the Deutschmark.

Stage 6 In order to hold prices firm for the whole period, the recommended rate of 3.50 is applied to £5.25 (the average sterling requirement), giving a price of DM18.375. This unit price of DM18.375 should be compared with the price based on spot at the date of quotation. This is calculated as:
a £5.00 × 3.7025 = DM18.5125 for 6 months, and
b £5.50 × 3.7025 = DM20.3637 for 6 months.
c Average rate for 1 year = DM19.438.

Exhibit 18.1   Indicated rates

Spot - Mid November 1978		3.7025	Quotation date
	28 February 1979	3.6110	
	31 March	3.5808	
	30 April	3.5507	
	31 May	3.5205	
	30 June	3.4925	
	31 July	3.4645	
	31 August	3.4365	
	30 September	3.4148	
	31 October	3.3932	
	30 November	3.3715	
	31 December	3.3590	
	31 January 1980	3.3467	

Average rate = 3.4618

The price reduction achieved by using the forward rates is 5.47 per cent. In this example it is, of course, assumed that British Widgets have to quote as low a price as possible to stand any chance of winning the business.

Operating forward contracts

If the order is obtained, the credit manager then has to make the forward sale. The procedure to adopt is as follows:

1   Check the *Financial Times* for a general idea of both spot and forward rates. If the rates have moved against him since the indications were obtained, he must decide whether to sell and obtain less sterling than anticipated, or to delay the sale in the hope that rates will improve. This is a dangerous practice, and the credit manager should not embark on this course without being very confident of the outcome — and also being prepared to accept sharp criticism if things go wrong! This point is examined in more detail further on.

2   Assuming the decision is to sell, the credit manager should then contact those banks he regularly uses for Deutschmark transactions and obtain spot and forward rates from each of them. The bank which offers the best combination of spot and forward rates will be asked to buy the Deutschmarks. Certain 'rules' should be noted in order to ensure good service from banks. First, it is not worth shopping around for rates on small amounts (say, under

$100,000). To do so is likely to cause annoyance. Secondly, it is wrong to go back and forth between banks trying to 'run an auction'. It follows from this that several telephones must be used simultaneously if an immediate decision between offered rates has to be made. If no immediate decision is to be made, it should be made clear at the outset and the bank told that an 'indication' is required. Thirdly, it helps the dealer if calls are made when the market of the country of the required currency is open, e.g. New York and other Eastern cities of North America at around 14.30 London time. Fourthly, always be precise in speech. If dollars are to be sold to the bank, say 'I will sell you X dollars' *not* 'Please buy X dollars'.

If good relations are to be maintained, all the banks which are asked to quote must be offered business from time to time. This really limits the numbers to, say, three or four — which should be sufficient for the needs of most companies.

For the purpose of this illustration we will assume that British Widgets' credit manager is very fortunate and makes his forward contracts at the same rates used in the quotation. However, the production department have now said that instead of an even flow of shipments, delivery will start at 6,000 for the first two months, increasing to 8,000 for the next two and then remaining at 9,000 for the next eight months.

Exhibit 18.2 shows the forward contracts made with the bank. The date at the start of the option period is known as the value date.

In the event, deliveries do not take place as scheduled and Exhibit 18.3 shows how a careful record must be kept so that each invoice and payment is matched to the appropriate contract.

While the invoices to the customer will be in Deutschmarks, there have to be sterling entries to the ledger. The conversion rate can either be that used to obtain the Deutschmark price at the quotation stage, or it can be the actual forward rate. There is much to be said for using the forward rate, since when payments arrive they will be converted into sterling by the bank at exactly the figure shown on the ledger.

It is often tempting to delay making a forward sale, especially when the credit manager knows that the business was obtained by quoting at a rate better than he can immediately obtain on a forward sale and if 'expert opinion' in the City is expecting the rates to improve in the exporter's favour. But no matter how strong are the reasons for delaying a forward sale, to do so is just as speculative as is deciding not to cover forward at all. Such a policy should not be adopted without the credit manager consulting with the sales manager concerned. To have any chance of success, the credit manager or one of his staff must have a permanent 'hot line' to his bank or other contact in the City so that any favourable movement in exchange rates can be acted on immediately.

If currency options were used in the above example instead of the forward exchange market, a great deal of time and effort would have been spared.

Exhibit 18.2 Forward contracts

Contract number	DM value	Option period	Rates
1	110,250	28 Feb – 31 May	3.6110
2	110,250	31 Mar – 30 Jun	3.5808
3	147,000	30 Apr – 31 Jul	3.5507
4	147,000		
5	165,375		
6			
7			
8			
9			
10			
11			
12		31 Jan – 30 Apr	3.3467

NOTES

1 Delivery is due to start in December and payment will therefore arrive in February at the earliest.

2 having fixed the beginning of the option period, there is nothing to be lost in arranging a three-month option to allow for late payments and/or late deliveries.

Whether or not the options would have been used depends on the spot rates ruling when the payments arrived.

Currency accounts

An exporter may choose to open and maintain a foreign currency account held either in the UK or overseas. Thus a Deutschmark account could be held in London or in Frankfurt (or in both). Currency payments are credited to the account, enabling the holder to pay for his imports without having to buy currency in the market. Quite apart from the obvious savings in bank charges and commissions, there are other benefits of particular interest to the credit manager.

Payments arriving early on a forward contract can be retained until the value date arrives. This enables the credit manager to obtain an extra month's premium. Looking back to Exhibit 18.2, if a Deutschmark account were held, the option period in Contract No. 1 could run from 31 March to 30 June, because if payment arrives in February (as it should) it can be held until

256

31 March. Currency accounts therefore allow considerably more flexibility in the planning of forward contracts.

It is very desirable to discuss the whole question of currency accounts in detail with specialist bankers.

Currency problems

A frequent problem results from currency payments not matching forward contracts because of changes in invoice value or the deduction of debit notes by the customer. The only remedy is to buy the shortfall at spot from the bank in order to deliver it to the bank to fulfil the forward contract.

Another very frustrating problem can occur if the UK bank which first receives a currency payment decides to convert it into sterling without checking with the beneficiary. Some of the clearing banks only refer to the payee if the payment exceeds a certain minimum, and the result can be that the exporter receives sterling at spot and he is unable to meet his forward commitment. This is very difficult to overcome when payments are sent by many different buyers whose own banks may be routing transfers through different UK correspondents. A possible solution is to give all currency customers very precise instructions about the disposal of their payments, and then to hope that these instructions are carefully noted and passed on by all the banks in the chain. Regrettably this does not always happen. A better solution, but not always practicable, is to arrange for currency payments to be made into a currency account in the country of the buyer. This was examined in Chapter 14.

Currency and credit terms

The fact that the cost of money varies from country to country is clearly important when credit terms are being considered.

When quoting in a currency with a high forward premium an exporter may be able to win business by offering extended credit because the cost of this can be offset by the forward premium. This could not be done in the example quoted of British Widgets, because the forward premium was used to reduce the price.

The alternative strategy — using the forward premium to offset the cost of credit — is illustrated in the following case study involving United Spares Ltd.

Foreign exchange/payment terms — case study

Your company is in the process of negotiating a contract for automotive spares with München Autopart GmbH, the value of which is £50,000 delivered to Munich. The buyer has indicated that the products are technically acceptable and he requires them to be delivered in one lot within 30 days of date of order.

You have calculated your price on the basis of being paid net cash within 30 days of shipment. This is due to the buyer having squeezed you on price, leaving very little profit margin for you. However, your company is very keen to get the business, as it will fit in very well with another order they have received and allow them to make some savings by economy of scale. The cost of credit is 1.5 per cent per month.

Shortly before the contract is about to be signed, the buyer states that 90 days' credit is required. A possible solution is to quote in Deutschmarks. The buyer indicates he will accept this. Using the rates given below, calculate whether the business can be accepted on these terms without eroding the profit.

QUOTATION DAY	DAY'S SPREAD	CLOSE	THREE MONTHS	% P.A.
DM	3.68–3.71	3.69–3.70	10–9 pf-pm	9.97%

The buyer also offers to pay in 30 days for 2 per cent discount, or in 60 days for 1 per cent. How do these alternatives compare? The answers are given in Exhibit 18.3.

ECGD Tender to Contract cover

Purpose To protect the exporter against exchange rate fluctuations between submission of a bid and signing of contract. Only US dollars or Deutschmarks or Japanese yen may be covered, with a minimum value of £5 million.

Operation
1 Exporter gives ECGD a rough estimate of the total sterling return expected if the contract is won, and the total payment period.
2 ECGD then calculates how much currency the exporter would need to sell forward to produce the required sterling figure.
3 The forward rates used by ECGD become guaranteed rates up to the date of contract.
4 The exporter prices his contract in the amount of currency indicated by

Exhibit 18.3

(i) 90 days

    (a) Cost of credit = £50,000 × 1.5% × 3 = £2,250
        LESS 30 days credit built into
        price (= £750)   = £1,500

    (b) Proceeds from forward sale: cost in DM using
        spot will be £50,000 × 3.7 = DM185,000
        Proceeds from selling forward <u>4 months</u>

```
                     Spot =  3.7000
LESS 3-month forward premium (0.0900)
                             3.6100
LESS estimated premium for
  fourth month              (0.0300)
            Forward rate 3.5800
```

        DM185,000 at 3.58 = £51,676
        Potential profit   = £1,676

    (c) Result
        Potential exchange profit = 1,676
        LESS Cost of credit   = (1,500)
              Net extra profit = <u>£176</u>

(ii) 30 days less 2%
     Payment will be DM181,300 (DM185,000 × 98%)
     This can be sold forward two months for a forward
     premium of 6pf, giving a forward rate of 3.64:

       181,300/3.64 = £49,808

     Net result = a loss of £192

(iii) 60 days less 1%
     Payment will be DM183,150 (DM185,000 × 99%)
     This can be sold forward three months for a
     premium of 9pf, giving a forward rate of 3.61:

       183,150/3.61 = £50,734

     Therefore exchange profit = £734
     LESS cost of one extra month's credit at 1.75
     per month = £750

     Result = Break even

(iv) Conclusion: the best alternative is net 90 days

ECGD. He is free to negotiate whatever payment terms he wishes, providing they fall within the overall framework given to ECGD.

5 If the contract is won, the exporter sells forward immediately. If the rates have altered and the sterling obtainable is different from that guaranteed by ECGD, any shortfall or surplus is covered as follows:

 a The exporter bears the first 1 per cent of loss on the agreed sterling figure and ECGD pays the balance up to a maximum of 25 per cent.

 b ECGD retains the first 10 per cent of any gain and the exporter keeps anything beyond that.

6 Premiums are charged on the total sterling proceeds, at rates dependent on the period of cover chosen by the exporter:

 a Up to 3 months 0.3 per cent

 b 4–6 months   0.1 per cent for each extra month

 c 7–9 months   0.15 per cent for each extra month

7 A deposit premium of £5,000 has to be paid on acceptance of ECGD's offer. This is non-returnable.

8 TTC cover is only available if the exporter applies for a Specific Guarantee.

9 At the end of nine months, if no contract has been signed, a further series of guaranteed rates will be issued by ECGD.

Costing currency contracts

In Chapter 17 an example was given of the calculations needed to cover interest costs, ECGD premium, bank charges, etc., in a sterling contract.

When currency is involved, a further set of calculations is necessary which will indicate any additional profit (or loss) to be offset against (or added to) the other costs.

Case study

The case study has been prepared with the aid of ECGD, whose co-operation and help is gratefully acknowledged. The basic data is shown in Exhibit 18.4 and the contract costs in Exhibit 18.5.

Currency income If ECGD TTC cover were obtained on this contract (at a cost of £36,000, see No. 7 in Exhibit 18.5) the exporter would be given dollar values, calculated from forward exchange rates available at the date of offer, which would *guarantee* the minimum sterling value of £6 million provided a contract was signed within six months.

A specimen quotation for this case study has been specially prepared by ECGD and is shown in Exhibits 18.6 and 18.7.

Exhibit 18.4 Basic data

1	Proposed Buyer	Acme Steel Co. Ltd
	Country	Nigeria
2	Currency of contract	US dollars
3	Maximum contract value	$12 million
4	Minimum required Sterling proceeds	£6 million
5	Payment terms	5% within 30 days of contract signature
		10% on shipment
		85% over 5 years (10 equal 6-monthly instalments)
6	Shipment	12 consignments at monthly intervals, commencing within 4 months of contract signature
7	Bond requirements	Advance payment bond (15%)
		Performance bond (10%)
8	Type of ECGD policy required	Supplier credit
9	Interest rate	7.5% p.a.
10	Estimated period to date of contract (from date of application to ECGD)	6 months

Paragraph 4.13 shows the forward rates presently available for each month throughout the contract period. Section 1 shows the amount of currency needed to produce the required sterling outcome at those rates. The bottom line on this exhibit shows that to guarantee a total sterling outcome of £6 million, using the forward rates available at the date of offer, the total contract value would have to be $11,180,962. These figures give an average forward rate for the contract of 1.8635.

If the exporter decides to take out TTC cover, he must, therefore, quote at minimum of $11,180,962 in order to obtain the ECGD guarantee of £6 million proceeds. If the exporter decides not to take up the TTC cover, he is gambling that exchange rates will not move against him, i.e. that the dollar will not weaken, *more* than will produce a shortfall equivalent to the cost of TTC cover (£36,000).

On the other hand, if he believes that a contract price of $12,000,000 will be acceptable to the buyer, there is no advantage in taking TTC cover.

With a price of $12,000,000 and the forward rates quoted by ECGD, the result would be a sterling figure of £6,439,495 — an extra 7.3 per cent profit. To obtain *less* than the minimum £6,000,000 with a contract price of $12,000,000, the average forward rate must be over $2 to the pound. On this example, expected to be signed within six months, this would be extremely unlikely. (*Written in March 1979.*)

A figure of $12,000,000 has been used in Exhibit 18.4 to calculate the contract costs.

Points arising from Exhibits 18.6 and 18.7

Exhibit 18.6, para. 5g 'Maximum period expressed in months . . . 69 months.' This is calculated by adding 5 years (60 months) to the ninth month after contract signature, which is the mean average delivery date.

Exhibit 18.7, para. 4.2 The rate of 0.6 per cent is calculated at 0.3 per cent for the first three months and 0.1 per cent for each subsequent month, making up the total estimated period from application to date of contract.

Exhibit 18.5 Contract costs

		$
1	ECGD premium (3% on $12 million)	360,000
2	ECGD premium for bank guarantee (0.32% on 85% of $12 million)	32,640
3	Bank fee (0.375% on 85% of $12 million)	38,250
4	Advance payment bond fee (1% on 15% of $12 million)	18,000
5	Performance bond fee (1% on 10% of $12 million)	12,000
6	ECGD premium for unfair calling cover (0.5% p.a. on 25% of $12 million for 15 months	18,750
		$479,640

(4% of contract value)

PLUS (if required)

7	ECGD Tender to Contract premium (0.6% of £6 million)	£36,000

PLUS (payable by the buyer)

8	Interest at 7.5% p.a. on Supplier credit	$2,103,750

$\frac{1}{2}$(10.2 million/10) × (7.5/100 × 55)
Formula given in Chapter 17.

Exhibit 18.6   Specimen proposal for ECGD Tender to Contract Agreement

1. We have read a specimen of your ECGD Tender to Contract Agreement (Revised October 1978) hereinafter called the "Agreement" and request you to inform us of the terms on which you are prepared to enter into such an Agreement in respect of the proposed contract (hereinafter called "the Supply Contract") specified in paragraph 5 below. We acknowledge that any such Agreement issued to us pursuant to this Proposal may only relate to the full 100% of the UK Element (as defined in the Agreement) of the Supply Contract and we certify that the details given in paragraph 5 herein refer only to such UK Element.

2. The form of this Proposal shall be incorporated as Schedule 1 to any Agreement subsequently issued in respect of this Proposal.

3. We have not entered into any contract of insurance or indemnity relative to the Supply Contract in respect of any cause of loss set out in the Agreement and we will not enter into any such contract of insurance or indemnity without your prior consent in writing.

4. All discussions and correspondence in connection with this Proposal and with any Agreement arising therefrom are to be treated by both sides as confidential and we undertake not to disclose without your prior consent in writing either the existence of the Agreement or any of the details thereof to our agents or to the Buyer or to any other person or firm other than in confidence to our bankers.

5. The Supply Contract details are as follows:
   a. Buyer   **The Acme Steel Co Ltd**
   b. Buyer's Country   **Nigeria**
   c. Purpose of the Supply Contract
      Supply of Engineering Equipment for new foundry
   d. Stage and date at which firm   **16 May 1979**
      foreign currency price needs
      to be set (state currency)   **US Dollars**

263

e. Maximum sterling requirement in
   respect of 100% of the UK Element
   only of the Supply Contract and   £6,000,000
   for which cover is required under
   the Agreement
f. Validity Period of Agreement
   required by us   6 months
g. Maximum period expressed in months
   from date of signature of the Supply
   Contract over which payments are to
   be received pursuant to the Supply
   Contract: **69** months

6. We certify that the representations made and
facts stated by us are true, and that we have not
misrepresented or omitted any material fact which
might have a bearing on the Agreement and that the
truth of such representations and facts and due
performance of each and every undertaking contained
herein or in the Agreement shall be a condition
precedent to any liability on your part thereunder.

APPLICANT'S SIGNATURE(S)

SIGNED   CAPACITY OF SIGNATORY   DATE

NOTES
1. In the case of incorporated companies this Proposal should be
   signed by an authorised officer for and on behalf of the company
   and should state the capacity in which the signatory acts (e.g.
   Managing Director, Secretary etc).
2. In the case of partnership this Proposal should be signed by one
   or more partners having authority to sign.

Exhibit 18.7, para. 4.5 The 'shortfall' and 'excess' margins refer to the percentage losses or profits borne by the exporter or retained by ECGD, respectively.

Exhibit 18.7, para. 4.6 The minimum payment of £500 is a figure set by ECGD, relating to the 'shortfall' and 'excess' margins.

Exhibit 18.7, para. 4.8 The 'largest figure' of £7,500,000 is an amount fixed by ECGD, as being the maximum sterling outcome the exporter can enter

Exhibit 18.7   Specimen offer of ECGD Tender to Contract Agreement

OFFER OF TENDER TO CONTRACT AGREEMENT
BUYER: THE ACME STEEL CO LTD
COUNTRY: NIGERIA

1   I have pleasure in informing you that ECGD has considered your
Proposal for Tender to Contract cover and is prepared to offer you
such cover in the form of the Tender to Contract Agreement (Revised
October 1978) a specimen of which you have read and on the terms
set out below. For the purposes of this Offer any expression
defined in the Tender to Contract Agreement (Revised October 1978)
shall have the same meaning when used in this Offer.

2   The form of this Offer shall be incorporated as Schedule 2 to
any such Agreement subsequently issued in respect of this Offer.

3   This Offer can only be accepted by payment of the sum of £5,000
on account of the Premium mentioned in paragraph 4.2 below so that
such sum is received by ECGD by the Expiry Date shown at paragraph
4.1 below. Such payment will not be refundable in any event. This
Offer is subject to withdrawal at any time before acceptance and
will in any event expire on the said Expiry Date.

4   Particulars of Offer
    4.1   Expiry Date 24th February 1979
    4.2   Premium shall be charged on the largest figure entered in
        Column 2 of Schedule 3 at a rate of 0.6%
    4.3   Declaration Date 14th day of each month
    4.4   First Declaration Date will be the 14th day of the month follow-
        ing date of signature of the Supply Contract.
    4.5   Margins 4.5.1 Shortfall Margin: $1\frac{1}{2}$%
                4.5.2 Excess Margin: 10%
    4.6   Minimum Payment £500
    4.7   Validity Period 24th February 1979 to 21st August 1979
    4.8   The largest figure to be entered in Column 2 of Schedule 3 shall not
        exceed £7,500,000
    4.9   The figure to be entered in Section 2 of Schedule 3 shall not exceed
        £1,762,500
    4.10   The figure to be entered in Section 3 of Schedule 3 shall not exceed
        £750,000
    4.11   Last date for Payments 26th February 1986
    4.12   Date of the Tender to Contract Agreement (Revised October 1978)
        shall, on acceptance of this Offer, be 24th February 1979

4.13 Forward Exchange Rates to be used to complete
     Currency Payments Schedule

List 1: Exchange Rate (US Dollars)	List 2: Periods (Month)	List 1:	List 2:
2.0071	1	1.8866	31
2.0025	2	1.8820	32
1.9994	3	1.8774	33
1.9967	4	1.8728	34
1.9941	5	1.8682	35
1.9913	6	1.8636	36
1.9879	7	1.8591	37
1.9850	8	1.8545	38
1.9829	9	1.8499	39
1.9787	10	1.8453	40
1.9755	11	1.8407	41
1.9716	12	1.8361	42
1.9671	13	1.8316	43
1.9627	14	1.8270	44
1.9583	15	1.8224	45
1.9539	16	1.8178	46
1.9495	17	1.8132	47
1.9451	18	1.8086	48
1.9406	19	1.8041	49
1.9362	20	1.7995	50
1.9318	21	1.7949	51
1.9274	22	1.7903	52
1.9230	23	1.7857	53
1.9186	24	1.7811	54
1.9141	25	1.7766	55
1.9095	26	1.7720	56
1.9049	27	1.7674	57
1.9003	28	1.7628	58
1.8957	29	1.7582	59
1.8911	30	1.7536	60
			(and for each subsequent month)

5. It is a condition of any Agreement to be entered into as a
result of your acceptance of this Offer that not later than your
delivery to ECGD of the Currency Payments Schedule pursuant to
Article 5.1 of the Agreement you shall have applied for, received
and accepted an offer from ECGD of an ECGD specific guarantee or an
ECGD buyer credit facility in respect of the business the subject
of this Offer. Failure by the Company to satisfy such condition
shall, unless ECGD at its sole discretion shall otherwise elect in
writing, render the Agreement null and void EXCEPT that ECGD shall
retain any Premium paid. This Offer should not be construed as any
indication of ECGD's willingness to consider any application or
make any offer in respect of an ECGD specific guarantee or an ECGD
buyer credit facility in respect of the business the subject of
this Offer.

Yours faithfully
for the EXPORT CREDITS GUARANTEE DEPARTMENT

(Continued)

CURRENCY PAYMENTS SCHEDULE
SECTION 1

Schedule of Currency and sterling cash flow position (becomes Schedule 3 when approved by ECGD and attached to Agreement)

Column 1	Column 2	Column 3	Column 4	Column 5
Sterling accounts corresponding to Currency accounts in Column 4	Accumulation of Column 1 accounts	Periods in Months for which Currency amounts in Column 4 will be sold forward in accordance with Article 5 of the Tender to Contract Agreement	Currency accounts which will be sold forward in accordance with Article 5 of the Tender to Contract Agreement *US$/DM	Accumulation of Column 4 accounts
300,000	300,000	1	602,130	602,130
50,000	350,000	4	99,350	701,965
50,000	400,000	5	99,705	801,670
50,000	450,000	6	99,565	901,235
50,000	500,000	7	99,395	1,000,630
50,000	550,000	8	99,250	1,099,880
50,000	600,000	9	99,145	1,199,025
50,000	650,000	10	98,935	1,297,960
50,000	700,000	11	98,775	1,396,735
50,000	750,000	12	98,580	1,495,315
50,000	800,000	13	98,355	1,593,670
50,000	850,000	14	98,135	1,691,B05
560,000	1,410,000	15	1,096,648	2,788,453
510,000	1,920,000	21	985,218	3,773,671
510,000	2,430,000	27	971,499	4,745,170
510,000	2,940,000	33	957,474	5,702,644
510,000	3,450,000	39	943,449	6,646,093
510,000	3,960,000	45	929,424	7,575,517
510,000	4,470,000	51	915,399	8,490,916
510,000	4,980,000	57	901,374	9,392,290
510,000	5,490,000	63	894,336	10,286,626
510,000	6,000,000	69	894,336	11,180,962

* Delete as applicable

SECTION 2

ECGD's Maximum Liability
to make Payments and
payments pursuant to
Articles 6.2 and 8.2
of the Agreement: $23\frac{1}{2}$% of the largest figure entered in Column 2

£ 1,762,500

SECTION 3

The Company's Maximum liability
to make Payments and payments
pursuant to Articles 6.2 and 8.2
of the Agreement: 10% of the largest figure entered in Column 2

£ 750,000

COMPANY'S SIGNATURE(S)

SIGNED

DATE

CAPACITY OF SIGNATORY

NOTES
1 In the case of incorporated companies this Proposal should be signed
  by an authorised officer for and on behalf of the company and should
  state the capacity in which the signatory acts (e.g. Managing Director,
  Secretary, etc).
2 In the case of partnership this Proposal should be signed by one or
  more partners having authority to sign.

when finalising his currency prices. (It represents a 25 per cent increase over the £6,000,000 minimum.)

Exhibit 18.7, para. 4.9 The figure of £1,762,500 is 23½ per cent of £7,500,000 and represents ECGD's maximum liability under this offer, i.e. 25 per cent of loss on £7.5 million less 1½ per cent borne by the exporter.

Exhibit 18.7, para. 4.10 The figure of £750,000 is 10 per cent of £7,500,000, representing the maximum amount of exchange profit the exporter would have to pay ECGD.

Exhibit 18.7, Currency payments schedule Column 3 identifies the period numbers (in months from contract signature), on which currency payments will be received according to the contract terms.

Chapter 19

Measuring and reporting credit performance

'A credit department is only as good as last month's results.' This comment is frequently applied to business operations of all kinds. It is perhaps not a bad motto to put on the wall, but the prudent credit manager will take care to estabish a pattern of reporting which will put each month's results into context.

Reporting to management takes many forms, ranging from a simple note of how much cash has been collected, to a detailed analysis of movements on the sales ledger, the ageing of major customer balances and the computation of ratios. Given a 'green field' situation — or at least a climate amenable to change — the principal recommendations are as follows:

1 Report monthly.
2 Balance statistics with narrative.
3 Be as brief as possible.
4 Identify trends.
5 Highlight problems.
6 Indicate progress towards objectives.

Monthly reporting is normal practice and particularly sensible where payment terms are monthly or similar, i.e. net 30 days. There are three measurements basic to the credit function:

1 Debtor level.
2 Cash.
3 Overdues.

While the relationship between cash and debtor level is so close as to be termed 'cause and effect', these items should be reported separately.

Debtor measurement

There are many possible ways of measuring the level of receivables, most of which are unsatisfactory because a change in sales volume or the incidence of holidays or shut-down periods prevents true comparisons being made over a period of time.

The system recommended is usually called the 'working back' method, referred to in Chapter 8. It is illustrated in Exhibit 19.1.

Exhibit 19.1 Debtor measurement

```
Total debtors - £10,000,000 at 30 June 1991

Information needed - Sales invoiced (including VAT)
in June, May and April


CALCULATION

Debtors                          10,000,000
Less June sales                  (4,500,000)  = 30 days
                                  5,500,000
Less May sales                   (4,850,000)  = 30 days
                      Balance       650,000
```

The balance of £650,000 has to be expressed as a percentage of the previous month's sales, i.e. April's:

$$\text{April sales} = 4,250,000$$

$$\text{Balance} = \frac{650,000}{4,250,000} = 15.2\% = 5 \text{ days}$$

The debtor level is therefore 65 days
Calculating each month as 30 days avoids minor fluctuations in ratios arising from months of unequal lengths.

There is little merit in quoting the current debtor level in a monthly report without putting it in context. This can be done in two different ways:

a   Showing a trend, and

b   Comparing with budget.

A trend in the debtor level can hardly be detected in under three months. To go beyond six months involves too many statistics.

Comparison with budget assumes a debtor's budget is set. If there is no debtor budget, the credit manager should himself be setting targets for at least three months ahead. It is important when establishing a budget or target level for debtors that ratios, i.e. so many days' sales, as in Exhibit 19.1, be used rather than actual monetary figures. These depend on sales achieved whereas a ratio is not affected by actual sales volume.

If the monthly report shows a trend (either improving or deteriorating) the credit manager should explain why, perhaps by identifying some major customers whose payments are slowing up. Similarly variations from budget should be explained.

Where several divisions or product groups are involved, it is very desirable to report separate debtor ratios for each unit because a satisfactory overall performance may conceal serious credit problems in some of the units. Another refinement is to show separate ratios for home and export debtors. This can logically be extended to the calculation of a ratio for every different payment term used by the company, since a ratio has limited significance unless it is compared to terms of payment.

Cash

Using the 'working-back' method means that the amount of cash collected is the key to the debtor level. It is not possible to set an annual 'cash budget' since the amount of cash collectable depends initially on the actual sales volume. Each month, therefore, the credit manager must calculate how much cash is needed to achieve the budget/debtor ratio. The method of doing this is shown in Exhibit 19.2.

Overdues

Measurement of debtor-level alone cannot give an adequate picture of the sales ledger. The ratio of 65 days given in Exhibit 19.1 gives no indication of the ageing of debtors, and indeed two totally different age analyses could produce the same ratio, as shown in Exhibit 19.3. The ageing of Column A is clearly far less satisfactory than Column B, but both represent 65 days.

In Chapter 7 an example was given of a computer age-analysis (Exhibit 7.2, page 85). This is intended for use within the credit department and is not

Exhibit 19.2 Cash target calculation

Using the same figures as in Exhibit 19.1:

A Budget debtor ratio for 31 July 1991 = 59 days
B 59 days at the end of July will mean the current
   month (July) plus 29 days of June sales
C Therefore the cash target for July will be total
   debtors at 30 June (£100,000,000) less 29 days of
   June sales (£4,350,000), which equals:

$$
\begin{array}{r}
10,000,000 \\
(4,350,000) \\
\hline
£5,650,000
\end{array}
$$

suitable for inclusion in a monthly report. The credit manager must decide
which overdue statistics to select. Two possible figures are:
a Percentage overdue of total debtors.
b Percentage over 90 days overdue of total debtors.
   If these results (or other similar figures) are reported, they should be
reported against a target or budget and shown with the figures for previous
months so that trends can be identified. Just as total debtor ratios should be
broken down into divisions and home and export, so should overdue figures.
An alternative to the percentage over 90 days overdue is to quote the actual
amounts. In contrast to total debtors and even total overdues, these are
hardly affected by sales volume and it may be more useful to monitor the
figures themselves.

Exhibit 19.3

	A	Percentage of	B
Current month	45	Total debtors	45
1st overdue month	23		35
2nd overdue month	9		20
3rd overdue month	4		–
4th overdue month	4		–
5th overdue month	3		–
6 months overdue and prior	12		–
	100%		100%

The drawback of the type of overdue measurement described is that no distinction is made between payments received, say on the 2nd of the month, and those arriving on the 30th of the same month. An account paid one day late is included under the same heading as one paid thirty days late. In Chapter 7, brief reference was made to an account history report which showed the number of days' credit taken against each month's sales (Exhibit 7.5, page 87). This is valuable as a reference on individual customers but of no use in any end-of-period measurement across the whole ledger.

There is another method of measurement which produces a total of 'overdue days' both for individual customers and for the total ledger. It is only practicable if operated by computer.

Stage 1   The computer must hold a record of the due date of every invoice.
Stage 2   The program compares the actual payment date of each invoice with the due date, and gives each item paid a weighting factor determined by the number of days overdue.
Stage 3   At the end of the period a calculation is made, giving the number of overdue days.

Example   Assume there are five customers on the ledger, named Brown, Jones, Smith, Black and Thomas. Their purchases in June (on net monthly terms) and payment record up to 30 August are as shown in Exhibit 19.4. Conventional debtor measurement would show that at the end of August, all the June accounts of these buyers having been paid, the debtor level would be 60 days (assuming no overdues exist prior to June and no July accounts are paid to terms), regardless of whether payments were received as shown or

Exhibit 19.4

Name	June pur- chases	Date paid	Number of days overdue	Weighted value		
Brown	2,000	5 Aug	5	10,000	(2,000 × 5)	
Jones	8,000	8 Aug	8	64,000	(8,000 × 8)	
Smith	5,000	13 Aug	13	65,000	(5,000 × 13)	
Black	3,000	20 Aug	20	60,000	(3,000 × 20)	
Thomas	4,000	30 Aug	30	120,000	(4,000 × 30)	
TOTAL	22,000			319,000		

Average overdue days for all five customers

$$= 319,000/22,000 = 14.5 \text{ days}$$

all together on 30 August. The additional measurement tells us that June accounts were paid in an average period of 45.5 days (31 days in July being the allowed period plus 14.5 overdue days).

The same principle is applied whether there are five customers each with one payment (as above) or one customer making five payments or five customers each making five payments. Any payments arriving ahead of due date can be given a negative weighting.

The merit of this method is that it produces a precise measurement of credit taken. If targets are based on it, the problem of a month-end cash scramble is largely avoided because payments received one or two days late are given a much more favourable weighting than those arriving a whole month late. The disadvantage is that a special computer program must be written, capable of matching every line item paid with the appropriate due date. Debit notes, credit notes and other adjustments must be ignored.

A further method of reporting overdues is given in Exhibit 19.5. By expressing the overdue balance at the end of month 2 as a percentage of the total account at the end of month 1, attention is focused on the slowest paying customers. Customers owing above an agreed minimum are listed individually, with a 'balancing' line for all those below the minimum. Other features can include the use of a target overdue percentage, the listing of customers in descending order of overdue percentage and the inclusion of the due date on items more than six months overdue.

Any measurement and reporting of overdues against a target is worthwhile if it prevents the efforts of the credit manager being concentrated too much on the achievement of a cash target, which might be reached solely by accelerating the flow of current and near-current money.

Beyond these three basic types of measurement — debtor level, cash and overdues — there are, of course, others which can be added. Some examples are as follows:

1 *Bad debts* Serious bad debts must be reported as they arise. It is wrong, however, to focus too much attention on the incidence of bad debts, unless an adverse trend is developing. On an annual basis, the amount written off must be reported but this should not be given undue importance. With most companies in most years, the amount of money tied up in overdue accounts is generally greater than that lost in bad debts.

2 *Disputes* If the level of items in query is a significant problem, the monthly volume should be reported. It can be helpful to turn the figure into a ratio. Thus, if 10 per cent of the debtors in Exhibit 19.1 are under dispute, this represents 6½ days. If the queries had been resolved, the debtor ratio would be 58½ days.

3 *Credit decisions* A relatively small number of companies endeavour to highlight the more positive side of credit activities by reporting the number

Exhibit 19.5 Home trade overdues as at 31 May 1991 (budget ratio is 40%)

Account at 30 Apr £	Customer	Credit limit £	Total account at 31 May £	Amount overdue at 31 May £	Ratio – Col.4 as % of Col.1	Age analysis, months				Comments
						1 £	2 £	3 £	3+* £	
10,509	J.Bloggs	15,000	18,904	10,509	100.0	7,304	1,615	1,590		
43,682	ABC Co.	50,000	57,311	23,907	54.7	12,633	11,274			
45,799	British Widgets	50,000	42,988	14,610	31.9	14,610				
	All others		51,087	16,342	32.0	9,503	3,412	2,916	511	
TOTALS			170,290	65,368	45.4	44,050	16,301	4,506	·511	

Note 1 – Overdue amounts in excess of £10,000 are to be shown separately together with a total for all other overdue amounts.

Note 2 – Customers would be ranked by ratio in descending order.

*If debt is more than six months overdue, the due date for payment should be noted.

or value of favourable to unfavourable credit decisions. This can be limited to new accounts or applied to all referred orders, in which case it may be worth relating the percentage rejections to each risk category. Whilst the credit manager may derive some satisfaction from this type of report, unless it is used in some way outside his department there is little point in producing it.

4 *Export ratios* Companies exporting to many different countries will be interested to see a debtor ratio (or 'collection period') for each major market. While each must be related to the primary payment terms in the market, the result will show how credit costs and the consequent effects on profits vary from market to market.

No form of report should consist entirely of statistics, or else it becomes virtually unreadable. In addition to the selective measurements, the credit manager should include brief references to any problems such as the worsening payment behaviour of a key customer, a request for extended credit by a major buyer or the continued lack of settlement in a large dispute.

Budgets

The credit manager will generally be asked to prepare a debtor or receivables budget for the following year. As already indicated it is preferable to budget ratios only because the inevitable variations in actual sales compared to budget sales will swiftly make a debtor budget using money values quite useless.

In preparing a budget, attention must be paid to regular 'seasonal factors', such as a rise in the debtor ratio at the end of August because of the holiday period affecting the throughput of invoices in customers' accounts payables. Another factor that must be checked is any expected change in the 'mix' of sales, e.g. an increasing proportion of exports on longer terms than home sales, or a switch from distribution sales to direct outlets, which may lead to difficulties in cash collections. Finally, any 'external' factor considered likely to affect credit operations should also be allowed for, e.g. computerising the sales ledger.

It follows from the above that if debtor budgets are to be prepared as painlessly as possible, the credit manager must educate the sales office to provide him with certain information which would probably not otherwise be prepared — for example, sales forecasts by different payment terms.

With the increasing emphasis being placed on cash-flow, credit managers can expect to be under pressure to reduce debtor ratios. What is achievable will depend very much on the starting point, and every credit manager will be aware of 'the law of diminishing returns'. As the debtor ratio reduces, so a further reduction requires an even greater effort. There may come a point where the credit manager has to use his commercial judgement to temper the demands of his financial masters. It may seem logical (and entirely reasonable) to persuade all customers to pay to terms, and a debtor ratio goal of 30 days (if everyone is on net monthly terms) should therefore be attainable. Quite apart from the existence of disputes and those customers unable to pay, the major obstacle will usually be a number of big customers who refuse to release their cheques those few days (or possibly weeks) earlier. Assuming that all approaches have failed, the credit manager is left with the choice of trying to force an improvement, through the holding of orders, or accepting defeat (without admitting it to the customer, of course).

As in so many situations, the 'right' decision will depend partly on the size of the gap between the actual and the required payment dates and partly on the relative strengths of buyer and seller in the market. A delay of up to, say, ten days will probably have to be accepted unless the supplier is in a monopoly or near-monopoly situation. On the other hand, payments regularly arriving three weeks or more late can reasonably be regarded as unacceptable. These are only intended as broad guidelines, and every credit manager has to determine what he believes is the ultimate or best debtor ratio he can achieve in the context of his own industry.

Similarly any budgets or targets prepared for the reduction of overdues must be realistic. If overdues aged 90 days or more are £10,000 at the end of December 1991, it is not very sensible to fix a target of nil for December 1992. The right target can only be established by reference to how that overdue figure has moved over the previous twelve months, or by how long it has taken to reduce from £20,000 to £10,000. Targets of this nature can usually be broken down into smaller units within the department. It is most important to set targets which, while difficult to achieve, are not impossible. Quarterly reviews of progress may be helpful, and the credit manager should be ready to change year-end targets in the light of events through the year.

Expense budgets

Credit department costs are subject to the same controls as those of any other department. In times of declining demand and rising unit costs, every area of the company must expect close scrutiny, which may result in expense cuts or even reductions in staff.

In this environment, the credit manager needs to be able to demonstrate the cost-effectiveness of his operation. A simple method is to calculate the cost of collecting every £1,000 of sales. This takes no account of how efficiently collections are being made. An alternative is to produce a kind of productivity ratio, using the following formula:

$$100 \, (SH/MAD) / R$$

where SH is the sales per head (in credit department) in the previous year,

MAD the mean average debtor level in the previous year and *R* the ratio in the base year. This is illustrated in Exhibit 19.6. (*Acknowledgement and thanks to Mr H. Edwards, who originated the basis of this ratio.*)

In this example, within two years the credit department has succeeded in reducing the debtor ratio by 13.6 per cent, while sales have increased by 40 per cent. Credit staff has actually decreased by 20 per cent. Using the formula, this indicates that credit department productivity has more than doubled. Had the number of staff remained constant (at 10), productivity would have increased by only 62 per cent.

The main weakness in this formula is that it assumes that increased sales result in a proportionate volume of work in the credit department. This is not always true. An alternative which perhaps gives a better indication is to replace the value of sales per head with the number of active accounts per head. This can be used to measure credit control efficiency on a monthly basis. The formula is as follows:

$$\frac{PR}{\text{(Performance ratio)}} = \frac{A}{S} \div DSO$$

Exhibit 19.6

	Year 1 (base year)	Year 2	Year 3
Number of credit department staff	10	9	8
Annual sales, £million	50	60	70
Sales/head £million	5.0	6.66	8.75
Mean average debtor level, months	2.2	2.0	1.9

Base year ratio = 5.0/2.2 = 2.27

Since this is the base year, 2.27 is treated as 100.

$$\begin{aligned}
\text{Year 2 ratio} &= (6.66/2.0) \div 2.27 \times 100 \\
&= (3.33/2.27) \times 100 = 1.466 \times 100 \\
&= \underline{147}
\end{aligned}$$

$$\begin{aligned}
\text{Year 3 ratio} &= (8.75/1.9) \div 2.27 \times 100 \\
&= (4.65/2.27) \times 100 = 2.048 \times 100 \\
&= \underline{205}
\end{aligned}$$

where A is the number of active accounts, S is the number of credit control staff actually at work during the month (net of sickness and holidays) and DSO is the number of days' sales outstanding. Whilst the number of active accounts is a better yardstick of credit control workload than sales volume, the results of this measurement are not always a true reflection of efficiency which can be affected by a number of other factors ranging from the number of invoicing errors to the level of bank interest rates. It does however have the merit of simplicity.

Bad debt provisions

In the absence of firm rules laid down by a company's auditors or accountants, the credit manager should draw up his own disciplines for determining the level of bad debt provisions.

Both the age and the 'quality' of a debt should be considered. Under the first heading, every item aged over a certain period should be examined with a view to reserving unless there is a valid reason to exclude it. Valid reasons would include a recent promise of payment (the customer being regarded as solvent), or an existing reserve for credit (goods having been rejected or returned). Quite apart from items selected on an age basis, there may well be other items of more recent date which must be regarded as doubtful quality. These will include customers under Receivership or in liquidation, customers in the hands of solicitors and possibly those in the hands of collection agents. A further category may include export debts 'frozen' by transfer delays.

Listings of this nature may only be required annually, but it is a good discipline to review quarterly. Where credit insurance policies (home or export) are held, a reduction in bad debt reserve may be possible. Credit insurance, however, is intended to protect against the unexpected failure, i.e. those which would probably not be identified in a bad debt provision exercise.

Further reading

Better Payment Practice, Dept. of Trade & Industry, Small firms division
Cash by express, SITPRO
Companies in Distress, Touche Ross & Co
Credit Analysis, J. Coleshaw, Woodhead-Faulkner
Credit Control and Debt Recovery, Gee Publishing
Credit in Europe, Cork Gully
Credit Insurance, D. Briggs and H. Edwards, Woodhead-Faulkner
Credit Management, Institute of Credit Management (monthly)
Credit Management Handbook, Gower Publishing
Credit Risk management, BPP Financial Publishing
Croner's Guide to Credit Management, Croner Publications
Debt recovery in Europe, Bermans
Disclosure of company documents in the EC, KPMG
Exports, Gee Publishing
Export Today, Institute of Export (monthly)
Finance of International Trade, A. Watson, Institute of Bankers
Getting paid for exports, H. Edwards, Gower Publishing
How to read a balance sheet, ILO, Geneva
Insolvency Law, S. A. Frieze
International Credit Management Handbook, Gower Publishing
International insolvency procedures, KPMG
International Trade & Documentary Credits, HSBC (Midland Bank)
Interpreting company reports and accounts, G. Holmes and A. Sugden, Woodhead-Faulkner
Success in International Trade — Foreign Exchange, Lloyds Bank Plc
The analysis of credit, A. Bathory, McGraw-Hill
The export trade, C. Schmittof, Stevens & Sons Ltd
The Forfaiting Manual, Finanz AG

281

Index